Microsoft® Project Server 2002

Microsoft® Project Server 2002

Qimao Zhang

Writers Club Press
New York Lincoln Shanghai

Microsoft® Project Server 2002

Writers Club Press
an imprint of iUniverse, Inc.

For information address:
iUniverse
2021 Pine Lake Road, Suite 100
Lincoln, NE 68512
www.iuniverse.com

ISBN: 0-595-24060-7

Printed in the United States of America

With my full heart of gratitude, I like to dedicate this book to all my family members and friends.

Contents

Preface

Managing projects using Project Server 2002 and Microsoft Project is a challenging and exciting experience. Collaboration is vital to successful project management in today's rapidly changing business environment. Project Server 2002 is a powerful tool set for collaborative planning and scheduling projects. This book strives to offer detailed and practical knowledge about Project Server 2002.

Target Users

This book is about Project Server 2002. If you are new to Project Server 2002, this book is for you. Project Server 2002 works with Microsoft Project. Microsoft Project details is not in the scope of this book. Users can reference other books about Microsoft Project 2000 and Microsoft Project 2002 features. It is essential for users to have good understanding of Microsoft Project in order to unleash the capabilities of Project Server 2002.

As a tutorial. You can use this book as a tutorial to learn Project Server 2002.

As a reference. You can use this book as a reference for Project Server 2002 installation, configuration, and customization.

The Special Features

This book includes many special features to maximize your understanding and comprehension of the material.

Formatting Conventions

Programming code. Programming code appears as this:

```
Dim strFirst As String
```

Icon and Sections

- **Hyperlink**

  🖳: This icon signals internet web sites.

- **Tip**

> *Tip*
>
> *This section contains a bit of advice or a hint to save you some headache.*

- **Note**

> This section provides additional information such as background information.

- **Caution**

> *! Caution*
>
> This section contains warnings.

How This Book Is Organized

This book is organized in the way you will use Project Server 2002. It begins with introduction and installation, progresses through customization. The later chapters provide more advanced information about Project Server 2002.

Chapter 1 Introduction to Project Server 2002

Project Server 2002 takes advantage of web technology that greatly enhances the Project functionality with instant project messaging, informative project views, and useful status reports. Project Server 2002 provides a centralized and dynamic location for key projects' stakeholders to analyze, communicate, and update projects.

Chapter 2 Install Project Server 2002

Installing Project Server can be a complex process, including many tasks that must be completed before, during, or after installing the product itself. This chapter is a step by step process for installing Project Server.

Chapter 3 Integrate with SharePoint Team Services

By integrating SharePoint Team Services with Project Server, Microsoft Project can leverage the document management technology (document library and list management technology) of SharePoint Team Services and provide a method that's easy to set up and use for sharing project-related documents and issues with team members and other stakeholders.

Chapter 4 After Project Server Installation

This chapter takes a detailed look at some of the changes occurred during the Project Server installation process.

Chapter 5 Project Server 2002 Database Structure

This chapter covers Project Server's database structure including permissions, configurations, DSN requirements, how to get aggregate information from the database, and accessing data from Project Server.

Chapter 6 Basic Features of Project Server

The basic features of Project Server is available for all authorized users such as: messages, password update, views, and timesheet.

Chapter 7 Advanced Features of Project Server

Some advanced features of Project Server only available to Administrator, other features available to both Project Manager and Administrator. This chapter covers rules, request status reports, manage user accounts, delete item from the database, manage views, and how to customize Project Server.

Chapter 8 Creating Powerful Projects Analysis

This chapter covers the techniques for an in-depth review of projects to supply a detailed analysis of your project portfolio. Combine the power of Office Web Components and the knowledge from previous chapters, you can extend Project Server data and create additional views, charts, and reports to meet the individual needs of all project stakeholders.

About the Author

Qimao Zhang is a senior software developer and Microsoft Certified Solution Developer (MCSD) at The Advisory Board Company in Washington, DC. He has MBA and M.S. in Computer Information Systems. In recent years, he has successfully delivered solutions to various clients such as ExxonMobil, USPS, Bank of

Columbia, PartyLite, Clarks England, and Verizon. He is the lead software engineer for Project Portfolio Management System at The Advisory Board Company. You can reach him by email at qimao@yahoo.com.

List of Abbreviations

Project Central—Microsoft ® Project Central
Project Server—Microsoft ® Project Server
Project—Microsoft ® Project
SQL Server—Microsoft ® SQL Server

1

Introduction to Project Server 2002

Project Server 2002 is a separate software product that integrates with Microsoft Project Professional to provide interactive web-based communications for managing a project. Since most projects are group endeavors, they require extensive communication between resources and project managers. The capabilities of Project Server 2002 can help you communicate project information to executives, managers, co-workers, or clients in an effective way.

Project Server 2002 takes advantage of web technology that greatly enhances the Project functionality with instant project messaging, informative project views, and useful status reports. Project Server 2002 provides a centralized and dynamic location for key projects' stakeholders to analyze, communicate, and update projects.

Successful project managers manage projects that produce desired results in established timeframes with assigned resources. Project Server works as a life-support system for project managers with powerful functionalities. The following table shows how Project Server's functionalities can avoid common project pitfalls:

Table 1.1: Avoid Project Pitfalls with Project Server

Project Pitfalls	Project Server's Functionalities to Avoid Them
Poor team communications	1. Delegate tasks to resources and resources receive prompt task alerts 2. Distributed project documents immediately available to all stakeholders 3. Instant project messaging and notification 4. Communicate project status with Status Reports 5. Address critical issues to key resources without delay
Inaccurate and late progress monitoring	1. Project progress can be updated dynamically as soon as users update their project status in Microsoft Project 2. Current project status available to all stakeholders immediately from Project Web Access
Not holding resources accountable for their performances	1. Project managers can analyze project status with a wide variety of customizable criteria such as task completion percentage and resource name 2. Project managers can review up-to-date individual timesheets 3. Project managers can generate reports for selected project and/or resource
Incomplete and inaccurate schedules and resource needs	1. Resources can update their work time changes according to their availability at anytime 2. Project schedule and status updated dynamically according to the latest changes

The key features of Project Server 2002 are:

- **Enterprise global template**

Project Server 2002 allows opening, editing, and saving an enterprise global template from the server database. Microsoft Project Professional users connecting to the server read the enterprise global template when starting up Project. This allows an organization to distribute and manage project and resource management standards.

- **Enterprise resources**

Project Server allows resources to be created, edited, and saved to the Project Server database.

- **Enterprise templates**

Project Server allows templates to be opened and saved to the Project Server database. Microsoft Project Professional users can view templates saved to the server database and create new projects based on the templates.

- **Integrated database**

Project Server integrates the Microsoft Project database and the Project Web Access database. The integrated database simplifies application and database management and provides Microsoft Project Professional users with a seamless user experience as they open and save projects and resources.

- **Integrated security**

Permission to access Microsoft Project and Project Web Access data is managed through the Project Server administrative features. Security for Project Server is supported per user per project and resource at both the application and database layers. Integrated security simplifies application management and significantly improves security.

- **Project Data Service**

Requests to access or update enterprise data are made to the Project Server PDS. The PDS provides a SOAP interface that allows third-party client applications to access the same Project Server features as Microsoft Project Professional and Project Web

Access. In addition, the PDS provides an extensibility model that allows third parties to extend the functionality of Project Server.

- **Portfolio Analyzer cube generation service**

The cube generation service creates the Portfolio Analyzer fact and dimension tables based on the Project Server database. The service then calls SQL Server Analysis Services to generate an OLAP cube based on the fact and dimension tables. Administrators can manage the service through Project Web Access. Third parties can include their own data in the Portfolio Analyzer cube[1].

Architecture

Microsoft Project enterprise project management features are based on an n-tiered application using the Microsoft .NET server platform. The client tier of the application is provided by Microsoft Project Professional and Project Web Access. Project Professional is a desktop application. This application is used to create, edit, and save projects, enterprise resources, and the enterprise global template. Project Web Access is a Web-based application that runs on Internet Explorer. Project teams use this Web-based application to access timesheets, status reports, project reports, and project analysis applications.

The middle tier of the architecture is provided by Project Server. Project Server combines aspects of an n-tiered Web server application with a two-tiered client-server database application.

Customers can also choose to use the document library and issue tracking features provided by the integration of Project Server with SharePoint Team Services (included with Project Server). This tier runs on Windows 2000 Server (or later).

The database tier of the solution is provided by SQL Server 2000. Project Server merges and extends the Microsoft Project 2000 and Project Server 2002 database schema[1].

Figure 1.1: Architecture overview

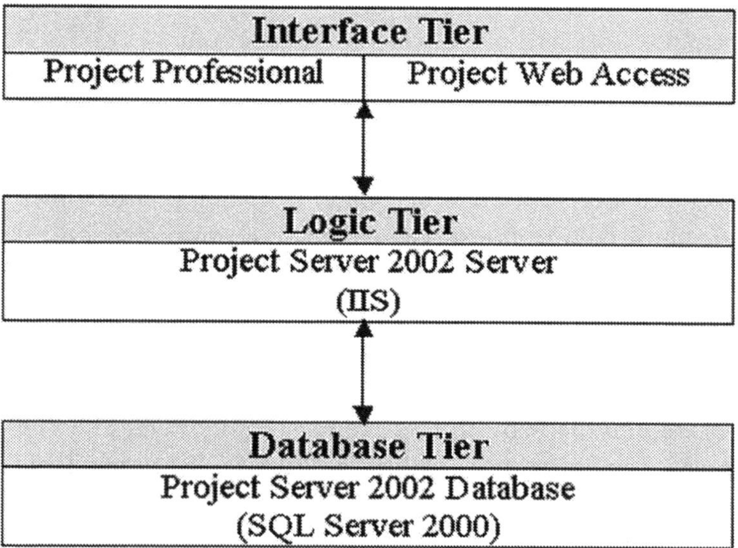

- Interface Tier

Project Web Access provides access to timesheet, project views, status reports, to-do lists, and document library and issue tracking (through SharePoint Team Services integration). Project Web Access consists of a set of ActiveX® controls (primarily a grid control) and HTML pages (provided through Active Server Pages [ASP pages]) running in Internet Explorer 5 or later. While Project Web Access provides limited offline features, it is primarily intended for users connected to Project Server.

Microsoft Project 2002 runs on Microsoft Windows 98 Second Edition and later as well as Microsoft Windows NT 4.0 Workstation and later. Microsoft Project Standard and Professional can publish information to Project Server and update information from Project Server into project plans. This is the workgroup functionality originally provided in Microsoft Project 2000. Microsoft Project Professional can also open and save enterprise projects and resources from Project Server[1].

- **Logic Tier**

  Project Server provides both workgroup and enterprise project management features to client applications. Workgroup features primarily interact with Project Server using the server business object. This object is called by Microsoft Project when project plans are published to the server. Clients communicate with the business object by posting XML documents to Project Server ASP pages.

  Enterprise features interact with Project Server using the Project Data Service (PDS). Requests from Microsoft Project Professional to read or save enterprise projects or resources to the server are first made by an XML request to the PDS. The PDS checks the permission for the authenticated user and then returns a list of available objects and/or connection string information. Microsoft Project then uses the connection string information to bind to the enterprise database using ODBC. Requests from Project Web Access for enterprise resource information are also made to the PDS. In this case, the PDS checks security and then directly queries the enterprise database and returns resource information to Project Web Access.

  The PDS is indirectly involved when administrators use Project Web Access to generate a Portfolio Analyzer OLAP cube or when users create and analyze models using Portfolio Modeler.

  Project Server runs on Windows 2000 Server or later and requires IIS 5.0 or later[1].

- **Database Tier**

  SQL Server provides the database layer services for Microsoft Project. Project Server merges and extends the Microsoft Project 2000 and the Project Server 2002 database schema. Microsoft Project Standard interacts exclusively with the workgroup tables.

Microsoft Project Professional and Project Web Access can work with both the workgroup and enterprise tables.

An important scalability improvement in the Project Server workgroup features is the use of view tables. When Project Server 2002 users accessed a project view, Project Server 2002 queried for the location of the project in the workgroup tables and then used the Microsoft Project OLE DB provider to bind to the project (saved as an .mpp file or in a database). This process occurred each time a user accessed the project. In Project Server, the OLE DB provider is invoked when a project is published to the server. The records produced by the OLE DB provider are written to a set of MSP_VIEW tables. These tables contain time-phased data for all projects published to the server. Project views are then created by performing SQL queries on these tables as opposed to views being created by invoking the OLE DB provider. The end result of the new architecture is that the load on Project Server and SQL Server is significantly reduced.

The enterprise features in Project Server include a significant revision in the way that Microsoft Project binds to the project database. When Microsoft Project 2000 opened a project from a database, it bound directly to the Microsoft Project tables in the database. If the user's Data Source Name allowed read/write access to the database, Microsoft Project could open and save changes to any project in the database even those projects managed by other project managers. Microsoft Project Professional uses connections that don't require Data Source Names to bind to SQL Server views of the project database. The SQL Server views contain only the information required to open the projects or resources selected by the user. This information only exists in the SQL Server views while Microsoft Project is opening or saving a project or resources. The Microsoft Project architecture provides application-level security through the PDS and database-level security through SQL Server views.

Classes of Users

Project Server 2002 contributes to the success of a project by ensuring clear communication of project data both up and down the management chain and by allowing project managers to capture the expertise of resources.

The involvement of both resources and senior management in the planning process is achieved through the Project Server 2002 client, which allows workers at all levels of the organization to view up-to-date project information and to interact with the project planner by providing input to the schedule and project plan[1]. Through Project Server 2002, even users with limited knowledge of project management methodology and no familiarity with Project can easily view, update, and provide input on the project plan and schedule.

The following table detail the features, benefits, and usage scenarios of Project Server 2002 by various classes of users within the organization.

Table 1.2: Classes of users

Classes of Users	Features and Benefits
Project managers	Project managers are responsible for planning and scheduling and for maintaining the project plan in Project 2000 or Project 2002. When using Project Server 2002 to involve the workgroup, project managers retain complete control of the master project plan; however, they also benefit from the increased involvement of others within the organization, leading to more synergistic planning and more informed decisionmaking.
Resources	Team members are identified as "resources" within the project plan. Resources' primary goals are to deliver on commitments and contribute to the success of a project. They are also expected to participate in planning tasks, estimating work, and tracking status. Project Server 2002 provides resources with a customizable, easy-to-use tool for keeping track of their own tasks and for seeing how their work contributes to the high-level projects or organizations.
Executives	Executives have an interest in the status of one or more projects across the enterprise. Executives can use Project Web Access to quickly access project status reports across their organizations. Reports are available at the portfolio, project, and resource level, so an executive can quickly identify projects in trouble. With the Portfolio Analyzer and easy access to online status reports and project documents stored on Sharepoint Team Services from Microsoft, executives can also analyze trends across projects and resources to understand the causes behind problems. The Portfolio Modeler allows executives to develop and evaluate solutions to problems by using interactive project staffing and scheduling tools. Project Web Access allows executives to see, understand, and resolve problems in projects across the enterprise.

Project Server 2002 includes options that provide precise control over the specific information available to each class of usera. These options can be set for an individual user or for entire class of users. These options can be set either from the administration module or from within Microsoft Project Professional.

Establish Rules

Project Server 2002 administration module enables an extremely detailed degree of control over the information and authority granted to each user or class of users. These options can be set and maintained by the project manager or by the server administrator:

- **Account management**

  Before users can access project data through Project Server 2002, they must have an account on the Project Server 2002 Server. User accounts may be set up by the project administrator or created automatically when the project manager sends the user a TeamAssign message. The project administrator oversees account management, adding and removing users from projects, assigning users to groups and roles, and determining what data will be available to each user.

- **Authentication**

  To ensure security, Project Server 2002 supports both Windows NT Authentication and its own authentication scheme, which uses username/password pairs maintained by Project Server 2002. The administrator can require either Windows NT Authentication, Project Server 2002 authentication (with or without password), or a mix of both types, which is the default behavior.

- **Views of project information**

  The administrator defines the views, including Gantt bar formatting, and specifies the views available to each workgroup member, the projects the workgroup member has access to, and the exact fields and data the workgroup member can see in each project. For example, resources may be allowed to view only their assigned tasks, tasks assigned to all resources, or tasks assigned to specific resources. By default, resources see information about the tasks assigned to them, but the administrator can also make other project information available to workgroup members, such as the status of tasks that they depend on.

- **Task delegation**

  The administrator determines whether to enable task delegation, and if so, specifies for which projects and resources it is allowed. All delegations must be approved by the project manager before the resources are reassigned in the master project plan.

Some Features of Project Server 2002

- **Making assignments**

  The project manager assigns work to resources. The project manager uses Project's TeamAssign function to notify the resources of the work assignments. Once a resource has been assigned a work assignment, the resource can log onto Project Server 2002 to check the details and update the status of the work assignment.

Figure 1.2: TeamAssign

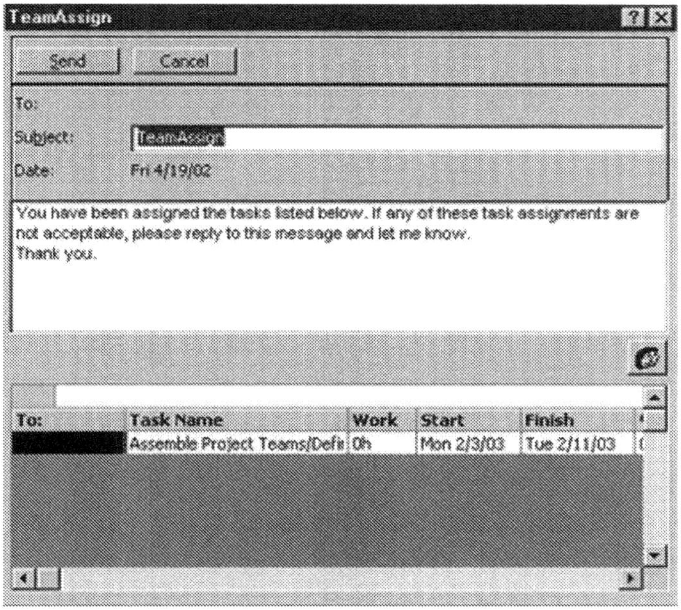

- **Status reports**

  Project Server 2002 includes the ability both to design templates for text-based status reports and to send status requests to resources. The project manager creates the report sections to be completed by the team, and may add text prompts to help resources fill out the report.

  The project manager determines the frequency of the status reports by setting up automatic requests or by issuing requests manually. Completed status reports can be reviewed and edited in Project Server 2002 and compiled to include information for the entire team in a single report.

- **Messaging**

  Updates to project information (such as task requests, delegations, and task updates) from resources are received as messages in the project manager's Project Server 2002 Inbox. The project manager can accept, reject, or edit the information contained in the message before passing the information to the master project plan.

  To expedite this process, the project manager creates rules that automatically accept specified changes when the project manager runs the rules on a set of messages. By carefully implementing rules, project managers can practice "management by exception," reviewing only those items that fall outside a set of pre-established criteria.

Figure 1.3: Messages

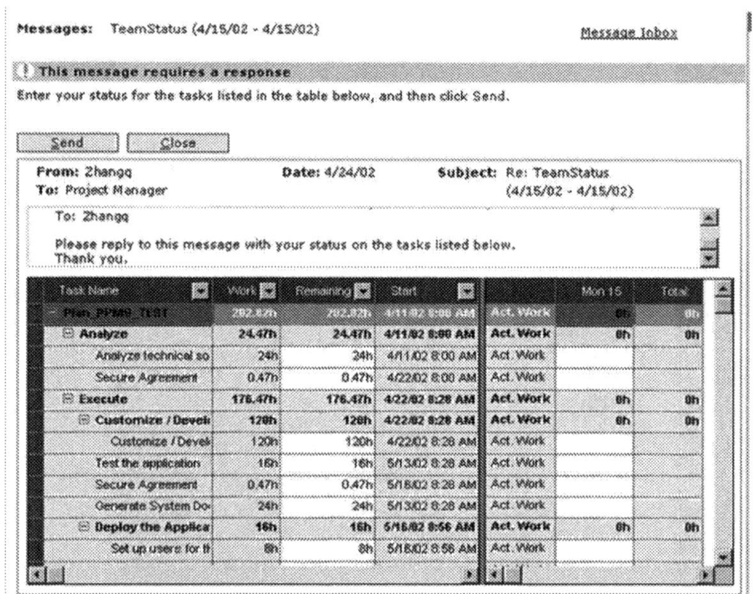

- Timesheet & Personal Gantt Views

  Project Server 2002 Timesheet provides a simple interface for everyone involved in a project to send updated information to the project manager. From the Timesheet, a resource can update hours, task percent complete, or any editable field for the tasks displayed. As in the Personal Gantt view, tasks shown in the timesheet can be filtered and grouped, allowing resources to organize the data the way they want.

  Personal Gantt view presents a graphical display of all project information available to a user. By default, resources see all tasks in which they have been assigned, for all projects in which they have been assigned a task. Users can choose from predefined views and chart styles made available by the project administrator or customize their view by reordering columns, filtering for specific tasks, and sorting or grouping tasks by project name, start date, or other task characteristics. This view can also be modified to include activities from the user's Outlook Tasks list.

Figure 1.4: Timesheet

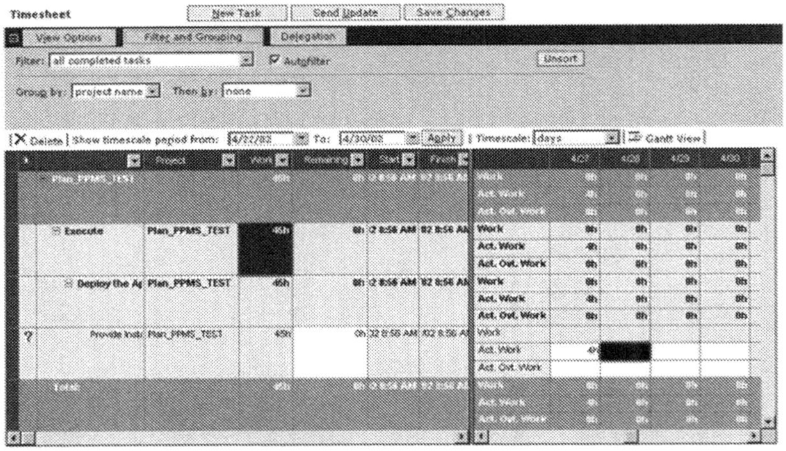

- Delegate tasks

  When enabled by the project manager, task delegation allows a Project Server 2002 user to assign a task to another resource and sends a message to the project manager indicating that the task has been reassigned.

  Delegation enables the project manager to make effective use of functional managers or leads, who can delegate a group of assigned tasks to their own team members or direct reports. Project Server 2002 supports this scenario by allowing the delegating resource to remain as the lead or intermediate manager of the delegated task, with responsibility to review and approve task updates and changes before they are forwarded to the project manager.

To ensure control over resource assignments, task delegation has three levels of control. The Project Server 2002 administrator can enable or disable delegation for the entire site. Once enabled for the site, the project manager can disable delegation on a project-by-project basis.

Finally, the project manager must approve any delegations submitted by resources or leads before the project plan is updated. The project manager can also control acceptance of delegations by implementing rules to automatically accept delegations that meet specified criteria.

- **Working offline**

  Project Server 2002's offline features allow resources to download their personal task lists and current status reports from the Project Server 2002 database to a local computer or laptop, working offline until they return to their desks or connect to the network and synchronize with the Project Server 2002 Server. On synchronization, updates and queued messages are sent to the project manager for review and incorporated into the master schedule.

  Resources can specify a range of dates, minimizing the storage requirements. Features available offline include timesheet data and task updates, Personal Gantt, and status reports.

  In addition, remote workers can access Project Server 2002 via dial-up or Remote Access Service (RAS) accounts. Windows NT and Project Server 2002 authentication ensure the security of remote connections.

- **SharePoint Team Services**

  Many project managers have been looking for better and more efficient ways to share information within their organization and with outside key stakeholders. The integration between Project Server and SharePoint Team Services significantly improved the way project team manages information and activities. Now project managers can easily create a Web site that serves as the central repository of all project information documents, contacts, tasks, discussions, and much more.

Using preprogrammed Web-authoring forms, SharePoint Team Services lets you instantly create a full-feature Web site that your team can begin using immediately. Once the site is launched, team members can add, edit, and delete information using their Web browsers. Automatic hyperlink management maintains links to new material, while templates protect the overall navigational structure, individual page layouts, and design elements[2].

Figure 1.5: SharePoint Team Services Home Page

Preformatted forms let your team members contribute to the SharePoint Team Services based Web site simply by filling out lists. You'll find forms for announcements, events, contacts, tasks, surveys, discussions, and links. SharePoint Team

Services also makes it easy to create custom lists by building on existing forms, or creating new ones from scratch[2].

The Document Library feature of SharePoint Team Services provides a single location for storing all your team's work. Transferring documents to the library is simple it just takes a Web browser. And when you assign templates to your document libraries, you guarantee that all documents are consistent and compatible. Powerful text-based search and a familiar folder view make it easy to find documents in the SharePoint team Web site library[2].

Figure 1.6: SharePoint Team Services Document Library

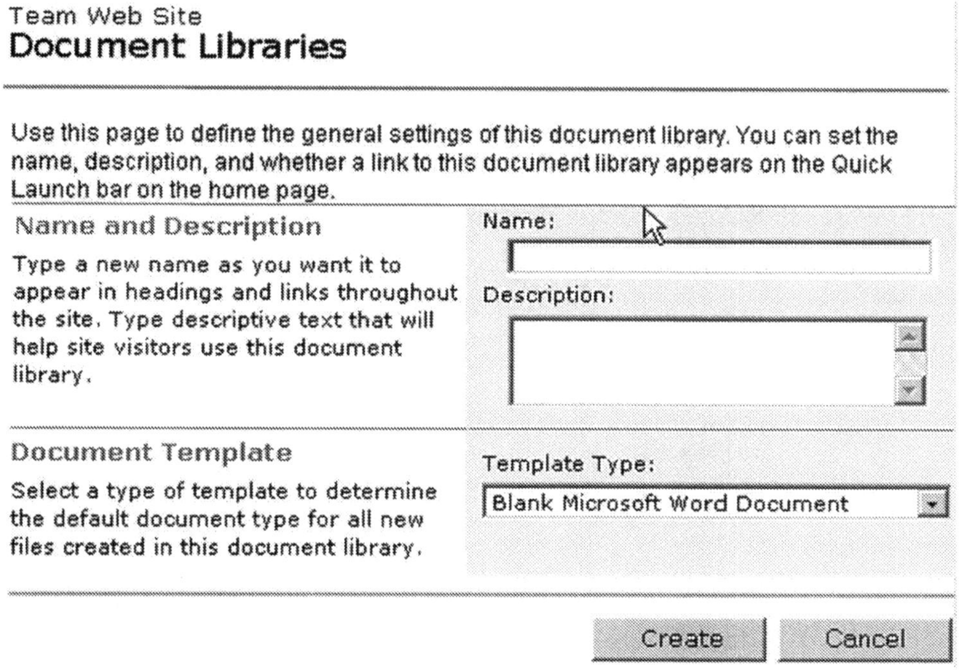

Team Web Site
Document Libraries

Use this page to define the general settings of this document library. You can set the name, description, and whether a link to this document library appears on the Quick Launch bar on the home page.

Name and Description

Type a new name as you want it to appear in headings and links throughout the site. Type descriptive text that will help site visitors use this document library.

Name:

Description:

Document Template

Select a type of template to determine the default document type for all new files created in this document library.

Template Type:

Blank Microsoft Word Document

Create Cancel

Table 1.3: Document List

File Name	Edit	Review Status	Last Modified
Upgrade SQL Server 7 to 2000	✍	Final	12/03/2002
Install Project Server 2002	✍	Approved	11/18/2002
Install SharePoint Team Services	✍	Draft	12/10/2002

SharePoint Team Services helps team members share ideas through subscriptions and notifications that alert everyone to Web site changes; inline document discussions that make it easy to collaborate on specific deliverables without altering original documents; discussion boards that serve as a central forum for specific topics; and surveys, which are a useful way to get targeted responses to key issues[2].

Figure 1.7: SharePoint Team Services Add Subscription

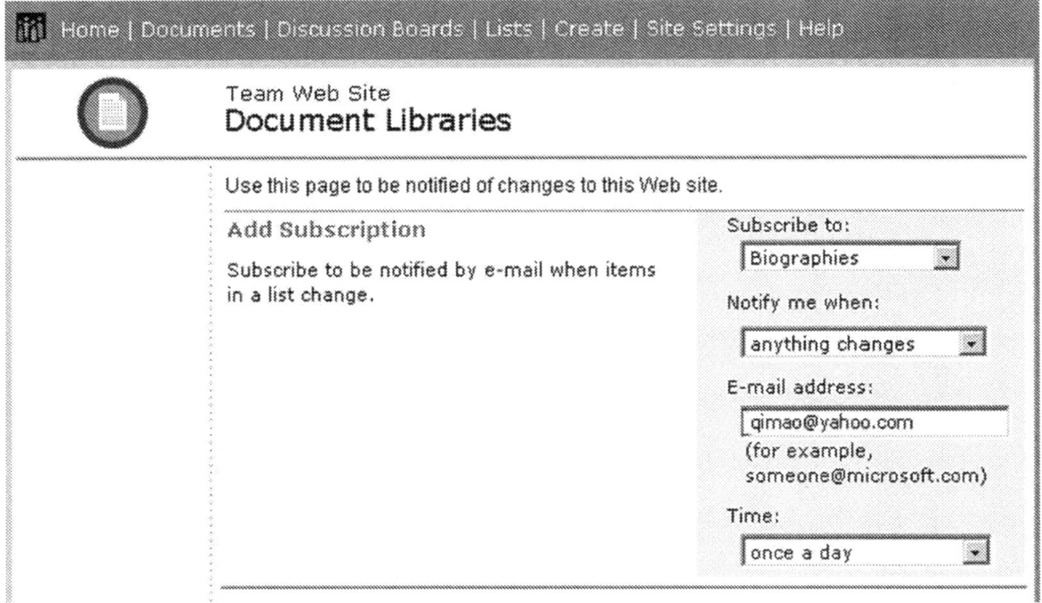

Figure 1.8: SharePoint Team Services Change Notification

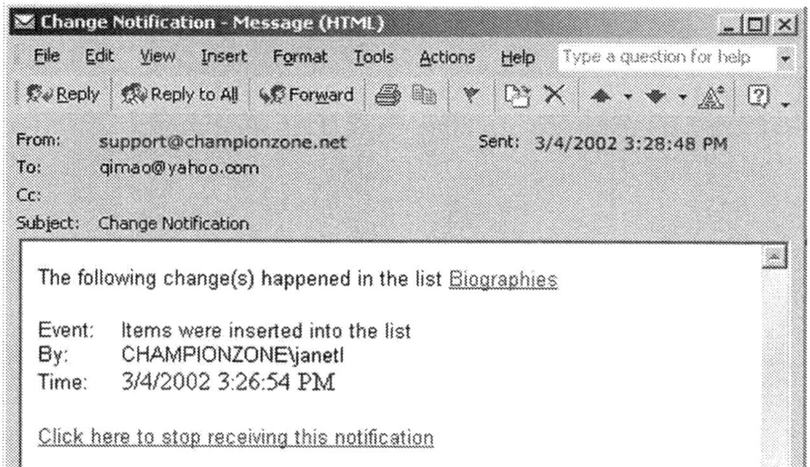

Figure 1.9: SharePoint Team Services Create Page

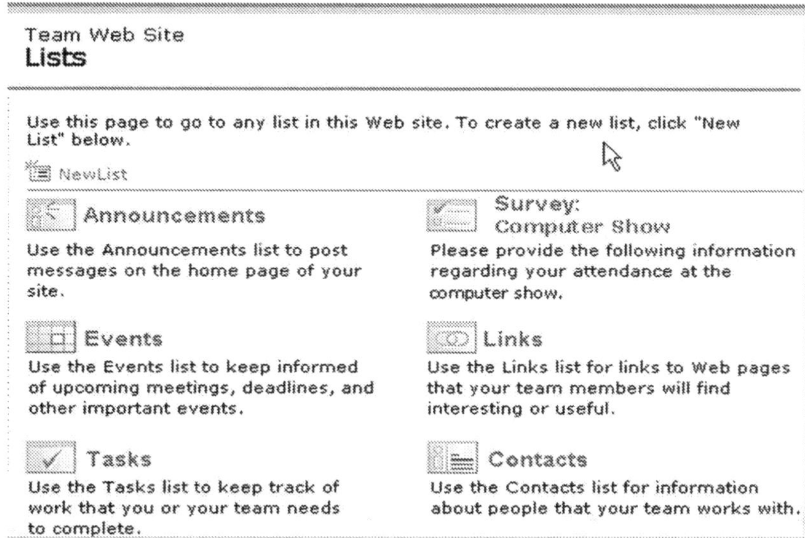

Office XP works seamlessly with SharePoint Team Services, so you can save documents from within any Office application and copy calendars and contact lists directly from Microsoft Outlook version 2002 and paste them directly into your team's Web site. Integration with Microsoft Excel version 2002 means you can also export lists and create Microsoft PivotTables and charts to analyze information or apply text formatting[2].

Extensibility and Interoperability

Microsoft Project 2002 provides customers and solution providers an extensible project management platform for both the client and server. A Microsoft Project Software Developer Kit (SDK) will be available shortly after Microsoft Project 2002 is available. The SDK provides detailed descriptions and sample code for extending Microsoft Project and Project Server. In addition, you can review selected extensibility features of Microsoft Project 2002 by reading the Microsoft Project 2002 Project Guide Architecture and Extensibility and Project Server Architecture and Extensibility white papers.

- **Microsoft Project Professional**

Microsoft Project 2002 continues to provide a rich object model and support for Microsoft Visual Basic for Applications. Developers can access and automate most of the features available from the Microsoft Project user interface, including the new enterprise project management features. New for Microsoft Project 2002 is the ability to open and save projects as XML documents. XML can be extremely useful when exchanging data between applications or systems. The Microsoft Project XML schema is provided in the document Microsoft Project XML (Projxml.xml) that is shipped on the Microsoft Project 2002 CD-ROM. In addition, Microsoft Project 2002 introduces the Project Guide, which integrates HTML pages with the Microsoft Project client. While Microsoft Project 2002 is shipped with a full set of Project Guide pages, developers can replace and extend Project Guide pages with full access to the Microsoft Project object model. Customizing Project Guide pages allows developers to integrate custom solutions into the Microsoft Project user interface.

- **Project Web Access**

  Project Web Access continues to support reuse of the Microsoft Project ActiveX grid controls and Web parts based on Project Web Access pages. New for Microsoft Project 2002 is the ability to extend or modify the Project Web Access menu structure directly from the Project Web Access administrative tools.

- **Project Server**

  The PDS is the key middle tier object for the Microsoft Project enterprise project management features. Developers can call PDS methods through its SOAP interface. PDS allows custom solutions for accessing many of the enterprise features of Microsoft Project Professional and Project Web Access. One key feature of the PDS is support for programmatically defining and updating enterprise outline codes. Where customers want to keep the Project Server enterprise codes consistent with the schema of other business intelligence or line-of-business solutions (such as general ledger, customer relations management, or employee relations), custom applications can be written to query for schema definitions in external systems and then use PDS calls to update the corresponding enterprise codes in the Project Server database. In addition, developers can extend the set of methods exposed by the PDS by registering extension objects on Project Server.

  Developers can extend the Project Server security system. This capability allows solution providers to extend the Project Server with new functionality (for example, risk management), yet allow access to the functionality to be controlled through the Project Server administrative tools.

  Developers can also extend the data used by the Portfolio Analyzer OLAP cube generation service, allowing integration of project data with other project or resource data in the Portfolio Analyzer views.

Licensing

Microsoft Corporation offers **Microsoft Solution for Enterprise Project Management** for medium-size and large businesses. This solution includes:

- Microsoft Project Professional 2002.
- Project Server 2002, which includes Project Web Access the Project Server Web interface.
- Project Server Client Access Licenses (CALs).

The following considerations apply to licensing the Enterprise Project Management solution:

- Project Server 2002 requires Microsoft Windows® 2000 Server.
- Project Server 2002 requires SQL Server 2000 for enterprise project management functionality.
- Project Web Access is the Web interface of Project Server. To create or fully interact with Portfolio Analyzer views in Project Web Access, you will need the Office Web Components that are available in Microsoft Office XP.

You can find more information about licensing from Microsoft's web site at:

💻 http://www.microsoft.com/office/project/howtobuy/default. asp#enterprise

Summary

Collaboration is vital to successful project management. Project Server 2002 continues this leadership by delivering a powerful set of collaborative planning and scheduling tools. As a Web-based companion to Microsoft Project, Project Server 2002 takes advantage of the accessibility and availability of information on Windows-based intranets to deliver collaborative features that encourage participation of the whole project team and provide unprecedented visibility to project information for the entire organization.

Project Server 2002 contributes to the success of a project by ensuring clear communication of project data both up and down the management chain and by allowing project managers to capture the expertise of resources. The involvement of both resources and senior management in the planning process is achieved through the Project Server 2002 client, which allows workers at all levels of the organization to view up-to-date project information and to interact with the project planner by providing input to the schedule and project plan. Through Project Server 2002, even users with limited knowledge of project management methodology and no familiarity with Project can easily view, update, and provide input on the project plan and schedule.

1. Microsoft Project 2002 Enterprise Project Management Architecture Guide. http://msdn.microsoft.com/library/default.asp?url=/library/enus/dnproj2002/html/entprojmgm.asp.

2. SharePoint Team Services Fast Facts. http://www.microsoft.com/frontpage/sharepoint/fastfacts.htm. Microsoft Corportation.

2

Install Project Server 2002

Installing Project Server can be a complex process, including many tasks that must be completed before, during, or after installing the product itself. Project Server can be used with Microsoft Project Standard and Microsoft Project Professional to enable efficient team collaboration between project managers, team members, and other stakeholders. Project teams can review and work with Project Server information by using a Web-based user interface called Project Web Access.

Project team members and other stakeholders can use Project Web Access, licensed separately, to view or work with project information on a Web site, and project managers can update changes to Microsoft Project to keep a project plan up to date.

Requirements

Hardware, system, and feature requirements for the Project Server installation are as follows[1]:

Hardware requirements

- Available hard-disk space: Approximately 70 megabytes (MB) for Project Server. For disk space requirements for additional products and components that are required for many Project Server features, refer to the documentation for those products and components.

- Processor: Intel Pentium 500 Megahertz (MHz) or higher (minimum Intel Pentium III 700 MHz recommended), or similar processor.
- Memory: 128 MB RAM or more (minimum 512 MB recommended).

These requirements are for a default installation. Your hard-disk and memory requirements may vary depending on your configuration and the options you choose.

System requirements

Microsoft Windows 2000 Server Service Pack 1 or later. Additionally, the following components must be installed:

Microsoft Internet Explorer 5 or later, included as a setup option for Microsoft Project 2002, is required for Project Web Access.

- Microsoft Internet Information Server (IIS) version 5.0 or later.
- The Microsoft Management Console (MMC) snap-in for IIS.

Feature requirements

In addition to the system requirements described above, many features of Project Server require additional products and components to be installed:

- SQL Server 2000 Service Pack 1 or later, or Microsoft Desktop Engine (MSDE) 2000 or later.

- SQL Server is required for the enterprise features of Project Server. It must be installed before installing Project Server.
- MSDE is included and installed during the Project Server installation when you use the install now option. MSDE is installed if it's not already on the system and SQL Server is not installed. Microsoft Data Access Components (MDAC) version 2.6 is also installed during the Project Server installation. Installing MDAC requires a reboot on Windows 2000 computers.
- Service packs installed for SQL Server must be the same version as those installed for Analysis Services.

- SQL Server Analysis Services is required for the Portfolio Analyzer feature of Project Server.

> **Note**
>
> - The Portfolio Analyzer feature is only available in association with Microsoft Project Professional.
> - Analysis Services is included with SQL Server.
> - Service packs installed for Analysis Services must be the same version as those installed for SQL Server.

- SharePoint Team Services from Microsoft is required for use of the documents library and issues tracking features of Project Server.

> **Note**
>
> - SharePoint Team Services is included with Project Server. You can install it either before or after you install Project Server.
> - To secure project documents on the server where SharePoint Team Services is installed, that computer must use the NTFS file system.

- Microsoft Office 2000 or later is required on computers using Project Web Access in order to use data access pages.
- Microsoft Office XP is required on computers using Project Web Access to get full advantage of the Office Web Controls (for example, to create new Portfolio Analyzer views).

Project Server is the successor of Project Central. Project Central has most functionalities of Project Server. If you are using Oracle database or your system configuration does not support Project Server, you may consider using Project Central. For more details, you can read the book *Microsoft Project Central: The Complete Reference* (ISBN: 0595232477).

Configuration Scenarios

Before installing Project Server, you need to decide on a configuration that suits your organization's needs. The most effective configuration, which can affect performance, security, ease of administration, and cost of equipment, is determined both by the expected number and types of concurrent users of Project Server and by how often you expect they will use specific features. For example, enterprise features like enterprise templates and enterprise resources may require more server resources than workgroup features.

This chapter provides general guidelines for determining a Project Server configuration that will provide suitable performance, given a set of organizational requirements. Performance is also influenced by hardware and software configurations and is likely to change significantly as a server's environment and configuration change. The proposed configuration should be thoroughly pilot-tested in your environment before you finalize the configuration of any server, including Project Server.

Basic configuration scenarios

Project Server is typically installed in some variation of either of two basic configurations. Either configuration may be suitable for your organization (or even a combination of both, for example, when temporarily supporting both Project Server 2002 2000 and Project Server 2002 during deployment of Project Server) .

Workgroup scenario

The workgroup server scenario is most similar to the average Project Server 2002 2000 configuration. This scenario supports a single workgroup, can be managed by individuals within the workgroup, and is installed on consumer-grade hardware.

Table 2.1: Workgroup scenario

Software	Typical Configuration
MSDE	Installed on local computer
SQL Server	Installed on local computer
SharePoint Team Services	Installed on local computer (installing on a separate, dedicated computer is recommended)
Load balancing	Not used
Clustering	Not used

Enterprise scenario

The enterprise server scenario describes an installation where the features of the workgroup scenario are insufficient; typically, this is an environment where the ability to scale to large numbers of users is required. The server is managed by professional IT staff and is installed on commercial-grade hardware. Project Server is installed on its own computer, and the Project Server database is installed on a separate database server computer. To support large numbers of users and heavier server loads, Project Server is likely to be configured to take advantage of load balancing techniques.

Table 2.2: Enterprise scenario

Software	Typical Configuration
Partitions	Two, with the operating system installed on one and Project Server (and other applications) on the other
MSDE	Not supported
SQL Server	Installed on a separate, dedicated computer
Analysis Services	Installed on a separate, dedicated computer
SharePoint Team Services	Installed on a separate, dedicated computer
Load balancing	Supported
Clustering	Supported

Usage scenarios

The number and type of users and amount of data refreshed to the client are the major factors that affect performance. In normal use of Project Web Access, many users are logged on performing different operations. This pattern of usage, simultaneous operations requiring the production or refresh of a page containing many records (such as assignments or task views), results in the highest response times. The amount of data presented by each operation to each user is a greater factor in performance than the total number of projects, tasks, and assignments in the database.

Therefore, the most effective way to determine your usage scenario is to determine how often per week each user connects to Project Server to view or update task assignments. Unless your organization requires a rigidly controlled timesheet processing cycle, each team member and project manager will probably connect to the server several times a week. Project managers will also spend significantly more time using Microsoft Project than Project Web Access. Other managers and executives using features such as Portfolio Modeler, Portfolio Analyzer, and the Project Center place less load on the system and are also less frequent users than project managers and team members.

Tip

For larger implementations, multiple Web servers using a load balancing system are recommended. In such situations, database server hardware should be considerably more robust than the hardware used for each Web server.

Installation

This section describes the steps required to install Project Server with the Setup program. Setup should only be run after verifying requirements and configuration scenarios.

Insert the Project Server CD into the CD-ROM drive, or connect to a network installation point. If you are installing from the Project Server CD with AutoPlay enabled, click Server installation in the Project Server 2002 Setup program, or, on the Project Server CD-ROM (or network install point), browse for and run the file named Setup.exe. You should see the Project Server 2002 Setup interface as shown in Figure 2.1.

Figure 2.1: Project Server 2002 Setup

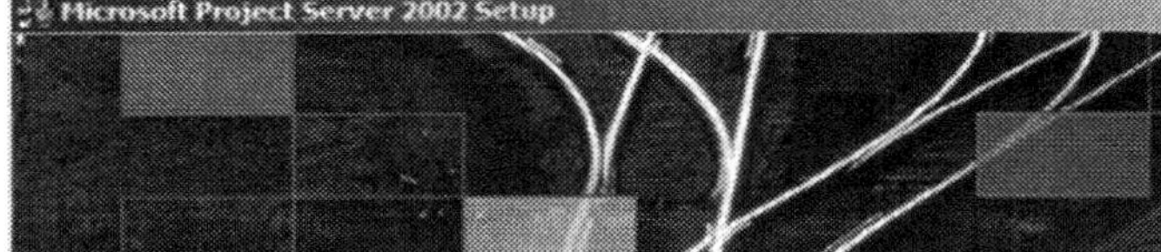

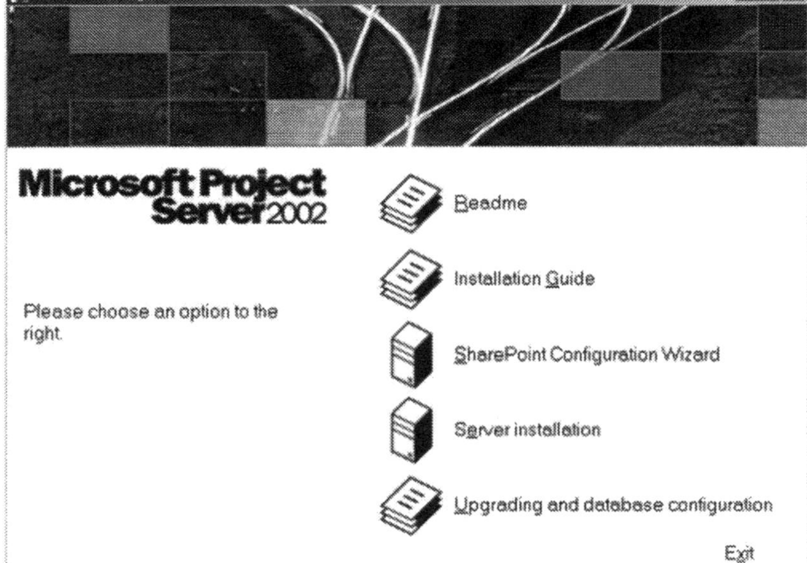

On the User information page of the Setup program, enter your user name, initials, organization, and Product Key, and then click **Next**. Read and accept the license agreement, and then click **Next**.

Figure 2.2: Project Server 2002 Setup

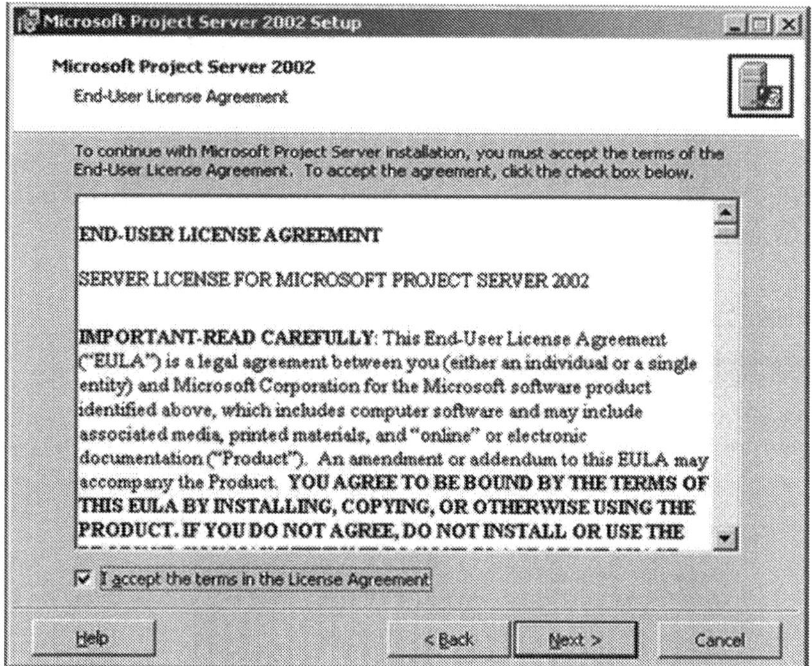

In the Install to box, specify where you want to install Project Server. The default location is C:\Program Files\Project Server.

Install using the **Custom** option if you have already installed SQL Server. In addition to the benefits gained by using SQL Server, this option allows you to take full advantage of enterprise features in Project Server.

This option makes it possible to install Project Server, the database, and SharePoint Team Services on separate computers.

Install using the **install now** option if you want to use Microsoft Desktop Engine (MSDE) as the database for Project Server and do not require the enterprise features of Project Server. MSDE is limited in areas such as the number of concurrent users it can support and does not include features like full-text indexing and database maintenance services. For a more secure and scalable solution, use the Custom option with a SQL Server database.

Project Server and the database are installed on the same computer. SharePoint Team Services can be installed to the same computer or a separate computer.

Figure 2.3: Project Server 2002 Setup

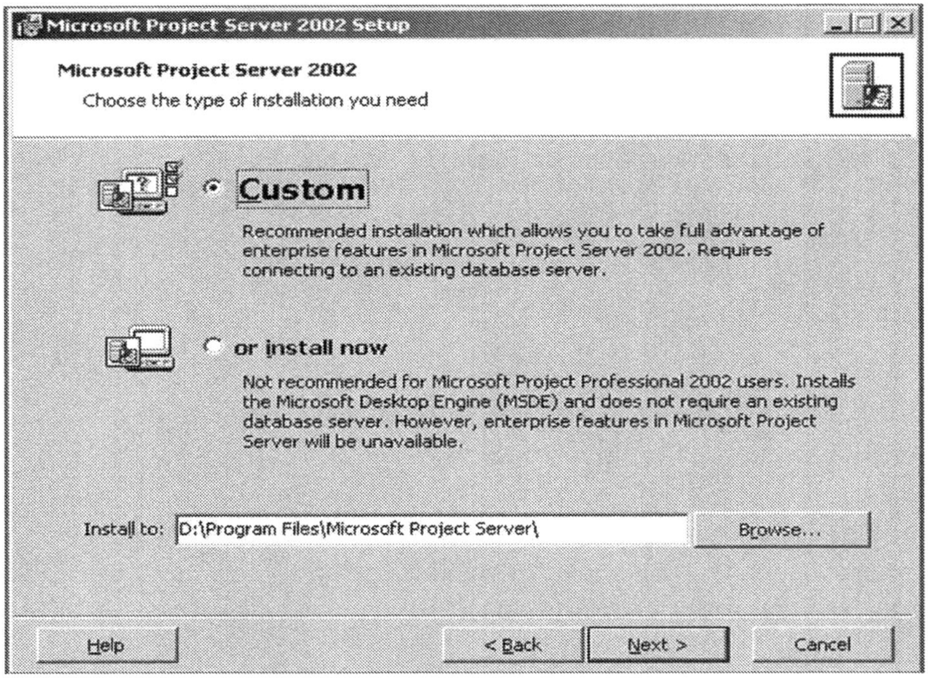

The following steps are using Custom option.

Step 1: Entering Database Server Information

- Choose Connect to an existing database if you have an existing Project Server database, for example, when upgrading from Project Server 2002 or after manually running the database setup scripts.
- You should choose Create a new database if you want the Setup program to automatically create a new database, tables, and default values, including user roles, on a SQL Server computer.

Figure 2.4: Project Server 2002 Setup

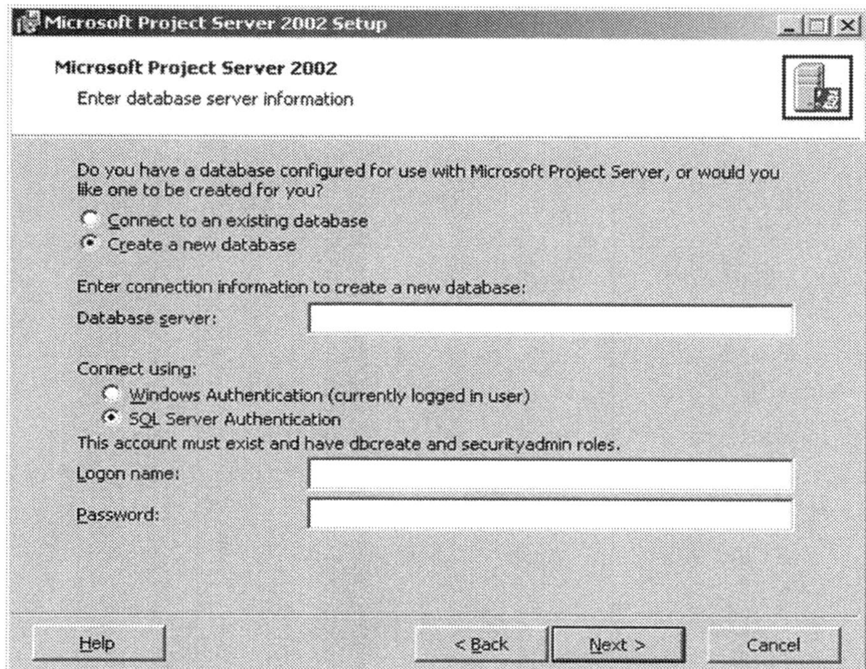

You can skip the information in Table 2.3 if you selected **Create a New Database.**

Table 2.3: How to Manually set up the Project Server database and tables (optional)

Project Server Setup automatically runs several SQL Server scripts when creating a new database as part of the installation process. If you would prefer to run those scripts manually, perhaps because of database policies or procedures in your organization, you can follow the steps listed below.
Caution These steps should only be followed if you are familiar with SQL and SQL Server.

1. Insert the Project Server CD into the CD-ROM drive, or connect to a network installation point.

2. From a command prompt, access the CD-ROM drive (or network installation point), and then go to the folder \SUPPORT\DATABASE.

3. Type the following commands to create the Project Server database and tables: the file Setupdb.cmd can be used to run all of the following scripts at once.

- To create the database:
  osql -S *server_name* -U *account_name* -P *password* -i "CREATE DATABASE *database_name*"
  where *server_name*, *account_name*, *password*, and *database_name* are placeholders. For example:
  osql -S ProjServer01 -U sa -P SApass*22 -i "CREATE DATABASE ProjectServer"
  Note The parameter letters S, U, P, and i are case sensitive.

- To create the Microsoft Project 2002 table schema (table names beginning with "MSP_"):
  osql -S *server_name* -U *account_name* -P *password* -d *database_name* -i Projtbls.sql
  where *database_name* is the name of the database you created in step 3.
  Note The parameter letters S, U, P, d, and i are case sensitive.
- To create the stored procedures that Project Server uses to ensure project data integrity:
  osql -S *server_name* -U *account_name* -P *password* -d *database_name* -i Projsps.sql
- To create the Project Web Access table schema (table names beginning with "MSP_WEB"):
  osql -S *server_name* -U *account_name* -P *password* -d *database_name* -i Webtbls.sql
- To create the tables that store the data used when viewing projects in the Project Center (table names beginning with "MSP_VIEW"):
  osql -S *server_name* -U *account_name* -P *password* -d *database_name* -i Viewtbls.sql
- To create the Project Server OLAP cube staging tables (table names beginning with "MSP_CUBE"):
  osql -S *server_name* -U *account_name* -P *password* -d *database_name* -i Cubetbls.sql
- To create the Project Server stored procedures:
  osql -S *server_name* -U *account_name* -P *password* -d *database_name* -i Websps.sql
- To create the Project Server security views:
  osql -S *server_name* -U *account_name* -P *password* -d *database_name* -i Secviews.sql

- To insert localized data into the Microsoft Project 2002 tables:
  osql -S *server_name* -U *account_name* -P *password* -d *database_name* -i Locdata.sql
  Note This script is found in the folder that corresponds to the locale ID (LCID) for your language. The English version, for example, can be found in the \SUPPORT\DATABASE\1033 folder.

- To insert the Enterprise Global and Enterprise Resources into the Microsoft Project 2002 tables:
  osql -S *server_name* -U *account_name* -P *password* -d *database_name* -i Eglobal.sql
  Note This script is found in the folder that corresponds to the locale ID (LCID) for your language. The English version, for example, can be found in the \SUPPORT\DATABASE\1033 folder.

- To insert localized data into the Project Web Access tables:
  osql -S *server_name* -U *account_name* -P *password* -d *database_name* -i Insdef.sql
  Note This script is found in the folder that corresponds to the locale ID (LCID) for your language. The English version, for example, can be found in the \SUPPORT\DATABASE\1033 folder.

- To insert language pack data into the Project Web Access tables:
  osql -S *server_name* -U *account_name* -P *password* -d *database_name* -i Insdeflp.sql
  Notes
  - This script is found in the folder that corresponds to the locale ID (LCID) for your language. The English version, for example, can be found in the \SUPPORT\DATABASE\1033 folder.

If you are installing a localized version of Project Server, you should also run the English version of this script after the version specific to your language.

4. In order for Microsoft Internet Information Server to have access to the Project Server database, create a SQL Server user account for it (or have an existing Integrated Windows authentication trusted account), grant it access permission to the database, and assign it the MSProjectServerRole role.

5. In order for Microsoft Project Professional to have access to the Project Server database, create a SQL Server user account for it, grant it access permission to the database, and assign it the MSProjectRole role.

6. Run the Project Server Setup program and click Custom. On the database connection page of the Setup program, click Connect to an existing database, and then enter the requested information for the database you manually created.

Note Using the OSQL tool is required because the lines in some of the scripts are too long for Query Analyzer. The OSQL tool can be found in the \SUPPORT\DATABASE folder. The previous steps may also be used to reset a Project Server database to the installed default values

Step 2: Entering Analysis Services Connection Information

The Windows user account that is used to connect to the Analysis Services computer must be a member of the OLAP Administrators group on that computer. This information must be entered in the format domain\account. (Analysis Services is used by the Portfolio Analyzer feature in Project Web Access. The Portfolio Analyzer feature is only available if you are using Microsoft Project Professional.)

Tip

If you choose to enter this information later, you can use Project Web Access to connect to Project Server, and then click Admin in the top link bar to go to the Admin center. In the side pane, click Manage enterprise features, and then select the Enable enterprise features check box. Next, in the side pane, under Enterprise Options, click Specify resource and OLAP cube updates. Click Yes to build an OLAP cube of project data, and then enter the name of the Analysis Services computer in the Analysis Server box and a name for the cube in the Cube name box.

Note

If you choose to enter information about this user account later, you must run PSCOMPlus.exe (found in the \Project Server\Bin\1033 folder of the Project Server computer) before you can build a cube. (This folder, 1033, contains the files for the English version. Files for other languages can be found in the folder that corresponds to the locale ID [LCID] for that language.) PSCOMPlus is used to provide the name of a user account (in the format domain\account) that should be impersonated by a COM+ application to allow Project Server to connect to the Analysis Services computer.

Figure 2.5: Project Server 2002 Setup

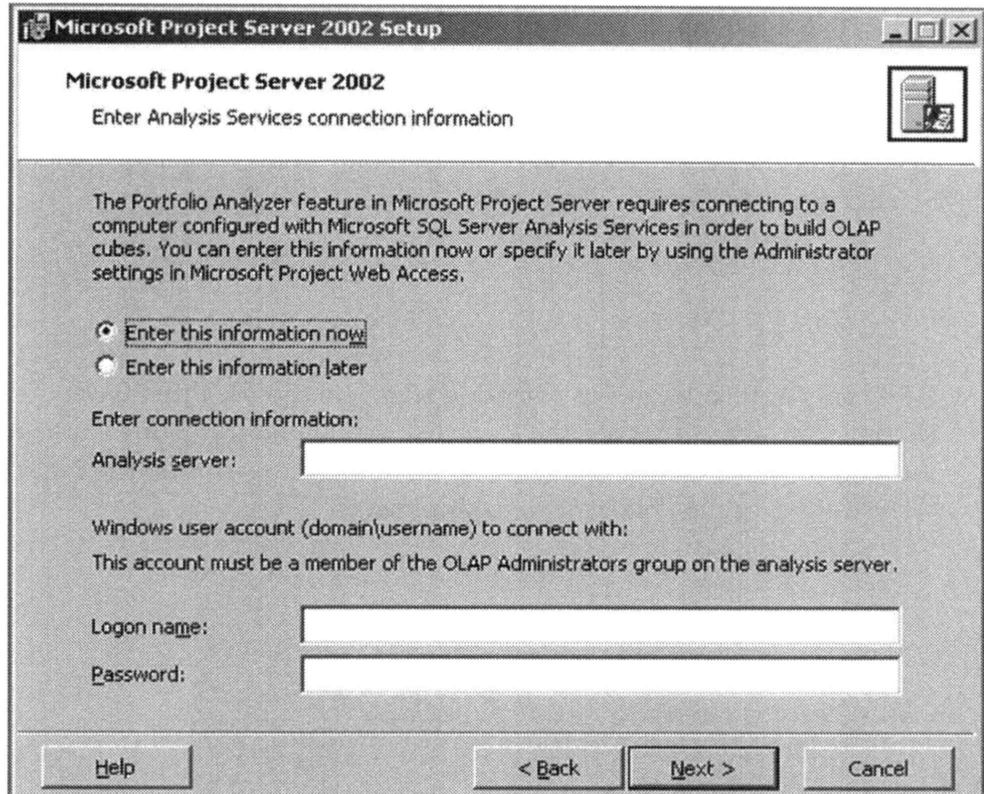

Step 3: Enter Web server information

You can enter email links and Web server information during this step:

- E-mail links in notifications and reminders will be incorrect until this information has been provided.

- The address for the Project Server computer that is accessible to users within your corporate network may point to a Web server that supports Secure Sockets Layer (SSL) encryption.
- If you provide an address for a Project Server computer that is accessible to users outside your corporate network, it should point to a Web server that supports SSL encryption for improved security.

Tip

If you choose to enter this information later, you can use Project Web Access to connect to Project Server, and then click Admin in the top link bar to go to the Admin center. In the side pane, click Manage organization to enter the Web address for the Project Server computer.

Figure 2.6: Project Server 2002 Setup

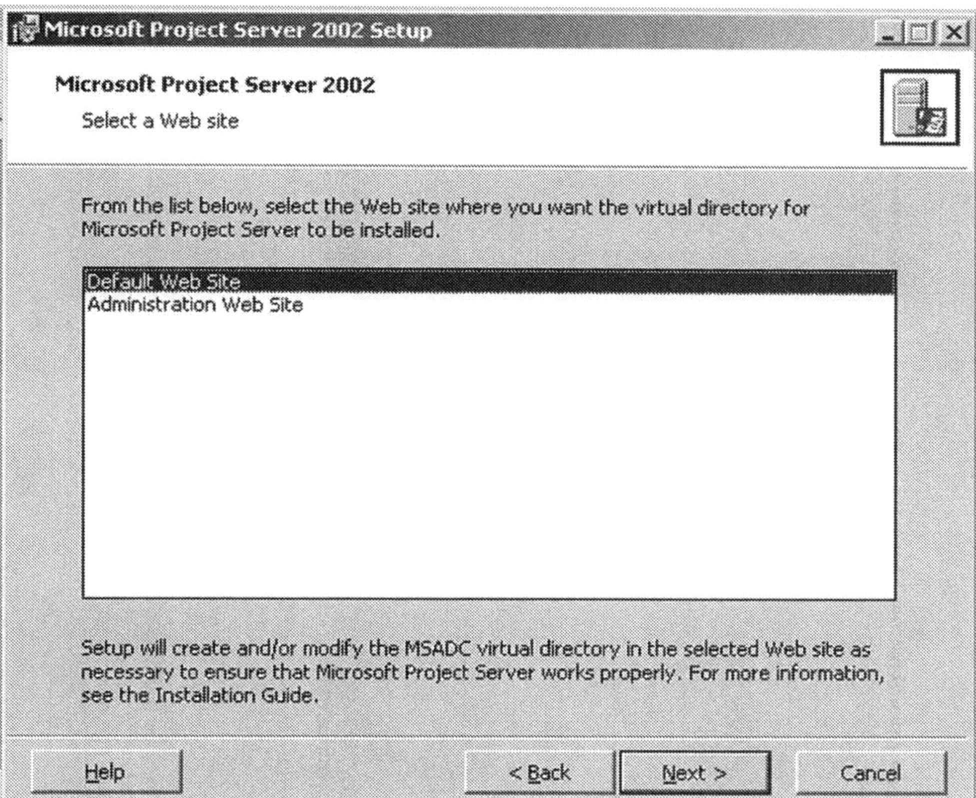

Figure 2.7: Project Server 2002 Setup

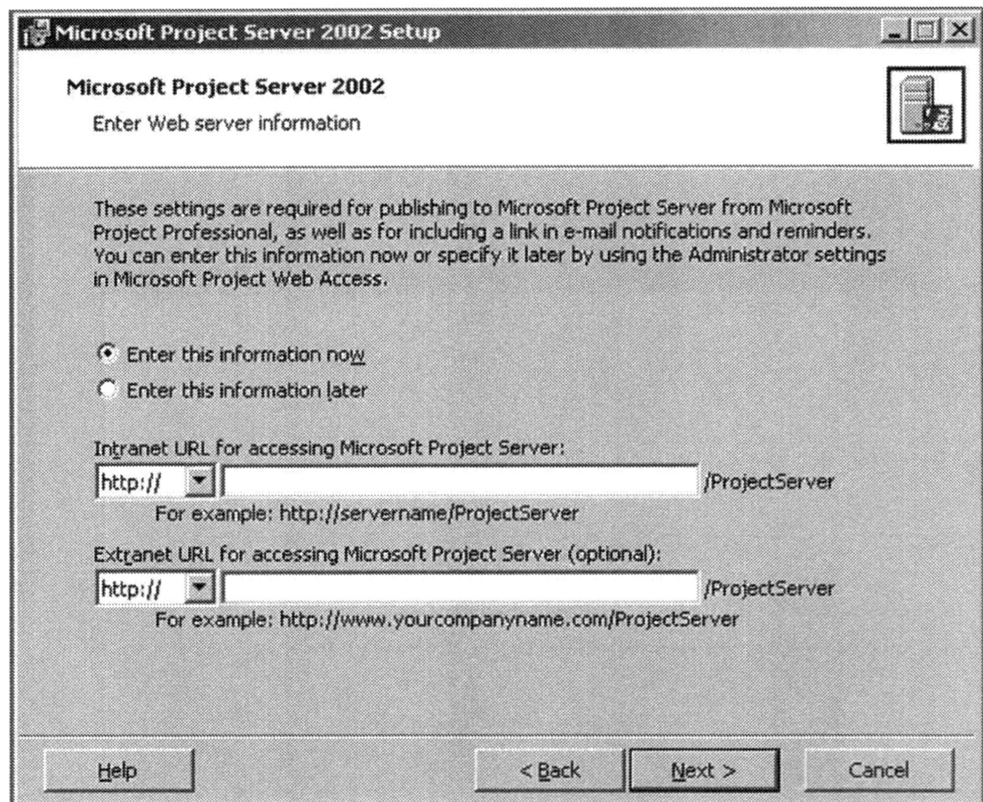

Step 4: Connect to a Web server running SharePoint Team Services

The following is additional information about connecting to a Web server running SharePoint Team Services when installing Project Server:

When entering information for the server running SharePoint Team Services

If SharePoint Team Services is already installed and configured to use the Secure Sockets Layer (SSL), the information for this step should be entered later by using Project Web Access.

- Web server port is the TCP port on the Web server that was opened for a site you created, in addition to the default Web site, for hosting SharePoint Team Services. The default Web site port is port 80.
- SharePoint administration port is the TCP port on the Web server running SharePoint Team Services that was opened so that the administrative features of SharePoint Team Services can be used from a remote computer.

Enter information about a Windows user account (in the format domain\account) that Project Server should use to connect to the computer running SharePoint Team Services in the Logon name and Password boxes. This user account must be a member of the Administrators group on the SharePoint Team Services computer.

If a new Windows user account was created for this purpose and the User must change password at next logon check box is set for the account, that user must log in and change the password before Project Server can be configured to connect with SharePoint Team Services.

Although a Windows domain user account is recommended, you can use a local account if the same account name and password are used on both the Project Server and SharePoint Team Services computers.

If you encounter an error that Project Server was unable to connect to the Web server running SharePoint Team Services, it may be because Project Server communicates with SharePoint Team Services by using the XMLHTTP protocol. In order for Project Server to communicate with the SharePoint Team Services computer successfully, the Project Server computer must be configured to connect through a proxy server if your organization uses one. (This requirement is true even when Project Server and SharePoint Team Services are installed on the same computer.)

To configure Project Server for a proxy server, run the WinHTTP proxy configuration utility by typing proxycfg -d -p *proxy-server-list optional-bypass-list* at a command prompt, where *proxy-server-list* is a space-delimited list of one or more proxy servers and *optional-bypass-list* is a space-delimited list of servers that should be accessed directly. If a proxy server is not specified for the given protocol, the -d option specifies that the server should be accessed directly instead. After running Proxycfg, restart Internet Services by typing iisreset at a command prompt. ProxyCfg.exe can be found by searching for "WinHTTP Proxy Configuration Utility" on MSDN. (After installing Project Server, the file can also be found in the Program Files\Project Server\Bin folder on the Project Server computer.)

For more information about Proxycfg, including details about the *proxy-server-list* and *optional-bypass-list* parameters, search for "Using the WinHTTP Proxy Configuration Utility" on MSDN.

If your organization does not use a proxy server, Proxycfg must still be used to set the default authentication policy.

When entering information for the SharePoint Team Services database

If SharePoint Team Services is already installed and configured to use SSL, the information for this step should be entered later by using Project Web Access.

Enter information about a Windows user account (in the format domain\account) that Project Server should use to connect to the SharePoint Team Services database in the Logon name and Password boxes. This user account only requires db_datareader access to the SharePoint Team Services database.

If a new Windows user account was created for this purpose and the User must change password at next logon check box is set for the account, that user must log on and change the password before Project Server can be configured to connect with the SharePoint Team Services database.

Although a Windows domain user account is recommended, you can use a local account if the same account name and password are used on both the Project Server and SQL Server computers.

Tip

If you choose to enter information about the server running SharePoint Team Services and the SharePoint Team Services database later, you can use Project Web Access to connect to Project Server, and then click **Admin** in the top link bar to go to the Admin center. In the side pane, under **Options**, click **Connect** to servers, and then click **Add server**.

If you choose to enter information about the server running SharePoint Team Services and the SharePoint Team Services database later, you should run PSCOMPlus.exe (found in the \Project Server\Bin\1033 folder of the Project Server computer) before connecting with Project Web Access to provide this information. (This folder, 1033, contains the files for the English version. Files for other languages can be found in the folder that corresponds to the locale ID [LCID] for that language.) PSCOMPlus is used to provide the name of a user account (in the format domain\account) that should be impersonated by a COM+ application to allow Project Server to connect to the SharePoint Team Services and SharePoint Team Services database computers.

Figure 2.8: Project Server 2002 Setup

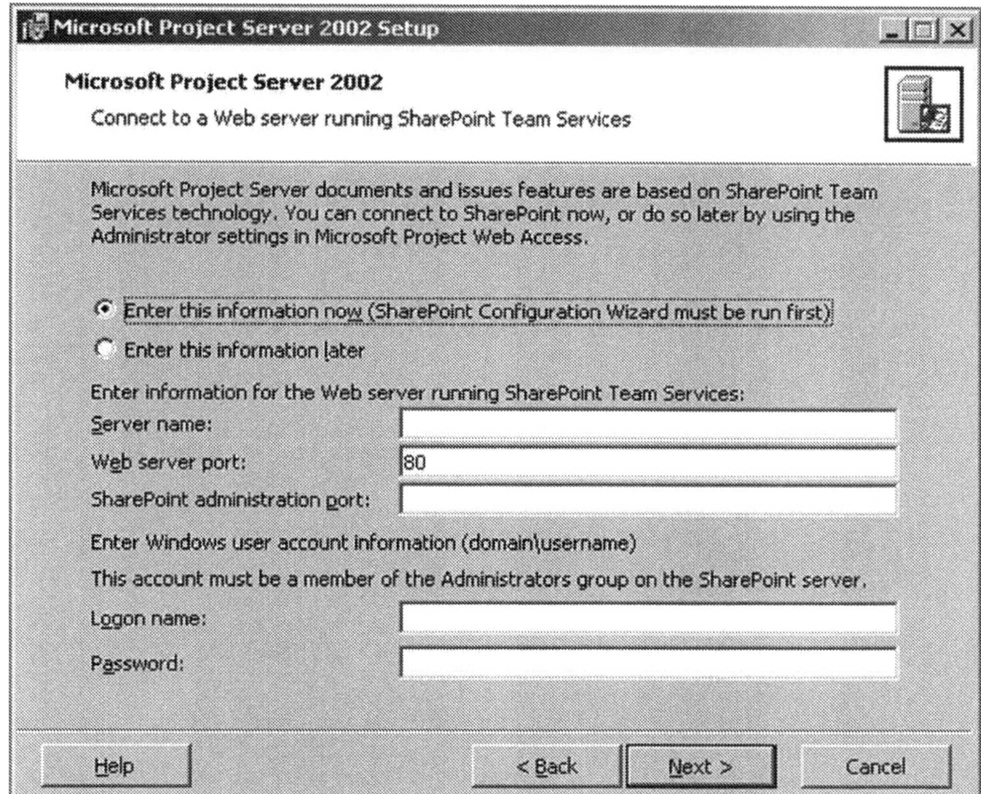

Step 5: Choose a Version of Project

During this step, you will choose compatible versions of Microsoft Project with Project Server 2002:

Figure 2.9: Project Server 2002 Setup

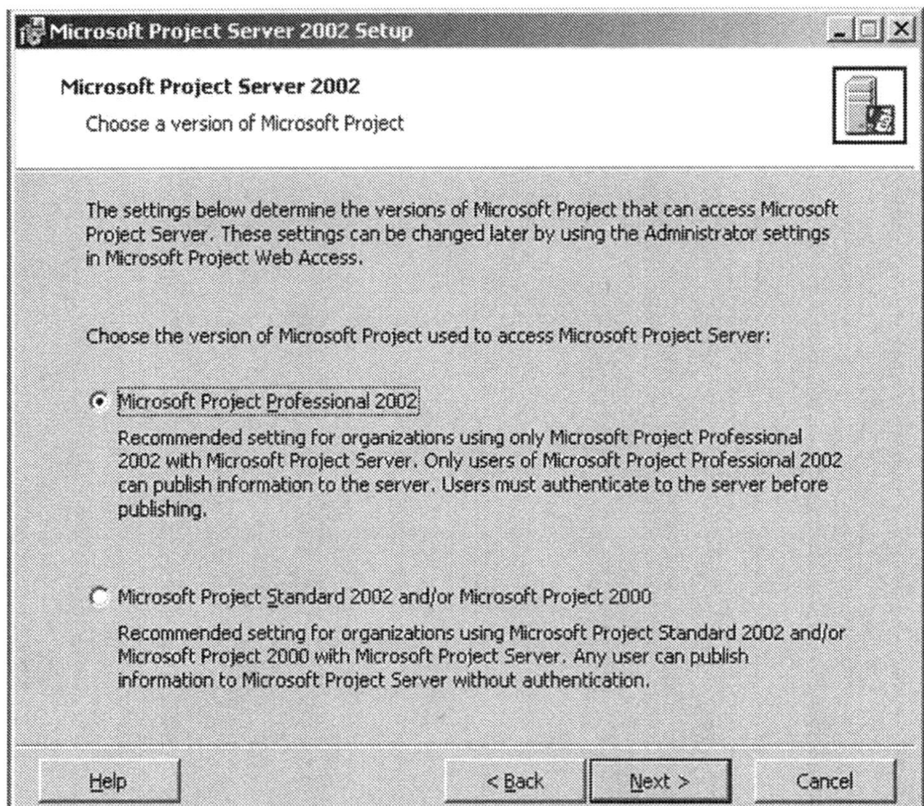

Step 6: Enter Administrator Password Information

During this step, you will enter administrator password information.

Figure 2.10: Project Server 2002 Setup

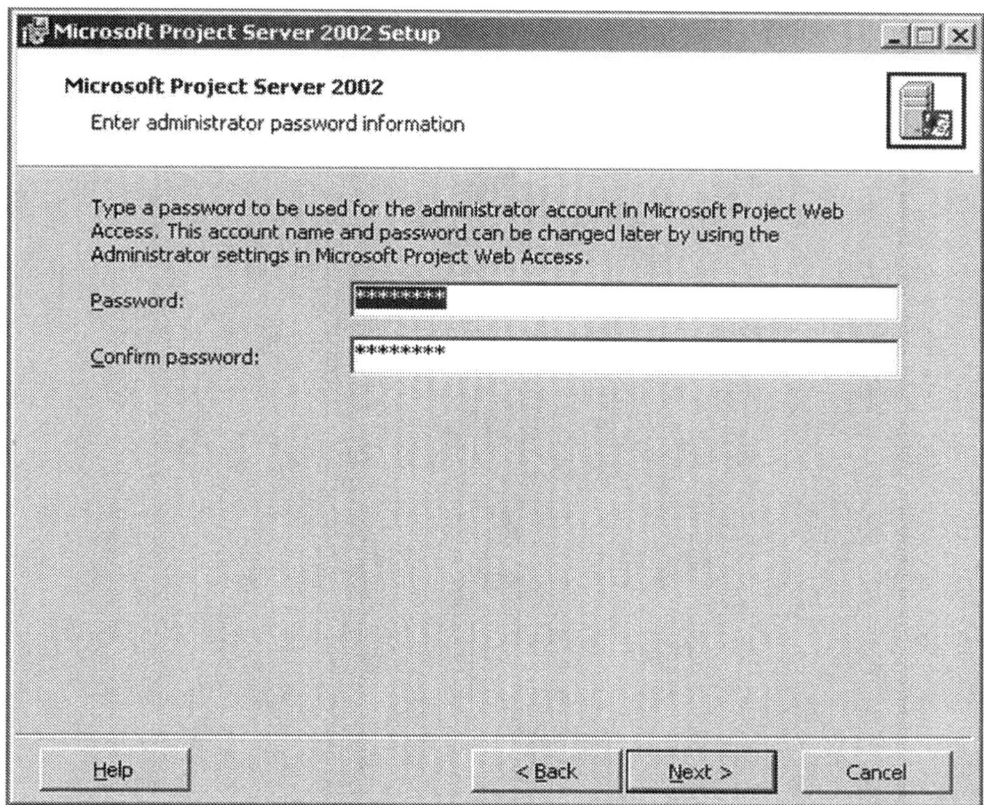

Step 7: Install

Click Install to install Project Server.

Figure 2.11: Project Server 2002 Setup

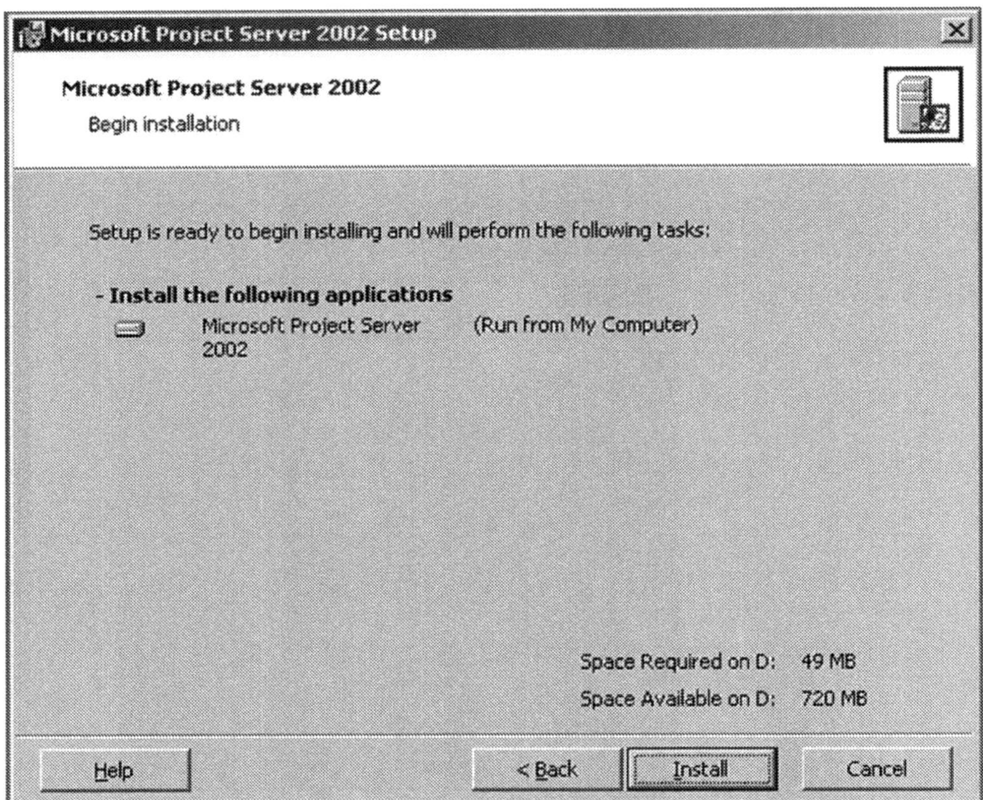

Figure 2.12: Project Server 2002 Setup

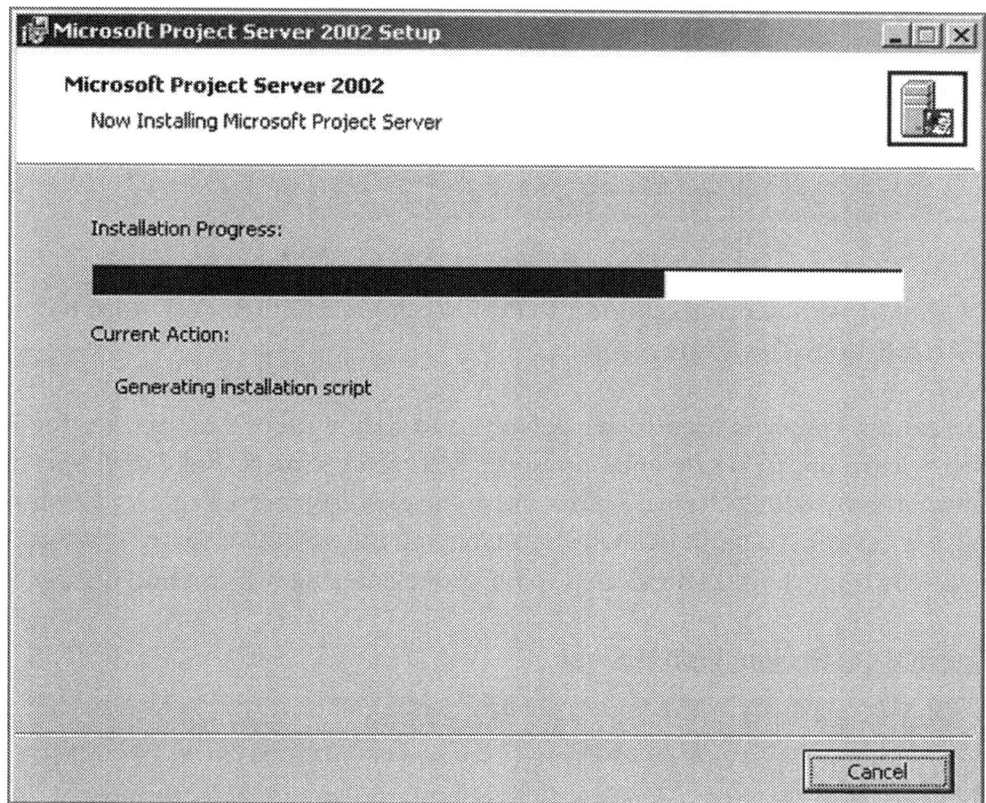

If you see the setup confirmation box, congratulations. You have successfully setup Project Server 2002.

Figure 2.13: Project Server 2002 Confirmation

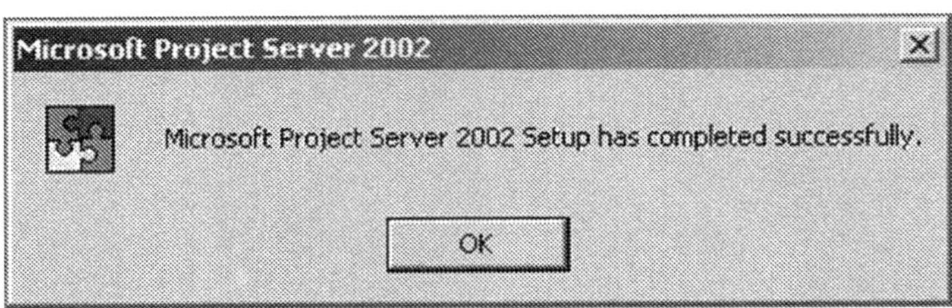

Use Project Web Access to connect to Project Server, and then click Admin in the top link bar to go to the Admin center.

The Admin center is used to set defaults and define users and security for Project Web Access and to set defaults for some Microsoft Project and Project Server features. After installing Project Server, finish the process by creating user accounts, setting permissions, defining views, and managing other Project Server settings. This is especially important if you elected to postpone entering information during setup.

Figure 2.14: Project Web Access

Microsoft Project
Web Access

What is Microsoft Project Web Access?

Setting up a Microsoft Project Server account

Log on using a different Microsoft Windows user account

Log on using your Microsoft Windows user account

Welcome to Microsoft Project Web Access

Please log on.

User name:

Password:

Type in your user name and password. If you do not have a user accou
Instructions on how to get an account set up on the Microsoft Project S

Copyright © 1990-2002 Microsoft Corporation. All rights reserved. Lice

Once you logged into Project Web Access, you should be able to see three function panes: top, left, and right.

The right pane has three lists: tasks, status reports, and issues. You should be alerted by any new items for tasks, status reports, and issues. The right pane gives users an overview of their to-do list:

Home

Welcome to Microsoft Project Web Access, Jennifer Schafer

Tasks

You have 2 new tasks assigned to you.

Status Reports

Upcoming status reports to submit:

- New Status Report Due on 06/16/03
- Windows.Net Status Report Due on 06/19/03

Issues

You have no active issues assigned to you.

Use the tabs across the top and the links on the left to navigate through Microsoft Project Web Access.

The top pane has links to all the major function areas: Home, Tasks, Projects, Status Reports, documents, issues, logout, and help. Users can click on any tab to work on that area:

Home | Tasks | Projects | Status Reports | Documents | Issues | Logout | Help

The left pane has a list of activities: change password, set my e-mail notifications and reminders, set e-mail reminders for my resources, and go offline:

Activities in Home:

Home Page
Change Password
Set my e-mail notifications and reminders
Set e-mail reminders for my resources
Go Offline

Install another language version

To install another language version of Project Server, do not use the Project Server setup program. If you attempt to run the installation program twice, you will not be able to install a second copy of Project Server. Use the Project Server Multilingual User Interface Packs to install different language versions of Project Server. These can be found in the Toolbox in the Microsoft Project 2002 Resource Kit:

http://www.microsoft.com/office/project/prk/2000/

Installing additional language versions of Microsoft Project will not affect the language used in the Documents and Issues centers of Project Web Access; the language for these centers is determined by the installation language of SharePoint Team Services from Microsoft.

Summary

This chapter covers the process of installing Project Server 2002. Depending on your organization needs, the installing process can be complex. You must ensure all the requirements are met prior to the installation. Next chapter covers the process of integrate SharePoint Team Services with Project Server 2002.

---

1. Project Server Installation Guide. Microsoft Corporation, 2002.

3

Integrate with SharePoint Team Services

By integrating SharePoint Team Services with Project Server, Microsoft Project can leverage the document management technology (document library and list management technology) of SharePoint Team Services and provide a method that's easy to set up and use for sharing project-related documents and issues with team members and other stakeholders. Because SharePoint Team Services is fully integrated with Microsoft Office XP, it's especially useful for storing Office XP documents[1].

Taking full advantage of the Web-based team collaboration features of Microsoft Project, SharePoint Team Services allows you to integrate documents and issues with the project management process[1].

Install SharePoint Team Services

You can install SharePoint Team Services from Project Server Setup interface. Read and accept the license agreement, and then click **Next**.

Figure 3.1: SharePoint Team Services Setup

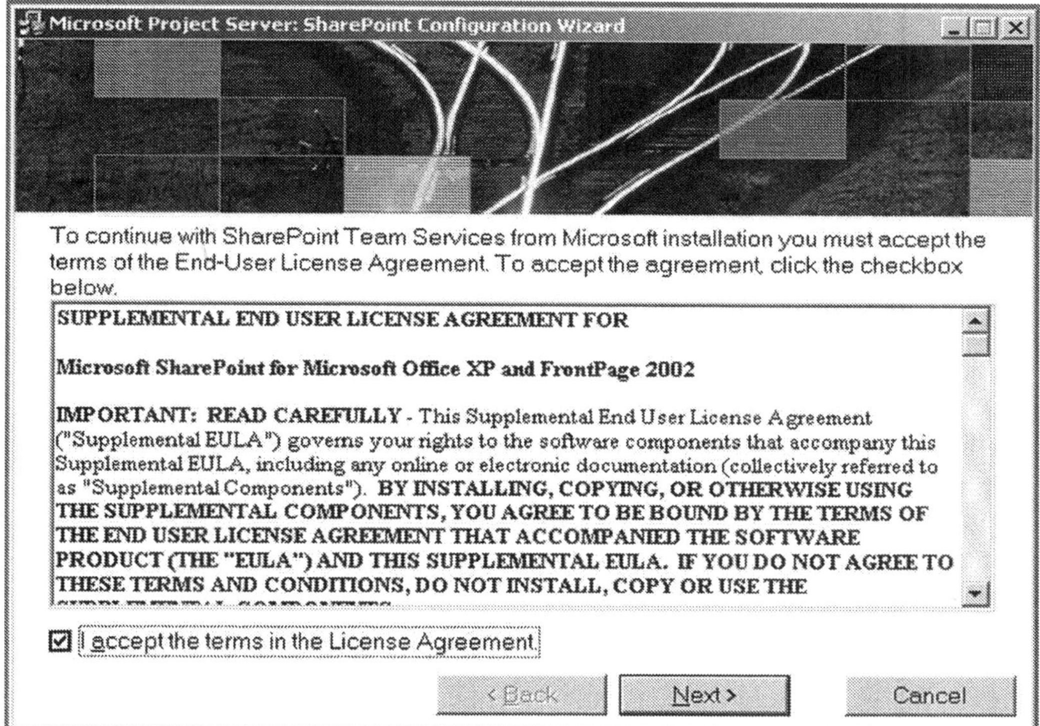

Enter the SQL Server database server name, database administration user name, and database administration password to use for any web sites running SharePoint Team Services:

Figure 3.2: SharePoint Team Services Setup

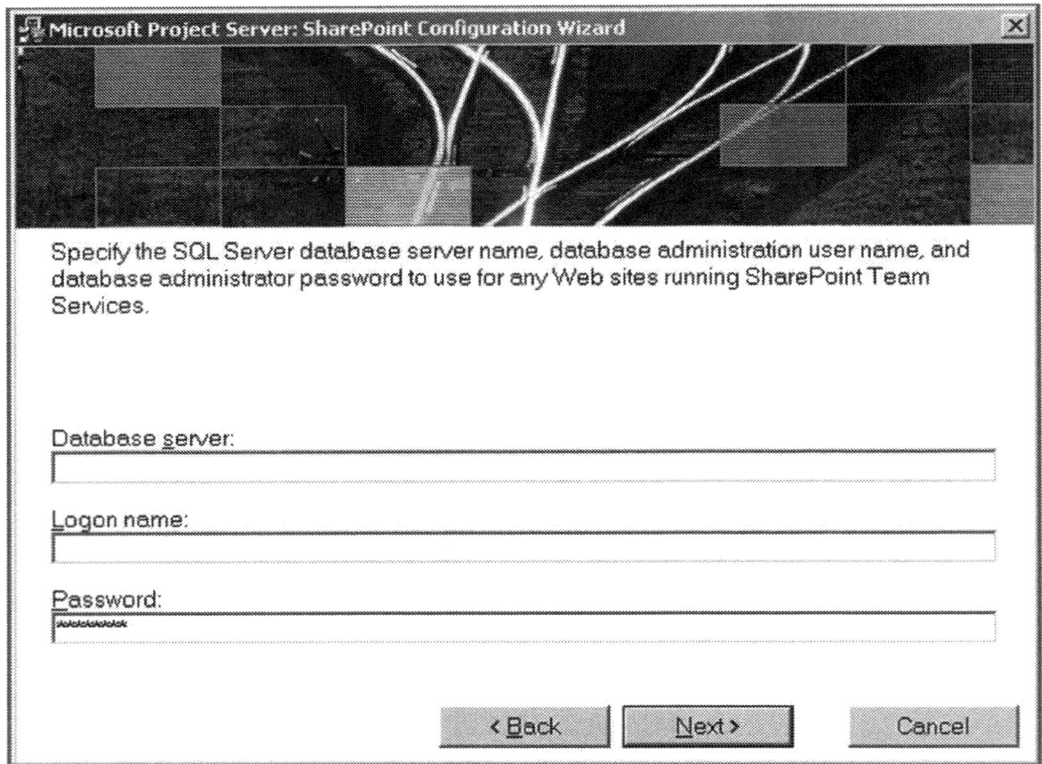

You will be prompted when the installation process completed.

Figure 3.3: SharePoint Team Services Setup

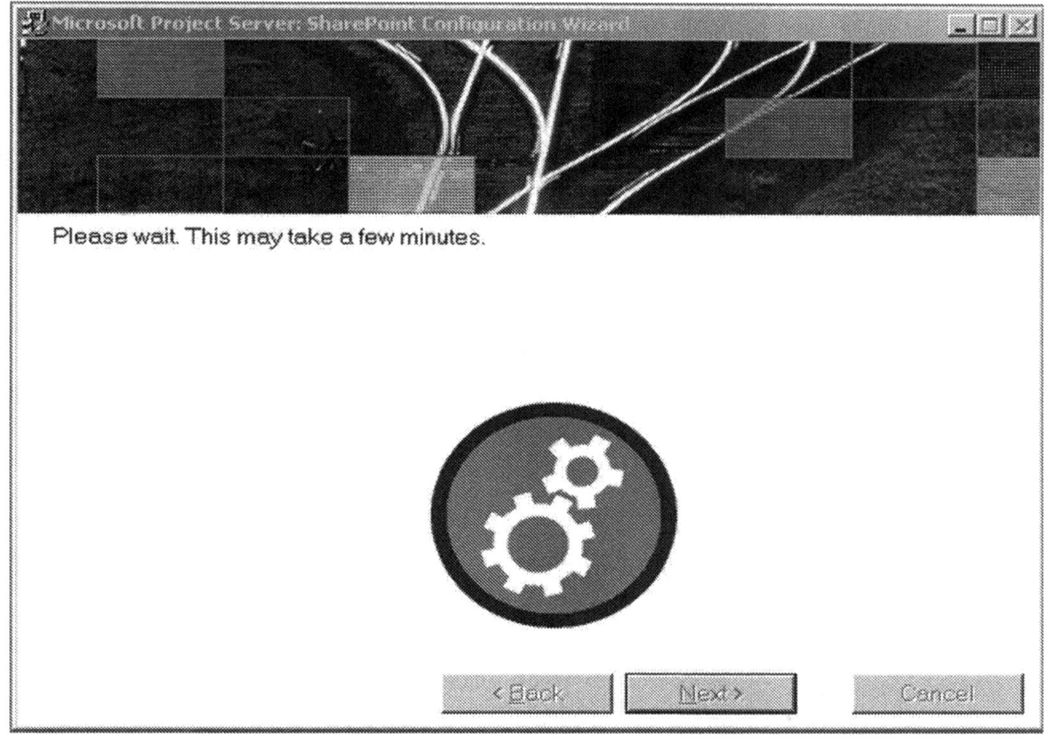

Note

If SharePoint Team Services is already installed with another program, such as Office XP with FrontPage or FrontPage 2002, Project Server Setup automatically configures SharePoint Team Services exclusively for Project Server. For this reason, it is recommended that you dedicate a physical server with SharePoint Team Services to Project Server.

Features of SharePoint Team Services

SharePoint Team Services is integrated with Project Server to make communicating and sharing project information easier. With Project Server, SharePoint Team Services works as a component of the server rather than a stand-alone program. Project Server automatically configures SharePoint Team Services, but some manual configuration and administration may be required as well. For SharePoint Team Services to work with Project Server, Microsoft Windows user accounts (domain and local) must be used.

Figure 3.4: SharePoint Team Services Home Page

When you use SharePoint Team Services with Project Server, it enables the Documents and Issues features in Project Web Access so that you can view and submit project-related documents and issues[1].

SharePoint Team Services Web sites include unique features that enhance collaboration with project document management and project issue tracking. Using SharePoint Team Services, you can:

- Create project document libraries to submit project documents and view documents quickly.
- Track issues in the predefined issue list and customize the issue template per project.
- Allow authorized users to create custom views with additional fields for document libraries and issue tracking lists.
- Secure documents and issues at the team Web site level to prevent unauthorized users from viewing and editing documents and issues.
- Secure remote administration from both the command line and Hypertext Markup Language (HTML) Administration pages to enable Project Server to programmatically and remotely administer SharePoint Team Services subwebs.
- Add users and perform other Web administration tasks by using an easy HTML interface.

You can find SharePoint Team Services Administrator's Guide at:

http://www.microsoft.com/technet/treeview/default.asp?url=/technet/prodtechnol/sharepnt/proddocs/admindoc/ows000.asp?frame=true

Create a Document Library

You can create a document library by clicking on **Documents** tab on the top pane, then type in the name, description and other information in the template.

Figure 3.5: SharePoint Team Services Document Library

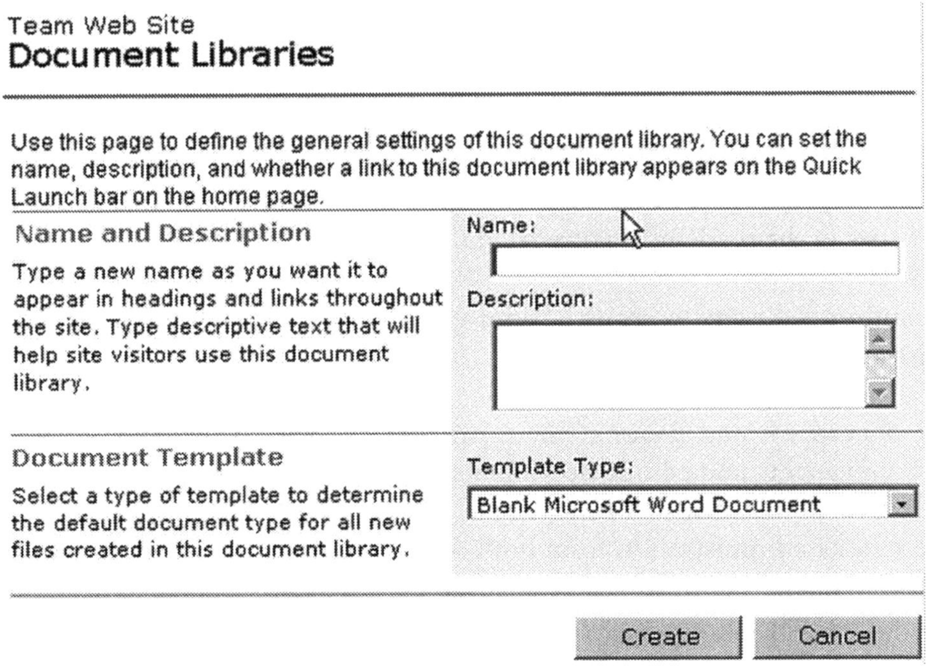

Team Web Site
Document Libraries

Use this page to define the general settings of this document library. You can set the name, description, and whether a link to this document library appears on the Quick Launch bar on the home page.

Name and Description
Type a new name as you want it to appear in headings and links throughout the site. Type descriptive text that will help site visitors use this document library.

Name:
Description:

Document Template
Select a type of template to determine the default document type for all new files created in this document library.

Template Type:
Blank Microsoft Word Document

Create Cancel

Then click on **Create** to create the document library.

Upload Files

In the document library section, you can upload, filter documents. You can also make subscription.

To upload a document, click on the **Upload** button. You can enter the following information for the document you are uploading:

- File name
- Description
- Review status (final, approved, draft)

Once you completed the upload process, you can either **Save and Close** or **Go Back to the Document Library**. You should be able to see the documents you have uploaded in the document library.

Table 3.1: Document List

File Name	Edit	Review Status	Last Modified
Upgrade SQL Server 7 to 2000	✍	Final	12/03/2002
Install Project Server 2002	✍	Approved	11/18/2002
Install SharePoint Team Services	✍	Draft	12/10/2002

Subscription and Notification

You can make a subscription for a document library. For example, you may want to be notified whenever files updated in that document library. To establish a subscription, you click on Documents, then select the document library you want to subscribe. You will see the subscription interface similar to Figure 3.6.

Figure 3.6: SharePoint Team Services Add Subscription

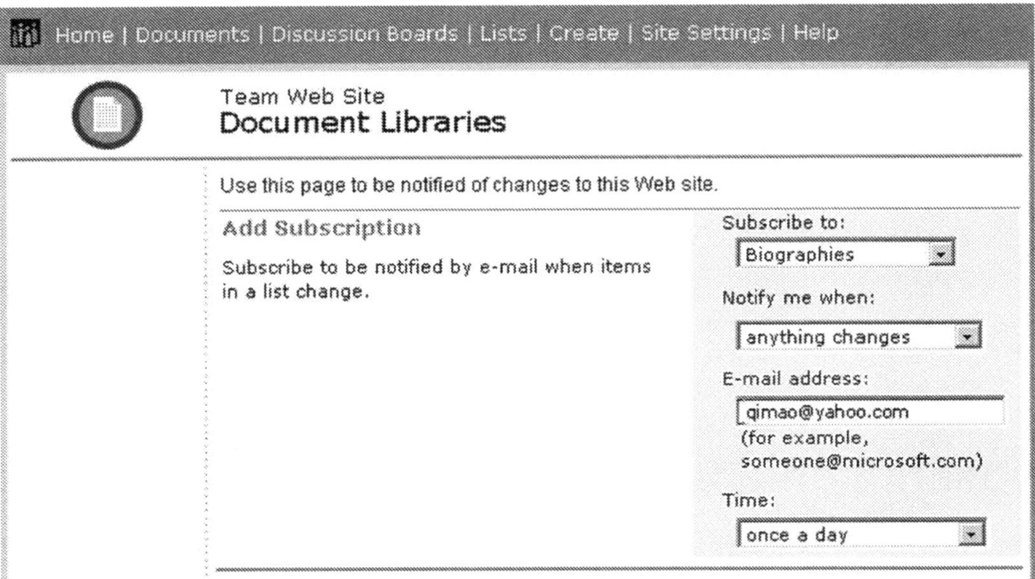

In the **Notify me when** selection box, the default value is anything changes. You can also specify the frequency you want to receive notice in the **Time** selection box. The default value is once a day. You can change it to other intervals such as once a week.

You will receive notification as shown in Figure 3.7.

Figure 3.7: SharePoint Team Services Change Notification

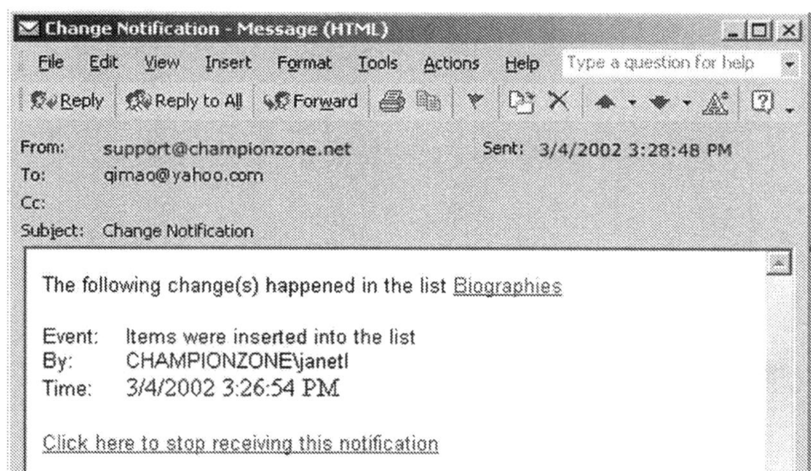

You can print, reply, or forward this notification just like an e-mail message.

SharePoint Team Services Architecture

The architecture of SharePoint Team Services is based on the architecture of Microsoft FrontPage Server Extensions 2002 and uses the Internet Server Application Programming Interface (ISAPI). Like FrontPage Server Extensions, SharePoint Team Services works with Microsoft Internet Information Services (IIS) on the Windows operating system and relies on a database, such as SQL Server or Microsoft Data Engine (MSDE) database. When created, a SharePoint Team Services Web site is immediately live on the server.

When SharePoint Team Services is installed on a Web server, SharePoint team Web site authoring and administration is available from any computer that has Microsoft Internet Explorer 5 or later. Authoring and administration features are also available from a client program compatible with SharePoint, such as the Microsoft Office

2000 client or the Office XP client, whether the computer is on the Internet or on an intranet[1].

Figure 3.8: SharePoint Team Services Architecture[1]

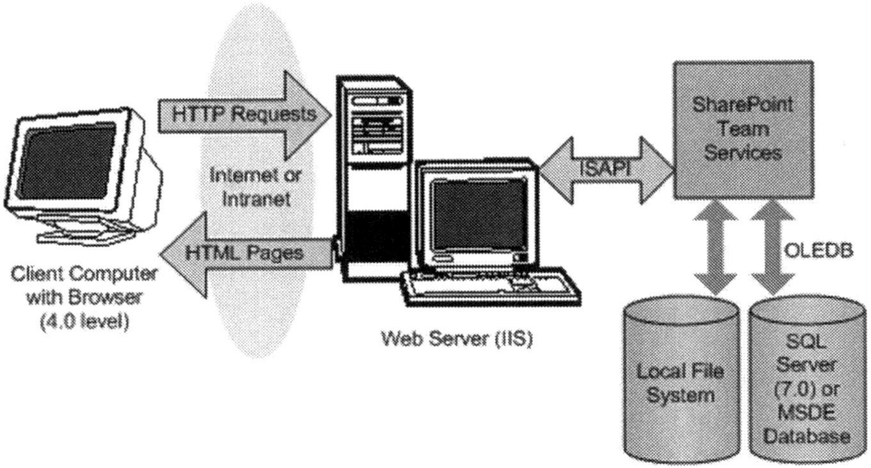

Communication between a client computer and a Web server running SharePoint Team Services uses the same open Hypertext Transfer Protocol (HTTP)-based protocol that Web browsers on a client computer use to interact with a Web server. No file sharing access on the Web server computer is needed, and neither File Transfer Protocol (FTP) nor telnet access is required. No proprietary file system sharing calls are necessary to use SharePoint Team Services[1].

Some features (such as exporting to a spreadsheet) use ActiveX components and require Microsoft Internet Explorer, but most content is returned to the client computer in HTML format.

Because SharePoint Team Services relies on both the file system and a database to track information about the Web site, these systems must be synchronized. For example, a list in a SharePoint Team Services Web site is a combination of data in the database and the HTML files. SharePoint Team Services provides tools for backing up the database but uses the usual operating system tools to back up the file system. Be sure to back up the file system whenever you back up the database. Keeping file system and database backups synchronized will help simplify the process if you ever need to restore your Web site.

A default SharePoint team Web site allows multiple document libraries to be created and multiple documents to be uploaded into each document library. SharePoint Team Services provides server-side schema template files to define fields and view schemas for storing or displaying list data, such as document properties and document library details. SharePoint Team Services schema files are modified for Microsoft Project to add specific document properties that are useful for project management[1].

An issue list is a customized SharePoint Team Services list file. When modifying SharePoint Team Services server-side template files for Microsoft Project, a default issue list is created for each team Web site; the default issue list provides specific fields for issue tracking for project management.

After the Project Server administrator has run the custom SharePoint Team Services setup and configuration program for Microsoft Project (Stswiz.exe), the SharePoint Team Services server-side template is automatically replaced with a specific template for Microsoft Project.

After a team Web site is provisioned on the Web server with the modified SharePoint Team Services template, document libraries and the issue list with the extended and modified fields are created for the site. Project Server displays the interface for interacting with project document libraries and the issue list to Project Web Access, and stores information about links between documents or issues and projects or tasks in the Project Server database[1].

Communication between Project Server and SharePoint Team Services

Project Server uses multiple means (based on variations of HTTP protocol) to communicate with Web servers running SharePoint Team Services.

- XMLHTTP

  Project Server requests and receives data from SharePoint Team Services through XMLHTTP. Project Server then parses the XML results returned by SharePoint and renders the data in Project Web Access. For example, Project Server displays data in custom view lists for documents and issues in the left navigation pane of Project Web Access, or on the linked documents or issues page that displays when you click the Link Documents or Link Issues buttons[1].

- HTTP

  Project Web Access pages display a portion of the SharePoint Team Services user interface in IFRAMES by passing the URL of the SharePoint Team Services form to the IFRAME. This occurs, for example, when a user opens a document library and is presented with the document list, or when a user drills down to project issues and is presented with the issue list in Project Web Access pages[1].

- **HTTP-based administrative protocol**

  Project Server remotely administers SharePoint Team Services Web sites using an HTTP-based protocol. Project Server implements the protocol within custom forms to pose requests to the ISAPI file Fpadmdll.dll in Microsoft Windows (Program

Files\Common Files\Microsoft Shared\web server extensions\50\isapi_vti_adm folder). Project Server uses this protocol to administer a server running SharePoint Team Services remotely for example, remotely creating a subweb when a project is published to Project Server, adding users to appropriate roles in the subweb, and deleting project subwebs[1].

Middle layer: Object Link Provider

The object link provider object (ProjObjProv.dll) resides in the middle layer of Project Server. It exposes interface methods for linking documents and issues to projects and tasks. The link information is stored in the Project Server database[1].

The objects related to tasks and projects are not limited to SharePoint Team Services documents and issue items. As long as the unique identifier of an object can be expressed in URL, XML or table IDs, an external object can be easily associated with projects and tasks, or with other external objects via the object link provider.

Front end: Project Web Access

Project Web Access is the single access point for project-related documents and issues. A user should always upload a document or create an issue by using Project Web Access.

When Project Server is used with SharePoint Team Services to enable document library and issue tracking features, it uses the following integration architecture.

Figure 3.9: SharePoint Team Services Integration Architechure[1]

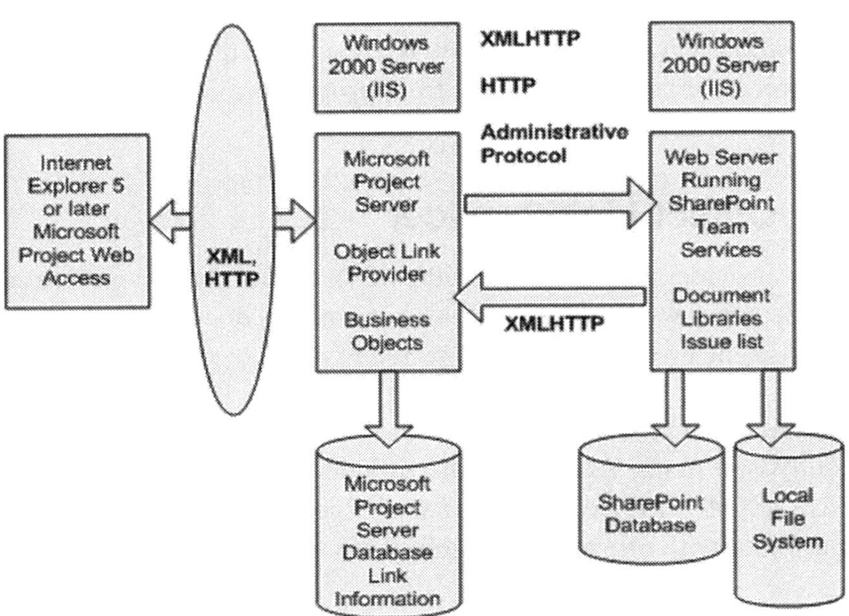

A SharePoint Team Services subweb is provisioned for each project published to the Microsoft Web Server database. When a project is published to Microsoft Project Web Server for the first time, Microsoft Web Server programmatically provisions the subweb. In enterprise mode, a project could have multiple versions. A subweb is created only for the published version of the project.

When a project subweb is provisioned, the following actions occur:

- The project subweb does not inherit security from its parent subweb. Therefore, users must be added into roles on each subweb to access project documents and issues in Project Web Access.

- A Windows user account that is specified during setup is the default administrator for each project subweb.

- Four custom roles are created on the subweb:

    - **Administrator** (Project Server) is a replica of the default Administrator role.
    - **Project Manager** (Project Server) is a replica of the default Advanced Author role.
    - **Team Member** (Project Server) is the Project Manager role minus the Design List right.
    - **Browser** (Project Server) is a replica of the default Browser role.

- Project Server users are added into their respective roles on the subweb based on their access to a project specified in Project Server.

    - Project Server users who have the global Manage SharePoint Team Services permission are added into the Project Server Administrator role of the subweb.
    - Project managers who have published a project are added into the Project Manager (Project Server) role of the subweb.
    - Users who have Save Project permission to save a project are added into the Project Manager (Project Server) role of the subweb.
    - Team members who have task assignments in a project are added into the Team Member (Project Server) role of the subweb.
    - Users who have Open Project permission on the project are added into the Browser (Project Server) role of the subweb.

The automatic subweb provisioning works seamlessly for an end user. A project manager creates a project plan, assigns tasks to resources, and publishes the project to Project Server. When the plan is published successfully, the project manager can immediately browse to the project document libraries and create project issues because the SharePoint Team Services subweb has already been provisioned, and the project manager has been given the appropriate rights to interact with the document and issues[1].

Document and issue security is set on the project level, not on the list level or list item level. Document and issue lists share the same security settings. A project manager can create document libraries, upload documents, create and modify issues, and add new fields to a document or issue list in the project subweb. A team member can create, upload, and modify documents and issues, but does not have permission to add new fields to a document or issue lists. A reviewer can view the documents and issues but cannot edit document properties or the content of documents and issues[1].

Public documents

When you use Project Server Setup to install and configure a Web server running SharePoint Team Services, the Setup program creates the subweb called MS_ProjectServer_PublicDocuments. Document libraries in this subweb serve as an organization's public document depository as defined in Project Server.

The following user roles are created for this subweb:

- Administrator (Project Server)
- Project Manager (Project Server)

Users are added to Project Server in appropriate roles, either through the Project Web Access Admin center or a project is published from Microsoft Project. Users with permission to manage SharePoint Team Services in Project Server are automatically added as Project Server Administrators. All other Project Server users are added as Project Server Project Managers so that every Project Server user can create document libraries, extend document properties, and upload documents into the public documents subwebs.

Like project documents, public documents are accessible in the Documents center of Project Web Access[1].

Other list items in the SharePoint subweb

A SharePoint subweb contains lists other than the documents and issues, such as events, announcements, discussions, and other custom lists. These other SharePoint lists are not accessible from Project Web Access. With their Web browsers, users can navigate directly to the specific subwebs that contain the other lists. For easier access, a URL pointing to the subweb link can be placed on the Project Web Access Home page[1].

Collaborating on Documents and Issues

When SharePoint Team Services is integrated with Microsoft Project, and the Documents and Issues centers have been enabled on Project Server, document libraries and issue lists can be created to provide easy access to project-related documents and issues. As soon as a project is published on Project Server, a SharePoint Team Services subweb is created for that project as a space for document libraries and issue lists. An administrator can also manually provide a SharePoint Team Services subweb for this purpose. Each project has its own subweb. There is also the public documents subweb that serves as the depository of documents public to the organization.

Document Libraries

Document libraries store a collection of documents like a file folder. These documents can be created based on document templates that are associated with document libraries. An authorized user (typically the project manager) defines document library properties, the default document template it uses, and access permissions to the documents published to a document library.

There are two types of document depositories in Project Web Access:

Project document library

This document library stores documents that are related to a specific project. Each project can have multiple document libraries, and authorized users can create additional document libraries for the project. Project managers, who by default have Design List permission on SharePoint Team Services, can make changes to specific document libraries.

Public document library

This document library stores documents that are accessible to all users in the organization. The server administrator defines who has access to documents in this document library. By default, all users in the Project Server can create document libraries and contribute documents.

When creating a document library, an authorized user, such as a project manager, can use default document library properties defined during Setup or specify new document library properties. A user may want to define a property that helps track documents in the project.

- To simplify document creation, an authorized user can define a template to be used for the document library.
- For ease of use, authorized users can create multiple views for a document library.
- Users can search document libraries for specific information. To find a document, the Search tool searches through all document libraries on the server and returns only documents that a user has permission to view.
- E-mail notifications can alert the project manager when a document is added to a document library or when a document has changed in a project.
- Documents in a document library are, by default, associated with a project. A project manager or a team member can associate documents with specific project tasks that have been published to Project Server as new or changed assignments.

- Documents are clearly marked by a document indicator and appear in the timesheet, Tasks center, and Project center of Project Web Access. For example, you can access documents submitted into a project lists in the Project center.

Tracking Issues

Issue tracking improves the efficiency and effectiveness of project management because it allows you to communicate about problems and related action items with team members and stakeholders. Issue tracking provides rich reporting, status indications, e-mail notifications, and alerts to help ensure that issues that come up during the completion of a project get attention and are resolved.

With SharePoint Team Services, each issue is treated as a documented collaborative discussion that typically has a process controlling its lifetime. Typically, someone starts the issue process by opening a new issue. Others can then add information to the discussion field of this issue. Eventually, helpful information can be entered in the resolution field, and, depending on the type of solution, the issue can be marked as closed or postponed.

SharePoint Team Services provides three levels of security on issues for a project:

- Read-only permission for stakeholders who need to review issues.
- Edit permission for authorized users, such as team members, who can create and edit issues.
- Edit and customization permission for project managers who can customize the specific fields (such as the priority, discussion, or resolution fields) and views (such as the issue list view) used for issues.

An administrator and a project manager can also define additional views for issues in a project. A new view is defined by specifying the visible fields in the issue list, the order of issues in the list, the filters applied, and the number of items displayed on a page.

Issues can be associated with projects, tasks, documents, and other issues. When an issue is linked to a task, it can affect the task directly, have the task as a work item, or be related to the task.

Issues are clearly marked by an issue indicator and appear in the timesheet, Tasks center, and Project center of Project Web Access. For example, newly assigned issues appear on the Home page, and you can access issue lists of projects in the Project center.

E-mail notifications can alert you when issues have been opened, assigned, or updated, and you can keep track of the status of issues. Depending on the actions taken to resolve them, issues appear as active, closed, or postponed.

Customization

Document and issue property lists can be customized to better meet your needs. By default, a Project Server administrator or a project manager can extend the properties of the document libraries and add additional tracking fields for issues.

- For a document library, an authorized user can change the name of the lists, security settings, and views; add new columns; and change the order of the fields in a column. For the issue list, an authorized user can add new columns, change the order of the fields in a column, and add additional issue views.
- For existing document columns, the title, status, and ownership settings can be changed.
- For existing issue columns, the title, status, priority, assignment, ownership, and due date settings can be changed.
- When creating or updating views, an authorized user can specify the columns to display, the order that the columns are displayed in, the criteria used to filter information displayed in the columns, and the number of items to be displayed.

Extensibility

In Microsoft Project 2002 SharePoint Team Services provides document library and issue tracking features. However, SharePoint Team Services may not meet an enterprise user's needs for a sophisticated document management or issue tracking process.

As an alternative, Project Server can function as a platform where solution providers can integrate third-party document management or issue tracking applications with Project Server. The Object Link Provider (OLP) object provides programmable interfaces for linking projects and tasks to generic external objects, such as documents residing in a third-party document management system and issues residing in a third-party issue-tracking application.

The following are scenarios for developing solutions that leverage the OLP object:

- Integration with an existing Microsoft product store (SharePoint Portal Server or Microsoft Exchange) for collaboration objects.
- Replacement of the Project Server document library solution and integration of Project Server with a third-party document store—for example, Documentum, DocShare, or Lotus Notes.
- Replacement of the Project Server issue tracking application and integration with a third-party issue tracking application.
- Customization of the existing integration of Project Server and SharePoint Team Services.

Summary

This chapter covers the integration between SharePoint Team Services and Microsoft with Project Server. Microsoft Project 2002 includes SharePoint Team Services to provide document library and issue tracking features. These two features greatly enhance collaboration in planning, executing, and closing a project. Together,

Microsoft Project 2002 and SharePoint Team Services provide an integrated collaboration solution that combines ease of use and end user flexibility.

Both Microsoft Project 2002 and SharePoint Team Services are built on the Microsoft .NET server platform and provide a rich middle-tier service. The OLP enables customers to replace solutions that are shipped with Microsoft Project 2002 and integrate project data with their preferred document management, issue tracking, or third-party collaboration applications.

---

1. Ying Wang and Frederique Klitgaard. Microsoft SharePoint Team Services Integration Architecture and Extensibility. Microsoft Corporation, June 2002.

4

After Project Server Installation

During the installation process, there are several things have been changed include:

- New file subfolders have been created and many files have been copied over
- New Registry Keys have been created
- New database has been created
- Some configuration changes have been made to IIS

We will take a detailed look at some of those changes. If you installed Project Server by using the Custom option and chose to provide some of the requested information later, you can use the instructions in this chapter for providing that information by using Project Web Access.

Project Server files and folders

Project Server installs files and uses registry keys much like Project. It installs its files in the local directory such as C:*Program Files\Project Server\IIS Virtual Root* directory. In this directory it places 24 sub-folders. The sub-folders and a general description of what each folder contains is shown in the table 3.1:

Table 4.1: Project Server sub-folders

Folder Name	Contains
Admin	Contains ASP pages that relate to Administrative tasks within Project Server.
CustError	Contains two HTML files that have custom error messages for Project Server.
DocLib	Contains document library tasks for Project Server.
Download	Contains the needed components for the browser to prepare to use OCX components.
Help	Contains on-line help information in HTML format
Home	Contains ASP pages that relate to the Home page within Project Server.
Images	Contains images used within Project Server.
Includes	Header files used by other ASP pages.
Isapi	Contains main DLL's for Project functionality
Issues	Contains issues related to Project Server.
Library	Additional ASP and VB Script info
Logon	Contains ASP related to logging on to Project Server.
Modeling	Contains modeling analysis tools for Project Server.
Notifications	Contains manager and self notification functions for Project Server
Objects	OCX Controls for browser to connect
PCNotes	Note pages
Shell	More ASP and JavaScript to support page shell related actions
StatusReports	ASP related to status reports
Styles	Cascading Style Sheets
Tasks	ASP pages related to tasks within Project Server
Templates	Contains templates used in generating web pages related to responding to messages.
Transactions	Contains calendar and tasks transaction pages.
Views	ASP pages related to views within Project Server
WebCalendar	ASP pages related to getting information from Outlook.

Internet Information Server (IIS)

During the installation process, Project Server also makes some configuration changes to IIS. First, installation creates a virtual directory (or application) with the name ProjectServer. This virtual directory is pointed at the local directory such as C:\Program Files\Project Server\IIS Virtual Root. Permissions on this virtual directory are set for Read only. For the application Project Server, Execute Permissions is set to Scripts and Executables.

Figure 4.1: Project Server virtual directory on IIS

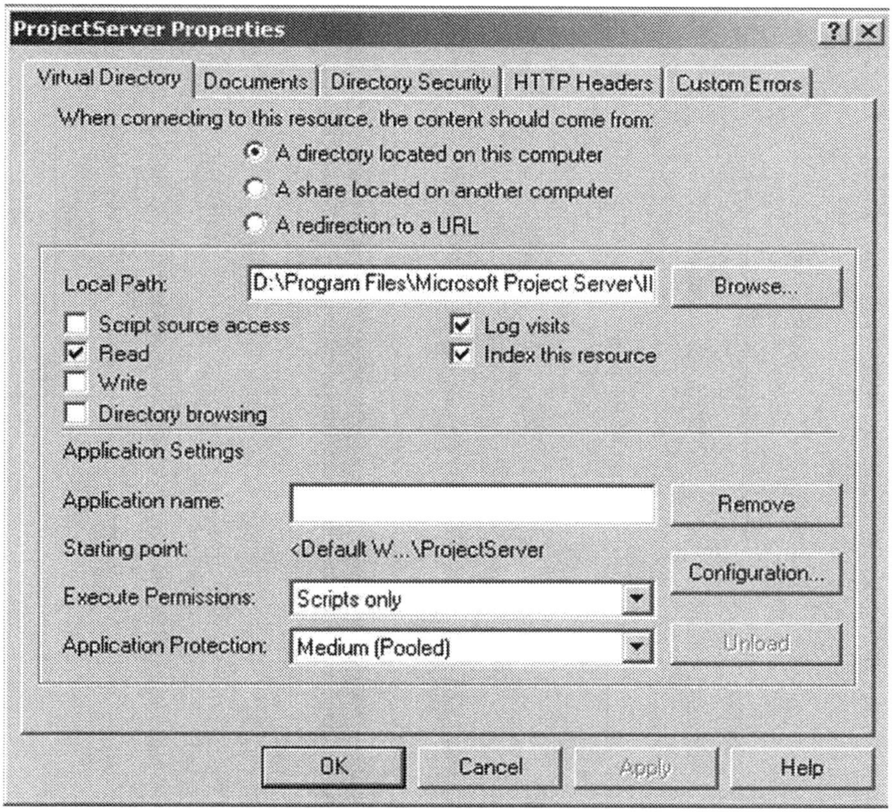

After the above are done, installation sets and enables default documents for the application. These files are located in the local directory C:\ProjectCentral. They are default.asp and default.htm. These documents are enabled as the default documents via the documents tab.

After the default documents have been enabled, authentication options are set for the application as a whole. These options are accessed via the Directory Security tab as shown below.

Figure 4.2: Project Server directory security on IIS

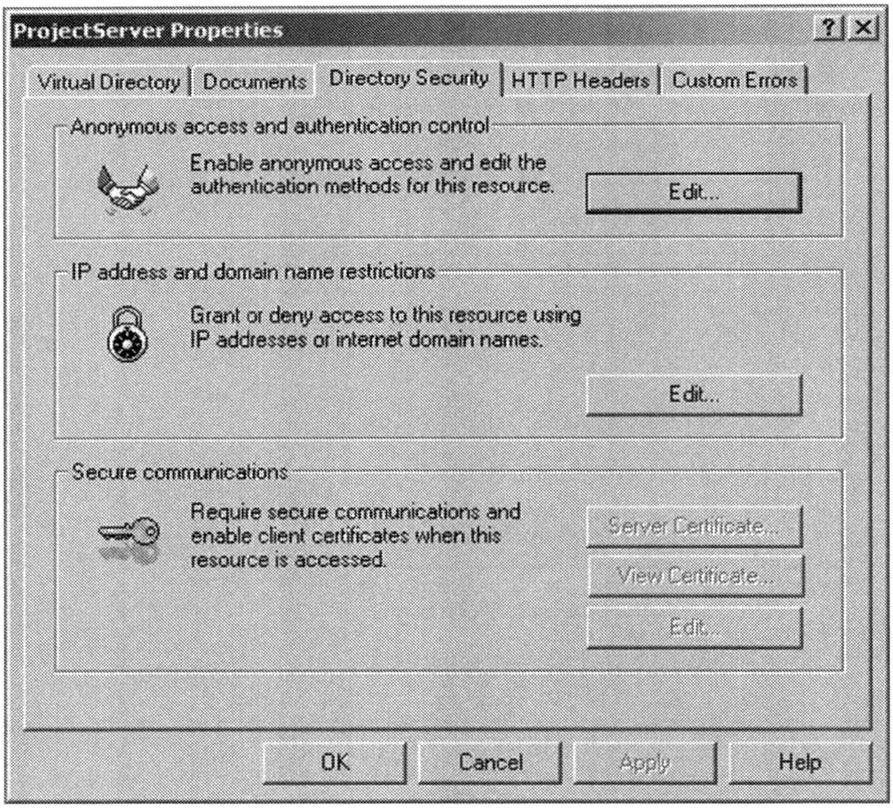

Clicking on the Edit button underneath Anonymous Access and Authentication Control takes you to the following dialog box as shown in Figure 3.4.

Figure 4.3: Project Server authentication methods

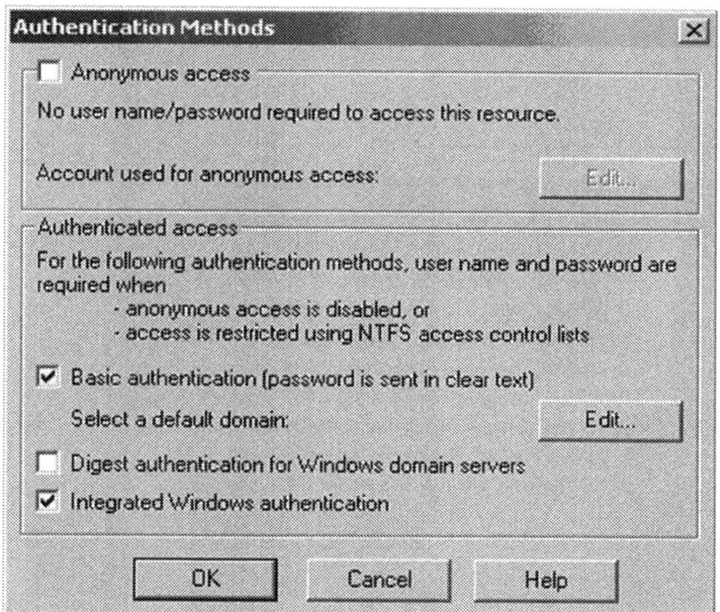

At the application level, only Basic Authentication and Integrated Windows authentication should be checked. In some cases where security issues dictate, it is possible to turn off Basic Authentication.

After Authentication options are set for the application as a whole, custom errors are set for the application. This is done via the custom errors tab shown below.

Figure 4.4: Project Server custom errors

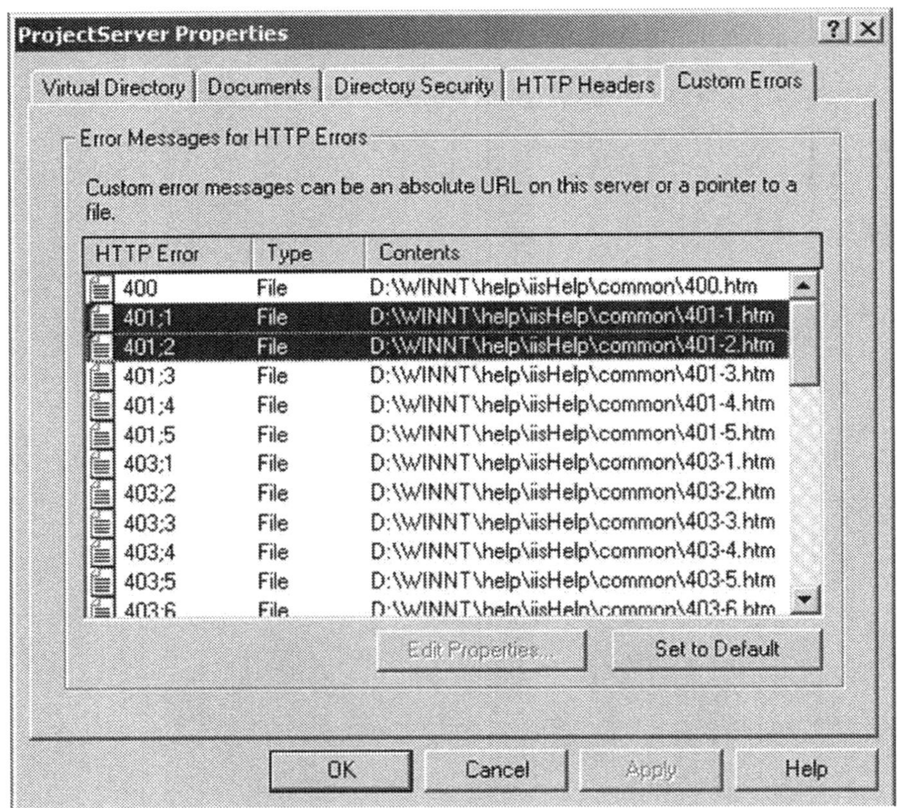

Once Custom Errors have been configured, Project Server Installation configures authentication options for individual files.

The **pjdbcomm.dll** located in the C:\ProjectCentral\ISAPI directory. Its authentication options are checked as:

- Anonymous access
- Basic Authentication
- Integrated Windows Authentication

Anonymous Access must be enabled. Basic Authentication and Integrated Windows Authentication are also both enabled. Basic Authentication may be disabled, however.

- Basic Authentication

Anonymous Access and Integrated Windows Authentication are not enabled. Basic Authentication is enabled.

Enter deferred setup information

If you installed Project Server by using the Custom option and chose to provide some of the requested information later, you can use the following instructions for providing that information by using Project Web Access.

Not all of the features and components described below may apply to your installation of Project Server.

Analysis Services connection

Use Project Web Access to connect to Project Server, and then click Admin in the top link bar to go to the Admin center. In the side pane, click Manage enterprise features, and then select the Enable enterprise features check box. Next, in the side pane under Enterprise Options, click Specify resource and OLAP cube updates. Click Yes to build an OLAP cube of project data, and then enter the name of the Analysis Services computer in the Analysis Server box and a name for the cube in the Cube name box.

Note You must run PSCOMPlus.exe (found in the \Project Server\Bin\1033 folder of the Project Server computer) before you can build a cube. (This folder, 1033, contains the files for the English version. Files for other languages can be found in the folder that corresponds to the locale ID [LCID] for that language.) PSCOMPlus is used to provide the name of a user account (in the format domain\account) that should be impersonated by a COM+ application to allow Project Server to connect to the Analysis Services computer[1].

Web server

Use Project Web Access to connect to Project Server, and then click Admin in the top link bar to go to the Admin center. In the side pane, click Manage organization to enter the Web address for the Project Server computer[1].

SMTP mail server

Use Project Web Access to connect to Project Server, and then click Admin in the top link bar to go to the Admin center. In the side pane, click Customize Project Web Access, and then click Notifications and reminders[1].

Web server running SharePoint Team Services from Microsoft

Use Project Web Access to connect to Project Server, and then click Admin in the top link bar to go to the Admin center. In the side pane, click Manage SharePoint Team Services. In the side pane under Options, click Connect to servers, and then click Add Server.

Note You should run PSCOMPlus.exe (found in the \Project Server\Bin\1033 folder of the Project Server computer) before connecting with Project Web Access to provide this information. (This folder, 1033, contains the files for the English version. Files for other languages can be found in the folder that corresponds to the locale ID [LCID] for that language.) PSCOMPlus is used to provide the name of a user account (in the format domain\account) that should be impersonated by a COM+

application to allow Project Server to connect to the SharePoint Team Services and SharePoint Team Services database computers[1].

Log on using a different Windows user account

By default, when Project Server attempts to authenticate a user with Windows authentication, it assumes that the user is using a computer where he or she has already logged on to the network using a Windows user account (Integrated Windows authentication). However, this may not always be the case. For example, a user may want to check Project Server information from someone else's computer or by using a common computer that is shared by several people and where the user has not logged on with his or her Windows user account[1].

In this case, when the user goes to a Project Server site, the Logon page opens instead of the Home page. The user must then click the Log on using a different Microsoft Windows user account link on the left side of the page. After entering his or her Windows user account information, the user is authenticated using Basic authentication and is then taken to the Home page.

However, to enable users to use the Log on using a different Microsoft Windows user account link on the Logon page, the administrator should perform the following steps on the Project Server computer:

- Enable Basic authentication for the Project Server virtual directory and for the Remote Data Services ISAPI Library (Msadcs.dll) using the Microsoft Managment Console (MMC) snap-in for IIS.

Note

- To enable Basic authentication for the Project Server virtual directory, right-click the virtual directory in the left pane of the Internet Information Services window and click Properties. Click the Directory Security tab and then click Edit in the section for Anonymous access and authentication control. Select the Basic authentication check box and then click Yes when asked if you want to continue. Click OK twice to apply your changes and close the dialog box, and then click OK to close the Inheritance Overrides dialog box without making any changes[1].

- To enable Basic authentication for the file Msadcs.dll, select the MSADC virtual directory in the left pane of the Internet Information Services window. Right-click msadcs.dll in the right pane and then select Properties. Click the File Security tab and then click Edit in the section for Anonymous Access and Authentication Control. Select the Basic authentication check box and then click Yes when asked if you want to continue. Click OK twice to apply your changes and close the dialog box[1].

- Set up the Secure Sockets Layer (SSL) features of Internet Information Server (IIS) for greater security[1].

Migrate Analysis Services repository to a SQL Server database

Each Analysis server has a repository to store metadata for the objects of the Analysis server (for example, cubes and dimensions). By default, this repository is a Microsoft Access (.mdb) database on the server computer where Analysis Services is installed.

In order for Project Server to successfully build the OLAP cube, you need to migrate the repository to a SQL Server (.mdf) database[1].

Note

- You can migrate the repository at any time after installing Analysis Services as long as SQL Server is installed and a database for the repository exists.

- If the SQL Server database supports Windows authentication, the OLAP Administrators group needs to be given DB_OWNER permission for the repository.

- If you prefer not to migrate the repository, you need to add the OLAP Administrators group to the list of users and groups that have Full Control permission for the \Program Files\Microsoft Analysis Services\Bin folder so that the cube can be built. (Right-click the folder name, click Properties, and then the Security tab.)

Tip

When you have migrated the repository to a SQL Server database, you can safely delete the old repository. By default, this database is \Program Files\Microsoft Analysis Services\Bin\msmdrep.mdb.

1 Log on to the Analysis Services computer with a user account that has permissions equivalent to either the Administrators group or OLAP Administrators group, and start Analysis Manager.

2 Right-click the name of your server under Analysis Servers, and then click **Migrate Repository** to start the Migrate Repository Wizard[1].

It is recommended that you choose the Analysis Services native format when migrating the repository.

Add users to cube database roles in Analysis Services

SQL Server Analysis Services uses Windows authentication to control access to online analytical processing (OLAP) cubes, for example, when using Portfolio Analyzer. By default, the OLAP cube database created by Project Server has no database roles defined so that only users or groups specifically added have access to the cubes[1].

This procedure can't be performed until an OLAP cube database has been built. To check the status of the cube database, open Project Web Access, and then click **Admin** in the top link bar to go to the Admin center. In the side pane, click **Manage enterprise features**, and then click **Specify resource and OLAP cube updates.** The status of the OLAP cube database is shown under **Current Cube Status**[1].

The process is:

1 Log on to the Analysis Services computer with a user account that has permissions equivalent to either of the Administrators or OLAP Administrators groups, and start Analysis Manager.

2. Expand the name of your server under **Analysis Servers** to see the cube databases on that computer.

3. Right-click the name of the database (as shown in the **Cube name** box of the **Updates to Resource Tables and OLAP Cube** page in Project Web Access), and then click **Manage Roles.**
4. Click **New**, and enter a name for the new database role in the **Role name** box.
5. On the **Membership** tab, click the **Add** button to add users and groups to the role.
6. Click **OK.**
7. On the **Cubes** tab, click **Check All** to enable access to all three cubes in the database.
8. Click **OK** to add the role[1].

Disable the Remote Data Services DataFactory object

Project Server uses the Remote Data Services (RDS) ISAPI Library (msadcs.dll). The RDS ISAPI Library exposes the DataFactory object (msadcf.dll), which has been identified as potentially insecure and which Project Server does not require. This procedure describes how to disable the RDS DataFactory object without also disabling the RDS ISAPI Library.

! Caution

Using Registry Editor incorrectly can cause serious problems that may require you to reinstall your operating system. Microsoft cannot guarantee that problems resulting from the incorrect use of Registry Editor can be solved. Use Registry Editor at your own risk.

For information about how to edit the registry, view the "Changing Keys and Values" Help topic in Registry Editor (Regedit.exe) or the "Add and Delete Information in the Registry" and "Edit Registry Data" Help topics in Regedt32.exe. Note that you should back up the registry before you edit it. If you are running Windows NT or Windows 2000, you should also update your Emergency Repair Disk (ERD) [1].

The following actions may disable Web applications that rely on the RDS DataFactory object.

If you have Web applications that use the RDS DataFactory object, follow the instructions in the article "Using the Customization Handler Feature in RDS 2.0," found on the Microsoft Universal Data Access site. The article can be found by clicking Technical Materials in the left pane under UDA Contents, and then scrolling to the RDS White Papers section under RDS Technical Materials[1].

Delete the following subkeys, if they exist:

```
\HKEY_LOCAL_MACHINE\SYSTEM\CurrentControlSet\Services\W
3SVC\Parameters\ADCLaunch\RDSServer.DataFactory
```

```
\HKEY_LOCAL_MACHINE\SYSTEM\CurrentControlSet\Services\W
3SVC\Parameters\ADCLaunch\AdvancedDataFactory
```

```
\HKEY_LOCAL_MACHINE\SYSTEM\CurrentControlSet\Services\W
3SVC\Parameters\ADCLaunch\VbBusObj.VbBusObjCls
```

Changes from uninstall Project Server

Uninstall Project Server is almost the reverse process of install it. The following changes that result from uninstalling Project Server:

- If Microsoft Desktop Engine (MSDE) was installed by the Setup program, it is removed during uninstall. Any database files created with it remain.
- If MSDE was installed by Setup, any Microsoft Data Access Components (MDAC) components that may have been upgraded remain.
- System files installed by Setup (such as the files for Microsoft XML) remain.
- Registry keys created for Project Server are removed.
- Additional products or components, such as SharePoint Team Services from Microsoft, are unaffected when uninstalling Project Server[1].

- If SharePoint Team Services was installed with the SharePoint Configuration Wizard included with Project Server, uninstalling by using the SharePoint Configuration Wizard also removes SharePoint Team Services. If the SharePoint Configuration Wizard was used to configure an existing installing of SharePoint Team Services for use with Project Server, uninstalling simply restores the SharePoint Team Services templates to their original state (existing subwebs are not affected) [1].
- Uninstalling Project Server, whether you've installed with the install now or Customize option, does not remove the database. Therefore, if you need to reset the database to the original condition, you can run the database scripts. When the scripts are run again, records in the database are automatically deleted before the new default records are created, giving you new tables with default records without deleting the database. Because all records are deleted when you rerun the scripts, you may want to back up any data before you rerun the scripts. Tools to back up and restore records in the database are contained in the Toolbox of the Microsoft Project 2002 Resource Kit at: http://www.microsoft.com/office/project/prk/2000/

The Microsoft Project 2002 Resource Kit is being updated constantly, it looks similar to Figure 4.5.

Figure 4.5: Microsoft Project 2000 Resource Kit

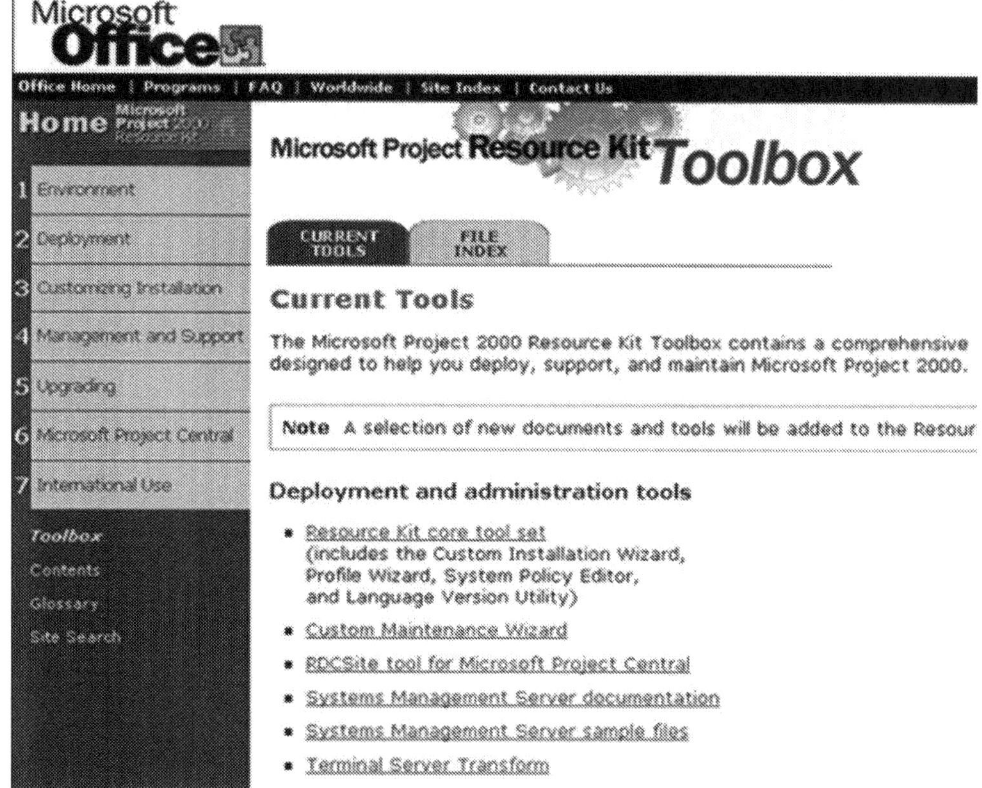

Summary

It is necessary to understand the configuration changes occurred during the Project Server installation process: new files and folders were created, new registry keys were added, some configurations changes occurred on Internet Information Server (IIS).

This chapter also covered the following topics:

- Enter deferred setup information
- Log on using a different Windows user account
- Migrate Analysis Services repository to a SQL Server database
- Add users to cube database roles in Analysis Services
- Disable the Remote Data Services DataFactory object
- Changes from uninstall Project Server

In next chapter, we will take a detailed look at the database structure for Project Server.

---

1. Project Server Installation Guide. Microsoft Corporation, 2002.

5

Project Server 2002 Database Structure

It is critical to know the database structure of Project Server 2002. Developers can access the business logic behind Project Server 2002 and incorporate the Project Server 2002 ActiveX controls to create solutions that combine the functionality of Project Server 2002 with database server. Project Server 2002 supports Microsoft SQL Server 2000 and Microsoft Data Engine 2000 or later.

Customized solutions could include adding new fields or tables to the Project Server 2002 database, or adding new databases, with corresponding updates to the query engine and business logic. To ensure the integrity of data, however, it is recommended by Microsoft that programmers focus on reading data from the Project Server 2002 database. For example, the schedule and resource data captured by Project Server 2002 could be incorporated into enterprise resource planning (ERP) systems or exported to a payroll accounting system.

There are three groups of tables in the Porject Server database: the MSP_WEB_ prefix to identify them as Microsoft Project Server tables, the MSP_CUBE_ prefix to identify Assignment and Resource cubes, and MSP_VIEW_ prefix to identify

Microsoft Project Web Access views. Table names are all uppercase with underscores separate all words.

Permissions and configuration

Project Server performs several types of operations on a database, each requiring DATA READER or DATA WRITER permissions in Microsoft SQL Server 2000. To save a new project to an empty database or to selectively export data to a database, a user must have **Create Table** permission. In addition to a valid logon ID, SQL Server users must be given access to the project database. Individual users access the data through Microsoft Project Web Access and therefore do not need permission for direct access to the Project Server.

> *! Caution*
>
> Placing triggers on Project Server database tables may cause data corruption or return unexpected results. It is important to note the following:
>
> - Any procedure fired by an INSERT or UPDATE trigger does not alter the @@identity property.
> - A procedure fired by an INSERT or UPDATE trigger must not perform an INSERT into a table with an Identity column or otherwise cause an Identity value to be generated by SQL Server 2000.

DSN requirements

Project Server supports an integrated database. For users of Microsoft Project Standard, the database is used to store data added or viewed through Project Web

Access. For users of Microsoft Project Professional, the database is used to store both Microsoft Project and Project Web Access data.

- Microsoft Project supports using a data source name (DSN) to connect to a server in the following instances:

- Microsoft Project Standard requires the use of a DSN to connect to a server.

- Microsoft Project Professional in offline mode requires the use of a DSN to connect to a server.

- Microsoft Project Professional in online mode cannot use a DSN to connect to a server.
  Connection information to the server is automatically communicated to Microsoft Project when the user identifies the correct server running Project Server. To connect Microsoft Project to a server using a DSN, do one of the following:

- If you are using Microsoft Project Standard:

  On the **Tools** menu, click **Options**. In the Options dialog box, click the **Collaborate** tab. Enter the name of the server.

- If you are using Microsoft Project Professional in offline mode:

  On the **Tools** menu, point to **Enterprise Options**, and then click **Microsoft Project Server Accounts**. Click **Add** to add the name of the server.

If multiple users need to access projects in the same database, not all users who change the data need to use the same DSN for connecting to the database. Microsoft Project stores both the combined DSN and project name (and alternatively the connection string) as the identifiers to locate a project using the following format: `<DSN>\ProjectName`.

DSN limitations in Microsoft Project

Here are the DSN limitations in Microsoft Project:

- You cannot use a DSN for project links such as resource pools, sharer files, external dependencies (cross-project links), or inserted projects.
- If multiple users modify the database, they should not save files by selecting the .mpd or .mdb file type from the Save as type list in the Save As dialog box.
- Microsoft Project caches logon passwords and other connection information. The same DSN cannot be used by more than one user ID on a single computer for different, simultaneous logons to the database. When a connection is established, that connection is reused even if a different logon name and/or password is entered at logon time. To log on with a different user ID, you must close all projects opened with the DSN. If there are simultaneous connections, you must create additional alternate DSNs for use with each user ID.

! Caution

You should never open the enterprise global template with a DSN. This can cause conflicts with the database and can cause data to be placed in unintended locations.

Accessing Data from Project Server

This group of scripts returns general statistical data about the information stored in the Project Server database tables. Chapter 8 covers how to visually representing statistical data with Chart component.

Find all projects

The following script extracts a list of all of the projects that are currently stored in the Project Server database, the name of the project manager for each project, and the total number of assignments for each project.

Tables	Fields	Description
MSP_WEB_PROJECTS	WPROJ_ID	The unique ID for the project
	WRES_ID	Refers to a valid ID in the MSP_WEB_RESOURCES table
	PROJ_NAME	The name of the project
MSP_WEB_RESOURCES	WRES_ID	The unique ID for the resource
	RES_NAME	The name of the resource
MSP_WEB_ASSIGNMENTS	PROJ_ID	Refers to a valid ID in the MSP_WEB_PROJECTS table

SQL Script is:

```
select
   PROJ_NAME as Project,
   RES_NAME as Project_Manager,
   (select count(*) from MSP_WEB_ASSIGNMENTS a
      where  a.WPROJ_ID = p.WPROJ_ID) as Assignments
from
   MSP_WEB_PROJECTS p,
   MSP_WEB_RESOURCES r
where
      p.WRES_ID = r.WRES_ID
and   p.WPROJ_ID <> 1
order by
   PROJ_NAME,
   RES_NAME
```

Find all resources that have assignments

The following script extracts a list of all of the resources that have assignments currently stored in the Project Server database, the name of the project that each resource is assigned to, and the total number of assignments for each project.

Tables	Fields	Description
MSP_WEB_PROJECTS	WPROJ_ID	The unique ID for the project
	PROJ_NAME	The name of the project
MSP_WEB_RESOURCES	WRES_ID	The unique ID for the resource
	RES_NAME	The name of the resource
MSP_WEB_ASSIGNMENTS	WPROJ_ID	Refers to a valid project in the MSP_WEB_PROJECTS table
	WRES_ID	Refers to a valid resource in the MSP_WEB_RESOURCES table

SQL Script is:

```
select
   RES_NAME as Resource,
   PROJ_NAME as Project,
   count(*) as Assignments
from
   MSP_WEB_PROJECTS p,
   MSP_WEB_ASSIGNMENTS a,
   MSP_WEB_RESOURCES r
where
      r.WRES_ID = a.WRES_ID
and   a.WPROJ_ID = p.WPROJ_ID
and   p.WPROJ_ID <> 1
group by
   PROJ_NAME,
   RES_NAME
```

Find all resources that have undeleted messages

The following script extracts a list of all resources that have undeleted Project Server messages currently stored in the Project Server database, the name of the project that is associated with the messages, and the total number of undeleted messages for each project.

Tables	Fields	Description
MSP_WEB_PROJECTS	WPROJ_ID	The unique ID for the project
	PROJ_NAME	The name of the project
MSP_WEB_RESOURCES	WRES_ID	The unique ID for the resource
	RES_NAME	The name of the resource
MSP_WEB_MESSAGES	WRES_ID_RECEIVER	Refers to a valid resource in the MSP_WEB_RESOURCES table
	WPROJ_ID	Refers to a valid project in the MSP_WEB_PROJECTS table

SQL Script is:

```
select
   r.RES_NAME as Receiver,
   PROJ_NAME as Project,
   count(*) as Undeleted_Messages
from
   MSP_WEB_PROJECTS p,
   MSP_WEB_MESSAGES m,
   MSP_WEB_RESOURCES r
where
      r.WRES_ID = m.WRES_ID_RECEIVER
and   m.WPROJ_ID = p.WPROJ_ID
and   p.WPROJ_ID <> 1
group by
   RES_NAME,
   PROJ_NAME
```

Find all requested status reports

The following script extracts a list of all status reports that have been requested and are currently stored in the Project Server database, the name of the project manager that requested the report, and the name of the resource who was requested to make the report.

Tables	Fields	Description
MSP_WEB_STATUS_REPORTS	WSR_ID	Refers to a valid ID in the MSP_WEB_STATUS_REQUESTS table
	WRES_ID_MGR	Refers to a valid ID in the MSP_WEB_RESOURCES table
	WREPORT_NAME	The name of the status report
MSP_WEB_STATUS_REQUESTS	WSR_ID	The unique ID for the status request
	WRES_ID_RECEIVER	Refers to a valid ID in the MSP_WEB_RESOURCES table
MSP_WEB_RESOURCES	WRES_ID	The unique ID for the resource
	RES_NAME	The name of the resource

SQL Script is:

```
select
   WREPORT_NAME as Report,
   m.RES_NAME as Project_Manager,
   r.RES_NAME as Resource
from
   MSP_WEB_STATUS_REPORTS p,
   MSP_WEB_STATUS_REQUESTS q,
   MSP_WEB_RESOURCES m,
   MSP_WEB_RESOURCES r
where
   p.WRES_ID_MGR = m.WRES_ID
and   p.WSR_ID = q.WSR_ID
and   q.WRES_ID_RECEIVER = r.WRES_ID
```

Find all status reports and their most recent responses

The following script extracts a list of all status reports and their most recent response dates before the @cur_date (current date) variable. Also, the status reports that are listed must have a frequency start date between the @start_date and @end_date variables.

Tables	Fields	Description
MSP_WEB_STATUS_REPORTS	WSR_ID	The unique ID of the status report
	WREPORT_NAME	The name of the status report
MSP_WEB_STATUS_RESPONSES	WSR_ID	Refers to a valid WSR_ID in the MSP_WEB_STATUS_REPORTS table
	WSUBMIT_DATE	The date a status report was submitted
MSP_WEB_STATUS_FREQUENCIES	WSR_ID	Refers to a valid WSR_ID in the MSP_WEB_STATUS_REPORTS table
	WREPORT_START_DATE	The date that status reporting is to begin

SQL Script is:

```
—declare the variables
declare @start_date as datetime
declare @end_date as datetime
declare @cur_date as datetime

—set the variable values
set @start_date = '2003-05-09'
set @end_date = '2003-06-10'
set @cur_date = '2003-05-09'

—select the fields
select
   s.WREPORT_NAME as 'Status Report',
   max(r1.WSUBMIT_DATE) as 'Last Response'
from
   MSP_WEB_STATUS_REPORTS s,
   MSP_WEB_STATUS_RESPONSES r1,
   MSP_WEB_STATUS_FREQUENCIES f
where
      s.WSR_ID = f.WSR_ID
and   s.WSR_ID = r1.WSR_ID
and   f.WREPORT_START_DATE between @start_date and @end_date
and   not exists (select r2.WSR_ID
      from MSP_WEB_STATUS_RESPONSES r2
         where r2.WSUBMIT_DATE > @cur_date
            and s.WSR_ID = r2.WSR_ID)
group by
   s.WREPORT_NAME
```

You can use the getdate() function instead of the cur_date variable if you want the date to be today's date.

Find the names of all resources assigned to each assignment in each project

The following script extracts a list of all projects that are currently stored in the Project Server database, the name of each assignment, and the team member assigned. The nonworking assignment time is excluded from the results.

Tables	Fields	Description
MSP_WEB_PROJECTS	WPROJ_ID	The unique ID for the project
	PROJ_NAME	The name of the project
MSP_WEB_RESOURCES	WRES_ID	The unique ID for the resource
	RES_NAME	The name of the resource
MSP_WEB_ASSIGNMENTS	WASSN_ID	The unique ID for the assignment
	WRES_ID	Refers to a valid WRES_ID in the MSP_WEB_RESOURCES table
	WPROJ_ID	Refers to a valid WPROJ_ID in the MSP_WEB_PROJECTS table
	WNWRK_ID	Refers to a valid ID in the MSP_WEB_NONWORKING table
	TASK_NAME	The name of the task

SQL Script is:

```
select
   PROJ_NAME as Project,
   TASK_NAME as Task_Name,
   RES_NAME as Team_Member
from
   MSP_WEB_PROJECTS p,
   MSP_WEB_RESOURCES r,
   MSP_WEB_ASSIGNMENTS a
where
      a.WRES_ID = r.WRES_ID
and   a.WPROJ_ID = p.WPROJ_ID
and   a.WNWRK_ID is NULL
order by
   PROJ_NAME,
   TASK_NAME
```

Find all time-phased data for a particular resource

The following script extracts a grouped, rolled-up list of time-phased data for a specified team member over a specified date range. The work type (scheduled, actual, or overtime) is also specified as a variable. The rolled-up data is grouped first by project name, then by task name, and finally by date with rolled-up work totals for each grouping level. The work values are displayed in hours.

Tables	Fields	Description
MSP_WEB_PROJECTS	WPROJ_ID	The unique ID for the project
	PROJ_NAME	The name of the project
MSP_WEB_RESOURCES	WRES_ID	The unique ID for the resource
MSP_WEB_ASSIGNMENTS	WASSN_ID	The unique ID for the assignment
	WPROJ_ID	Refers to a valid ID in the MSP_WEB_PROJECTS table
	WRES_ID	Refers to a valid ID in the MSP_WEB_RESOURCES table
MSP_WEB_WORK	WASSN_ID	Refers to a valid ID in the MSP_WEB_ASSIGNMENTS table
	WWORK_START	The start date for the work
	WWORK_FINISH	The finish date for the work
cursor		Used for initial filtering and computation for the process of expanding the compact time-phased data
temporary table		Used to store, group, sum, and roll up the expanded time-phased data

SQL Script is:

```
declare @res_name as nvarchar(510)
declare @begin_date as datetime
declare @end_date as datetime
declare @work_type as int

— set these variables
select @res_name = 'Team Member'
select @begin_date = '2001-09-09'
select @end_date = '2001-12-09'
select @work_type = 0 — 0=scheduled, 1=actual, 2=overtime
— end user variables

— function variables
declare @assn_id as int
declare @td_start as datetime
declare @total_days as int
declare @td_value as decimal(25,6)
declare @td_cur_date as datetime
declare @p_name as nvarchar(510)
declare @t_name as nvarchar(510)
— end function variables

— create temporary table
create table #tp_data ( td_date datetime, td_hours deci-
mal(25,9),
   task_name nvarchar(510), proj_name nvarchar(510) )

— create cursor for data collection
declare td cursor for
select
   a.WASSN_ID,
   WWORK_START,
   datediff(day, WWORK_START, WWORK_FINISH)+1,
   WWORK_VALUE
```

```
from
   MSP_WEB_WORK w,
   MSP_WEB_RESOURCES r,
   MSP_WEB_ASSIGNMENTS a
where
      a.WRES_ID = r.WRES_ID
and   a.WASSN_ID = w.WASSN_ID
and   r.RES_NAME = @res_name
and   w.WWORK_TYPE = @work_type
and   (@begin_date <= WWORK_FINISH or @end_date >=
WWORK_START)
order by
   WWORK_START

— loop through cursor to explode time-phased data
open td
fetch next from td into @assn_id, @td_start, @total_days,
@td_value
while @@fetch_status <> -1
begin
   select @td_cur_date = @td_start
   while @total_days > 0
   begin

      — get the task name
      select @t_name =
         ( select TASK_NAME
         from MSP_WEB_ASSIGNMENTS
         where WASSN_ID = @assn_id )

      — get the project name
      select @p_name =
         ( select PROJ_NAME
         from MSP_WEB_PROJECTS p, MSP_WEB_ASSIGNMENTS a
         where a.WASSN_ID = @assn_id and a.WPROJ_ID =
p.WPROJ_ID )
```

```
        — insert the data row into the temp table
        insert #tp_data values ( @td_cur_date, @td_value,
           @t_name, @p_name )
        select @td_cur_date = DATEADD(d, 1, @td_cur_date)
        select @total_days = @total_days - 1
     end

     — get next row from cursor
     fetch next from td into @assn_id, @td_start,
@total_days, @td_value
end
close td
deallocate td

— display data from temporary table with grouping and
rollup
select
   proj_name as Project,
   task_name as Task,
   td_date as 'Date',
   SUM(td_hours/60000) as 'Total_Work'
from
   #tp_data
group by proj_name, task_name, td_date with rollup

— clean up that temporary table
drop table #tp_data
```

Find all time-phased data for a particular project

The following script extracts a grouped, rolled-up list of time-phased data for a specified project name over a specified date range. Also, the work type (scheduled, actual, or overtime) is specified as a variable. The rolled-up data is grouped first by team member name, then by task name, and finally by date with rolled-up work totals for each grouping level. The work values are displayed in hours.

Tables	Fields	Description
MSP_WEB_PROJECTS	WPROJ_ID	The unique ID for the project
	PROJ_NAME	The name of the project
MSP_WEB_RESOURCES	WRES_ID	The unique ID for the resource
	RES_NAME	The name of the resource
MSP_WEB_ASSIGNMENTS	WASSN_ID	The unique ID for the assignment
	WPROJ_ID	Refers to a valid WPROJ_ID in the MSP_WEB_PROJECTS table
	TASK_NAME	The name of the task
MSP_WEB_WORK	WASSN_ID	Refers to a valid WASSN_ID in the MSP_WEB_ASSIGNMENTS table
	WWORK_START	The start date for the work
	WWORK_FINISH	The end date for the work
	WWORK_VALUE	The number of hours worked, measured as minutes * 1000
	WWORK_TYPE	Indicates the type of work

SQL Script is:

```
declare @proj_name as nvarchar(510)
declare @begin_date as datetime
declare @end_date as datetime
declare @work_type as int

— set these variables
select @proj_name = 'Microsoft Project'
select @begin_date = '2003-09-09'
select @end_date = '2003-12-09'
select @work_type = 0 — 0=scheduled, 1=actual, 2=overtime
— end user variables

— function variables
declare @assn_id as int
declare @td_start as datetime
declare @total_days as int
declare @td_value as decimal(25,6)
declare @td_cur_date as datetime
declare @tm_name as nvarchar(510)
declare @t_name as nvarchar(510)
— end function variables

— create temporary table
create table #tp_data ( td_date datetime, td_hours deci-
mal(25,9),
   task_name nvarchar(510), team_member nvarchar(510) )

— create cursor for data collection
declare td cursor for
select
   a.WASSN_ID,
   WWORK_START,
   datediff(day, WWORK_START, WWORK_FINISH)+1,
   WWORK_VALUE
```

```
from
   MSP_WEB_WORK w,
   MSP_WEB_RESOURCES r,
   MSP_WEB_ASSIGNMENTS a,
   MSP_WEB_PROJECTS p
where
      a.WPROJ_ID = p.WPROJ_ID
and   a.WASSN_ID = w.WASSN_ID
and   p.PROJ_NAME = @proj_name
and   w.WWORK_TYPE = @work_type
and   (@begin_date <= WWORK_FINISH or @end_date >=
WWORK_START)
order by
   WWORK_START

— loop through cursor to explode timephased data
open td
fetch next from td into @assn_id, @td_start, @total_days,
@td_value
while @@fetch_status <> -1
begin
   select @td_cur_date = @td_start
   while @total_days > 0
   begin
      — get the task name
      select @t_name =
         ( select TASK_NAME
         from MSP_WEB_ASSIGNMENTS
         where WASSN_ID = @assn_id )
      — get the team member name
      select @tm_name =
         ( select RES_NAME
         from MSP_WEB_RESOURCES r, MSP_WEB_ASSIGNMENTS a
         where a.WASSN_ID = @assn_id and a.WRES_ID =
r.WRES_ID )
```

```
        — insert the data row into the temp table
        insert #tp_data values ( @td_cur_date, @td_value,
           @t_name, @tm_name )
        select @td_cur_date = DATEADD(d, 1, @td_cur_date)
        select @total_days = @total_days - 1
     end

     — get next row from cursor
     fetch next from td into @assn_id, @td_start,
  @total_days, @td_value
  end
  close td
  deallocate td

  — display data from temporary table with grouping and
  rollup
  select
     team_member as Team_Member,
     task_name as Task,
     td_date as 'Date',
     SUM(td_hours/60000) as 'Total_Work'
  from
     #tp_data
  group by team_member, task_name, td_date with rollup

  — clean up that temporary table
  drop table #tp_data
```

Find a list of assignments and assignment data for a team member

The following script extracts a list of all of the assignments and related, associated assignment data for a specified team member over a specified date range. The results script will include summary assignments that may be excluded by adding MSP_WEB_ASSIGNMENTS.TASK_IS_SUMMARY = 0 to the where clause of this script.

Tables	Fields	Description
MSP_WEB_PROJECTS	WPROJ_ID	The unique ID for the project
	PROJ_NAME	The name of the project
MSP_WEB_RESOURCES	WRES_ID	The unique ID for the resource
MSP_WEB_ASSIGNMENTS	WASSN_ID	The unique ID for the assignment
	ASSN_START_DATE	The start date for the assignment
	ASSN_FINISH_DATE	The finish date for the assignment
	WASSN_COMMENTS	Contains user comments about the assignment
	WASSN_PCT_COMP	The current status of the assignment, expressed as the percentage of the assignment's work that has been completed
	ASSN_WORK	The total amount of work scheduled to be performed by a resource on a task
	ASSN_REM_WORK	The amount of time required by a resource assigned to a task to complete the assignment
	WRES_ID	Refers to a valid WRES_ID in the MSP_WEB_RESOURCES table
	WPROJ_ID	Refers to a valid WPROJ_ID in the MSP_WEB_PROJECTS table
	TASK_IS_SUMMARY	Indicates whether the task is a summary task
	TASK_NAME	The name of the task

SQL Script is:

```
declare @res_name as nvarchar(510)
declare @begin_date as datetime
declare @end_date as datetime

 — set these variables
select @res_name = 'Team Member'
select @begin_date = '2001-09-09'
select @end_date = '2001-10-10'
 — end variables

select     WASSN_ID as Assignment_ID,
      TASK_IS_SUMMARY as Summary,
   TASK_NAME as Task_Name,
       ASSN_START_DATE as Start,
      ASSN_FINISH_DATE as Finish,
       WASSN_COMMENTS as Comments,
      WASSN_PCT_COMP as Percent_Complete,
       ASSN_WORK/60000 as Assigned_Work,
      ASSN_REM_WORK/60000 as Remaining_Work,
       PROJ_NAME as Project
from     MSP_WEB_ASSIGNMENTS a,
      MSP_WEB_PROJECTS p
where     a.WRES_ID = (Select WRES_ID from MSP_WEB_RESOURCES
        Where RES_NAME = @res_name)
and     a.WPROJ_ID = p.WPROJ_ID
and     ASSN_START_DATE Between @begin_date And @end_date
```

Find all overdue assignments

The following script extracts a list of all assignments that are late as of a specific date. The date for determining a late assignment is a variable, so any date can be inserted.

The variable @days_late determines how late the assignment is; the script can be changed to report only those assignments that are five or ten days late, for example. An assignment is considered late when remaining work and the @check_date occur after the assignment's finish date.

Tables	Fields	Description
MSP_WEB_PROJECTS	WPROJ_ID	The project names from the project IDs
	PROJ_NAME	The name of the project
MSP_WEB_RESOURCES	WRES_ID	The team member names from the resource IDs
	RES_NAME	The name of the resource
MSP_WEB_ASSIGNMENTS	WASSN_ID	The task names, assignment IDs, project IDs, and the resource IDs
	WPROJ_ID	Refers to a valid WPROJ_ID in the MSP_WEB_PROJECTS table
	WRES_ID	Refers to a valid WRES_ID in the MSP_WEB_RESOURCES table
	ASSN_WORK	The total amount of work scheduled to be performed by a resource on a task
	ASSN_REM_WORK	The amount of time required by a resource assigned to a task to complete an assignment
	ASSN_FINISH_DATE	The finish date for the assignment
	TASK_NAME	The name of the task

SQL Script is:

```
declare @check_date as datetime
declare @days_late as int

 — set these variables
select @check_date = GETDATE()
select @days_late = 0
 — end variables

select
   PROJ_NAME as Project,
   TASK_NAME as Task,
   RES_NAME as Resource,
   ASSN_WORK/60000 as Work_Assigned,
   (ASSN_WORK/60000 - ASSN_REM_WORK/60000) as
Work_Complete,
   ASSN_REM_WORK/60000 as Work_Remaining,
   ASSN_FINISH_DATE as Scheduled_Finish
from
   MSP_WEB_PROJECTS p,
   MSP_WEB_ASSIGNMENTS a,
   MSP_WEB_RESOURCES r
where
      a.ASSN_REM_WORK > 0
and   DATEDIFF(day, a.ASSN_FINISH_DATE, @check_date) >
@days_late
and   a.WPROJ_ID = p.WPROJ_ID
and   a.WRES_ID = r.WRES_ID
```

Find all assignments that have been delegated to another user

The following script extracts a list of all assignments that have been delegated from one user to another, including the task name, delegator, delegatee, and the project manager. The script lists all delegations, approved or not, and could easily be extended to list only approved delegations or those delegations awaiting approval.

Tables	Fields	Description
MSP_WEB_ASSIGNMENTS	WASSN_ID	The unique ID for the assignment
	WPROJ_ID	Refers to a valid ID in the MSP_WEB_PROJECTS table
	TASK_NAME	The name of the task
MSP_WEB_RESOURCES	WRES_ID	The unique ID for the resource
	RES_NAME	The name of the resource
MSP_WEB_DELEGATION_ ASSIGNMENTS	WASSN_ID	Refers to a valid ID in the MSP_WEB_ASSIGNMENTS table
	WDELEG_ID	Refers to a valid ID in the MSP_WEB_DELEGATIONS table
MSP_WEB_DELEGATIONS	WDELEG_ID	The unique ID for the delegation
	WRES_ID_DELEGATOR	Refers to a valid ID in the MSP_WEB_RESOURCES table
	WRES_ID_DELEGATEE	Refers to a valid ID in the MSP_WEB_RESOURCES table
MSP_WEB_PROJECTS	WPROJ_ID	The unique ID for the project
	WRES_ID	Refers to a valid ID in the MSP_WEB_RESOURCES table

SQL Script is:

```
select
   TASK_NAME as Task_Name,
   r1.RES_NAME as Delegator,
   r2.RES_NAME as Delegatee,
   r3.RES_NAME as Project_Manager
from
   MSP_WEB_ASSIGNMENTS a,
   MSP_WEB_RESOURCES r1,
   MSP_WEB_RESOURCES r2,
   MSP_WEB_RESOURCES r3,
   MSP_WEB_DELEGATION_ASSIGNMENTS da,
   MSP_WEB_DELEGATIONS d,
   MSP_WEB_PROJECTS p
where
   a.WASSN_ID = da.WASSN_ID
and   da.WDELEG_ID = d.WDELEG_ID
and   d.WRES_ID_DELEGATOR = r1.WRES_ID
and   d.WRES_ID_DELEGATEE = r2.WRES_ID
and   a.WPROJ_ID = p.WPROJ_ID
and   p.WRES_ID = r3.WRES_ID
```

Tables used for global Project Server 2002 Settings

There are six tables used for global Project Server 2002 settings: MSP_WEB_GANTT_STYLES, MSP_WEB_GANTT_SETTINGS, MSP_WEB_GANTT_SCHEMES, MSP_WEB_ADMIN, MSP_WEB_ADMIN_LINKS, MSP_WEB_NONWORKING_CATAGORIES.

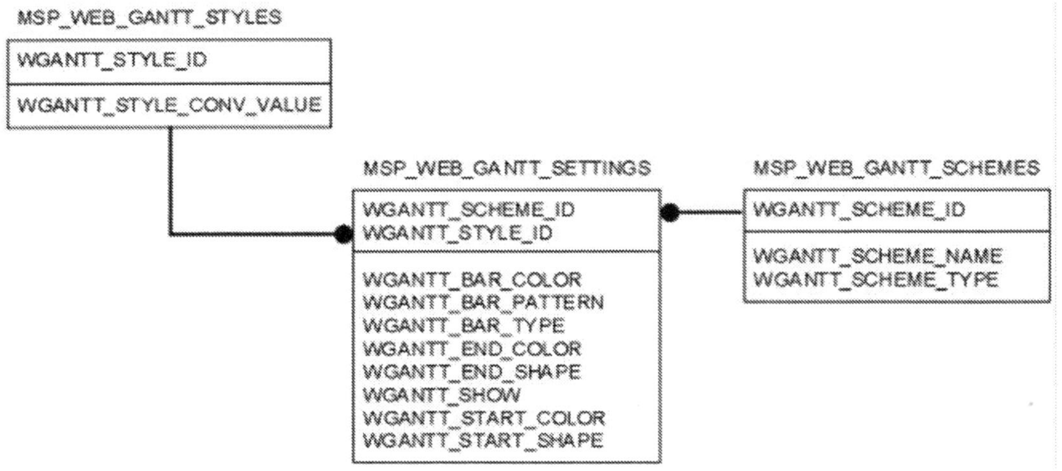

MSP_WEB_ADMIN

WADMIN_AUTHENTICATION_TYPE
WADMIN_IS_DELEGATION_ALLOWED
WADMIN_MIN_PASSWORD_LENGTH
WADMIN_NEW_ACCOUNT_PRIVILEGE
WADMIN_WEEK_STARTS_ON

MSP_WEB_ADMIN_LINKS

WLINKS_ID

WLINKS_HEIGHT
WLINKS_HREF
WLINKS_NAME
WLINKS_TITLE
WLINKS_TYPE

MSP_WEB_NONWORKING_CATEGORIES

WNWRK_ID
WNWRK_NAME

WNWRK_CODE
WNWRK_ORDER

Tables used for Project Server 2002 only

The table MSP_WEB_CONVERSIONS and MSP_WEB_STRING_TYPES deal with localized strings for international language versions of Project Server 2002. The table MSP_WEB_RESERVED_DATA is used for storing reserved data.

MSP_WEB_CONVERSIONS

STRING_TYPE_ID CONV_VALUE LANG_ID
CONV_STRING

MSP_WEB_STRING_TYPES

STRING_TYPE_ID STRING_LANG_ID
STRING_TYPE

MSP_WEB_RESERVED_DATA

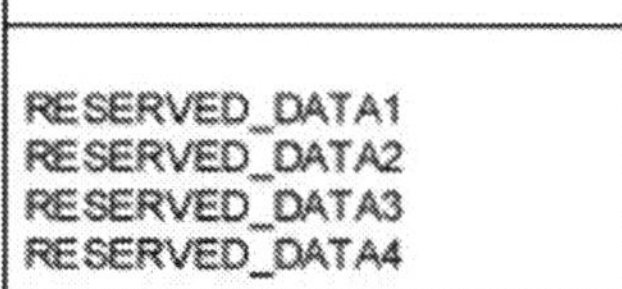

Status Tables

There are five status tables: MSP_WEB_STATUS_REQUESTS, MSP_WEB_STATUS_REPORTS, MSP_WEB_STATUS_FREQUENCIES, MSP_WEB_STATUS_DISTRIBUTION, MSP_WEB_STATUS_RESPONSES. These five status tables store all relevant status report information including the reports, requestor, requestee, and frequency.

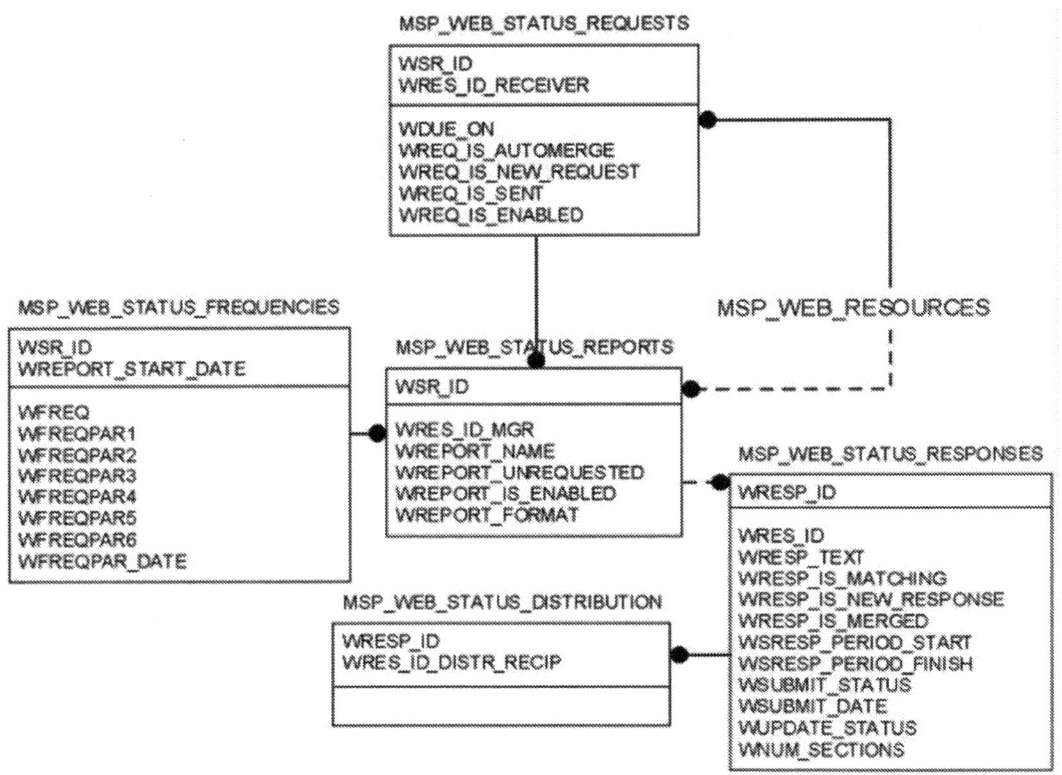

Resources and categories

The MSP_WEB_RESOURCES table contains all user accounts. Any record deleted from this table will be permanently deleted from Project Server 2002.

There are three categories tables: MSP_WEB_RESOURCE_CATEGORIES, MSP_WEB_VIEW_CATEGORIES, and MSP_WEB_VIEW_PROJECTCATEGORIES. The categories tables control which categories resources belong to, which projects the category has access to, and which views the category has access to.

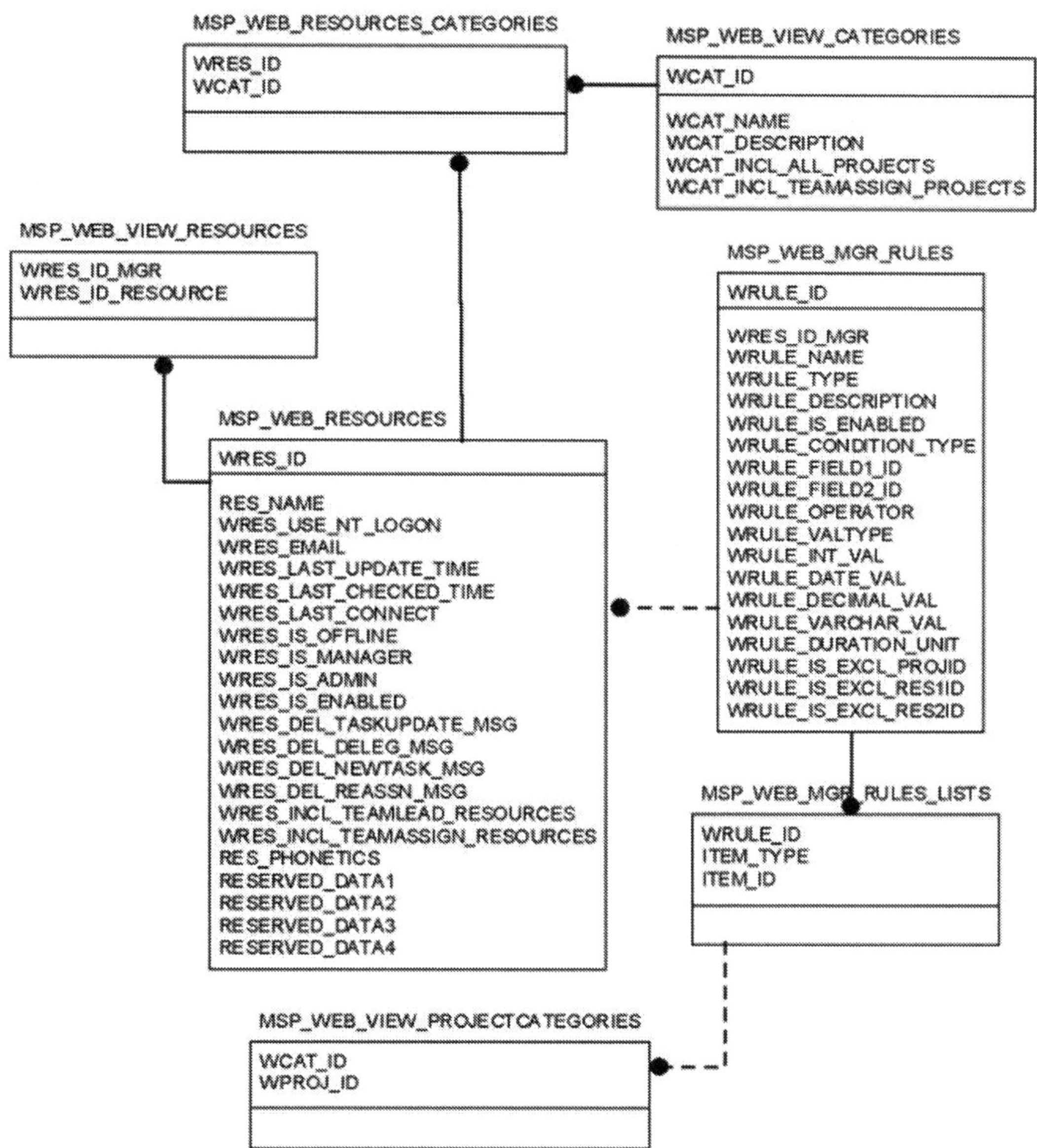
MSP_WEB_RESOURCES_CATEGORIES
WRES_ID
WCAT_ID
MSP_WEB_VIEW_CATEGORIES
WCAT_ID
WCAT_NAME
WCAT_DESCRIPTION
WCAT_INCL_ALL_PROJECTS
WCAT_INCL_TEAMASSIGN_PROJECTS
MSP_WEB_VIEW_RESOURCES
WRES_ID_MGR
WRES_ID_RESOURCE
MSP_WEB_MGR_RULES
WRULE_ID
WRES_ID_MGR
WRULE_NAME
WRULE_TYPE
WRULE_DESCRIPTION
WRULE_IS_ENABLED
WRULE_CONDITION_TYPE
WRULE_FIELD1_ID
WRULE_FIELD2_ID
WRULE_OPERATOR
WRULE_VALTYPE
WRULE_INT_VAL
WRULE_DATE_VAL
WRULE_DECIMAL_VAL
WRULE_VARCHAR_VAL
WRULE_DURATION_UNIT
WRULE_IS_EXCL_PROJID
WRULE_IS_EXCL_RES1ID
WRULE_IS_EXCL_RES2ID
MSP_WEB_RESOURCES
WRES_ID
RES_NAME
WRES_USE_NT_LOGON
WRES_EMAIL
WRES_LAST_UPDATE_TIME
WRES_LAST_CHECKED_TIME
WRES_LAST_CONNECT
WRES_IS_OFFLINE
WRES_IS_MANAGER
WRES_IS_ADMIN
WRES_IS_ENABLED
WRES_DEL_TASKUPDATE_MSG
WRES_DEL_DELEG_MSG
WRES_DEL_NEWTASK_MSG
WRES_DEL_REASSN_MSG
WRES_INCL_TEAMLEAD_RESOURCES
WRES_INCL_TEAMASSIGN_RESOURCES
RES_PHONETICS
RESERVED_DATA1
RESERVED_DATA2
RESERVED_DATA3
RESERVED_DATA4
MSP_WEB_MGR_RULES_LISTS
WRULE_ID
ITEM_TYPE
ITEM_ID
MSP_WEB_VIEW_PROJECTCATEGORIES
WCAT_ID
WPROJ_ID

Projects, Messages, and Non-Working

The MSP_WEB_PROJECTS table has all the project summary information such as start date and finish date.

All Project Server 2002 messages are stored in the MSP_WEB_MESSAGES table. Some specific message information for assignments, delegations, and nonworking time are stored in corollary tables.

The FIELD_ID column in MSP_WEB_WORKGROUP_FIELDS_INFO table points to a localized string that can be extracted from the index in the MSP_WEB_CONVERSIONS table.

These MSP_WEB_NONWORKING and MSP_WEB_MESSAGES_NONWORKING tables store the data about nonworking time including the messages.

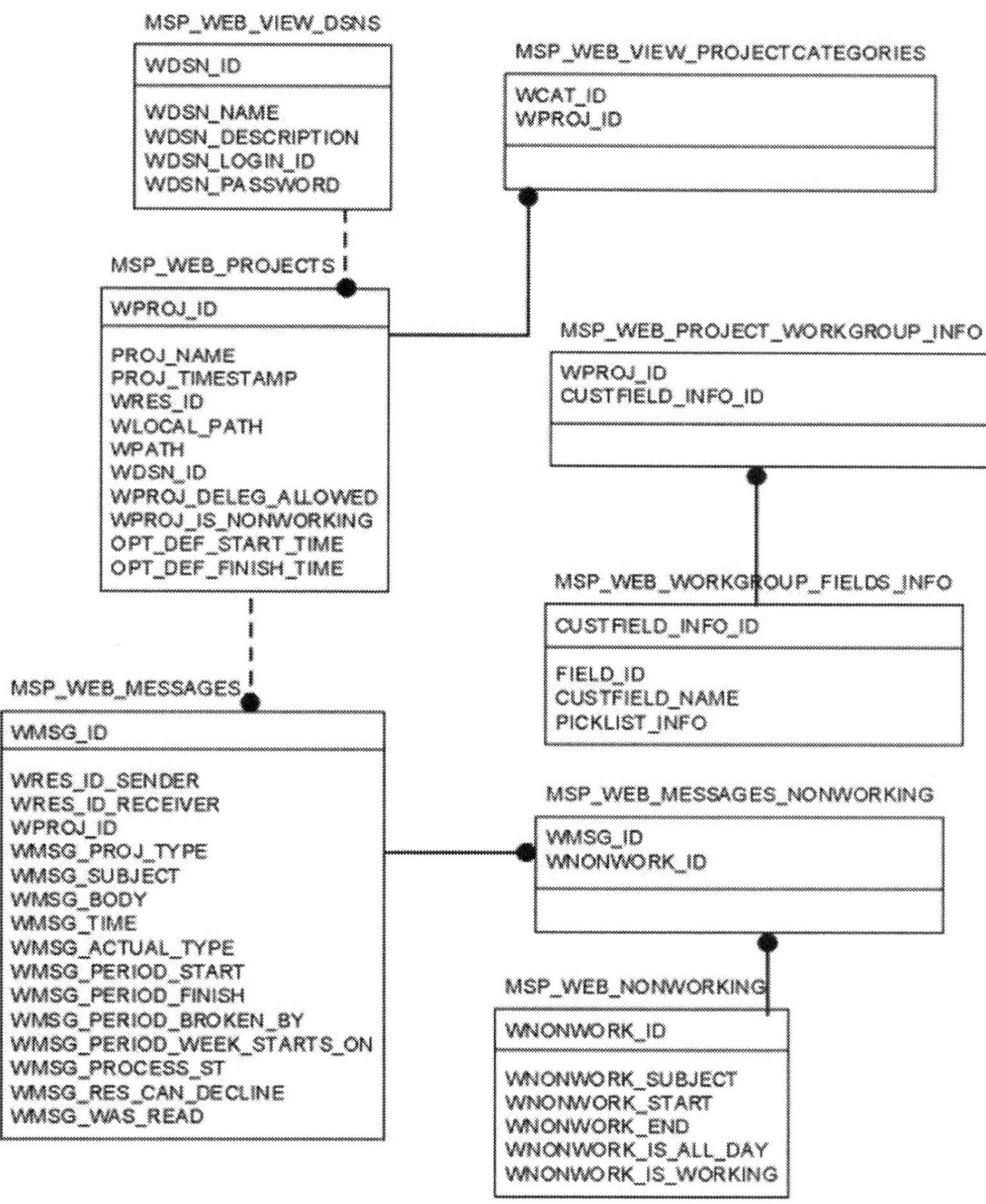
MSP_WEB_VIEW_DSNS
WDSN_ID
WDSN_NAME
WDSN_DESCRIPTION
WDSN_LOGIN_ID
WDSN_PASSWORD
MSP_WEB_VIEW_PROJECTCATEGORIES
WCAT_ID
WPROJ_ID
MSP_WEB_PROJECTS
WPROJ_ID
PROJ_NAME
PROJ_TIMESTAMP
WRES_ID
WLOCAL_PATH
WPATH
WDSN_ID
WPROJ_DELEG_ALLOWED
WPROJ_IS_NONWORKING
OPT_DEF_START_TIME
OPT_DEF_FINISH_TIME
MSP_WEB_PROJECT_WORKGROUP_INFO
WPROJ_ID
CUSTFIELD_INFO_ID
MSP_WEB_WORKGROUP_FIELDS_INFO
CUSTFIELD_INFO_ID
FIELD_ID
CUSTFIELD_NAME
PICKLIST_INFO
MSP_WEB_MESSAGES
WMSG_ID
WRES_ID_SENDER
WRES_ID_RECEIVER
WPROJ_ID
WMSG_PROJ_TYPE
WMSG_SUBJECT
WMSG_BODY
WMSG_TIME
WMSG_ACTUAL_TYPE
WMSG_PERIOD_START
WMSG_PERIOD_FINISH
WMSG_PERIOD_BROKEN_BY
WMSG_PERIOD_WEEK_STARTS_ON
WMSG_PROCESS_ST
WMSG_RES_CAN_DECLINE
WMSG_WAS_READ
MSP_WEB_MESSAGES_NONWORKING
WMSG_ID
WNONWORK_ID
MSP_WEB_NONWORKING
WNONWORK_ID
WNONWORK_SUBJECT
WNONWORK_START
WNONWORK_END
WNONWORK_IS_ALL_DAY
WNONWORK_IS_WORKING

Views

The four view tables store all relevant view information including view types, view fields, and column order. These tables link to the categories tables that are used for security.

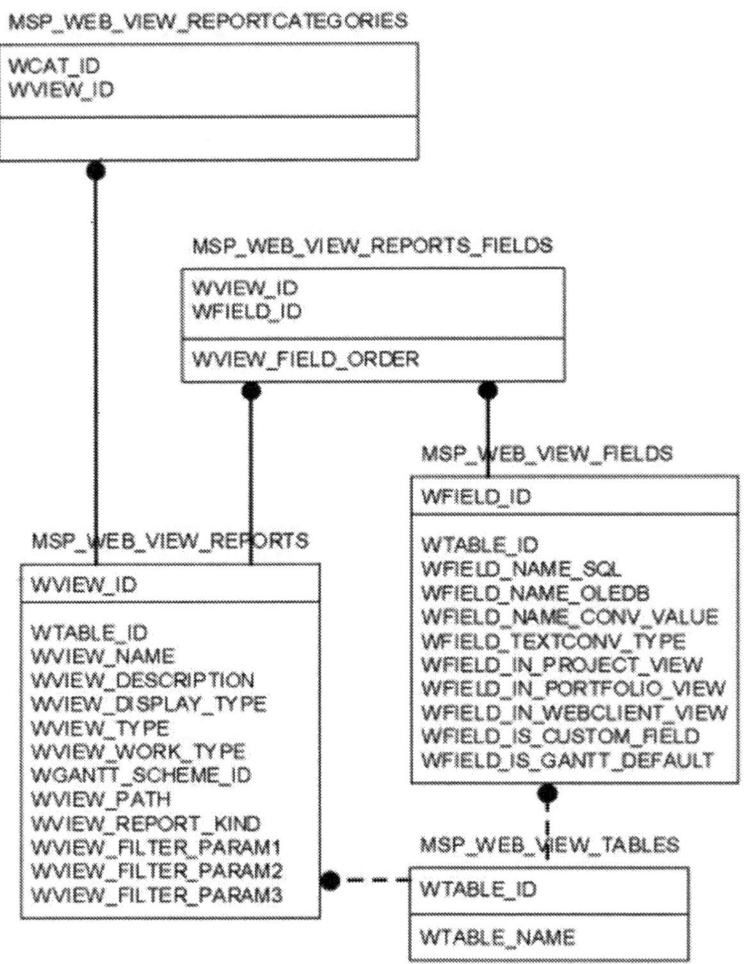

Assignments and delegations

The MSP_WEB_ASSIGNMENTS table stores the data about assignments including task information and update information. The three delegations tables store the data about delegated assignments including the messages. The MSP_WEB_MESSAGE_DELEGATIONS table links to the MSP_WEB_MESSAGES table.

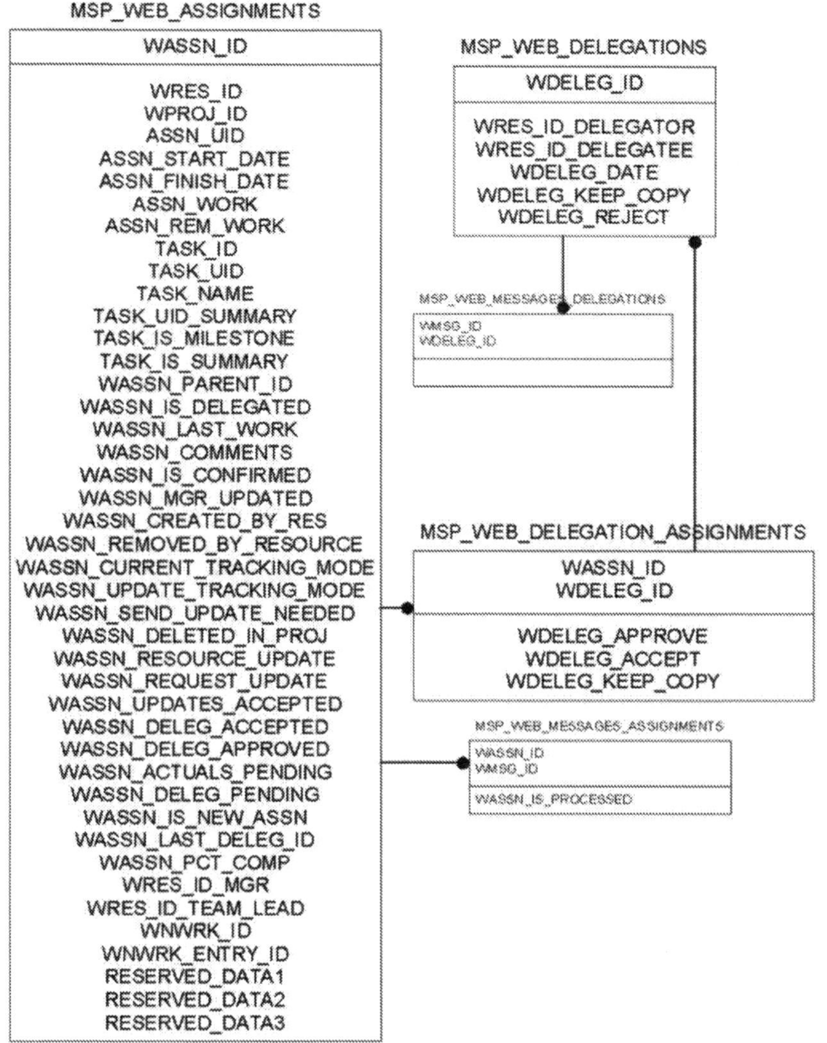

Security Tables

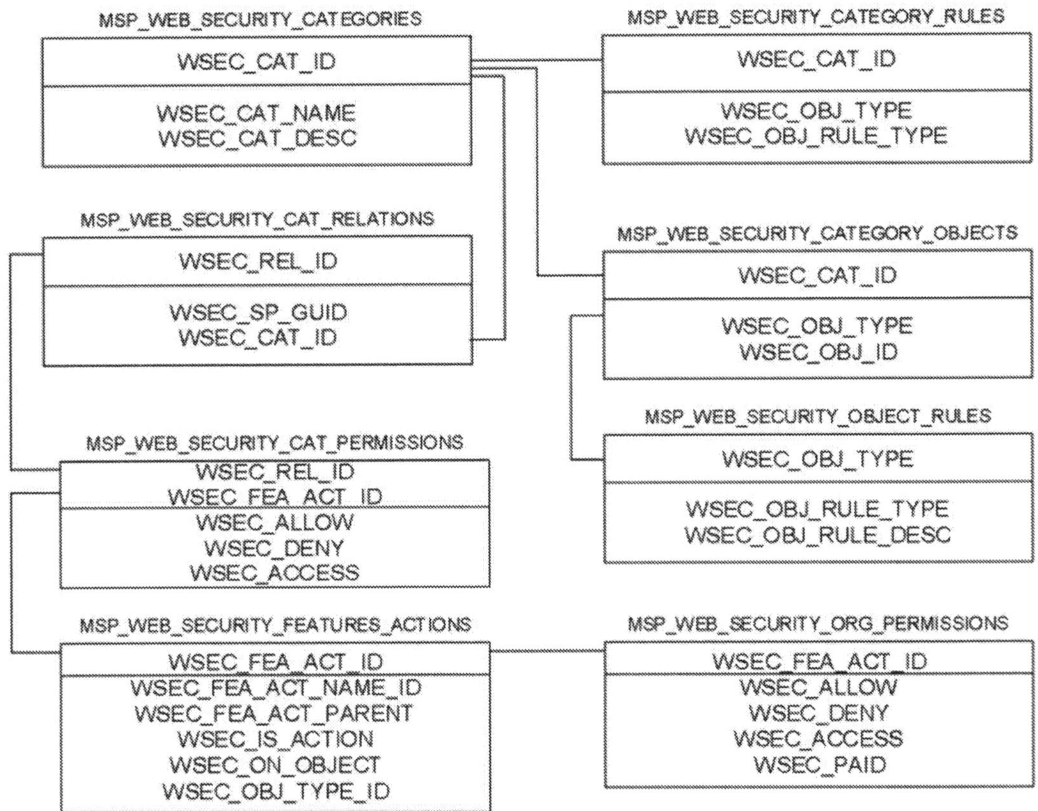

MSP_WEB_SECURITY_OBJECT_TYPES

WSEC_OBJ_TYPE_ID
WSEC_OBJ_TYPE_NAME

MSP_WEB_SECURITY_GROUP_MEMBERS

WSEC_GRP_GUID
WRES_GUID

MSP_WEB_SECURITY_GROUPS

WSEC_GRP_ID
WSEC_GRP_GUID
WSEC_GRP_NAME
WSEC_GRP_DESC
WSEC_GRP_DASHBOARD_URL

MSP_WEB_SECURITY_TEMPLATE_PERMISSIONS

WSEC_TMPL_ID
WSEC_ACT_ID
WSEC_ALLOW
WSEC_DENY
WSEC_ACCESS

MSP_WEB_SECURITY_TEMPLATES

WSEC_TMPL_ID
WSEC_TMPL_NAME
WSEC_TMPL_DESC

MSP_WEB_SECURITY_MENUS

WSEC_MENU_ID
WSEC_MENU_NAME_ID
WSEC_MENU_CUSTOM_NAME
WSEC_MENU_PARENT_ID
WSEC_MENU_SEQ
WSEC_MENU_DESC_ID
WSEC_MENU_CUSTOM_DESC
WSEC_MENU_PAGE_ID
WSEC_MENU_IS_CUSTOM
WSEC_MENU_IS_TOP_LEVEL
WSEC_MENU_LINK_GROUP_NAME_ID

MSP_WEB_SECURITY_PAGES

WSEC_PAGE_ID
WSEC_PAGE_MENU_ID
WSEC_PAGE_URL
WSEC_PAGE_CUSTOM_URL
WSEC_PAGE_HELP_URL
WSEC_PAGE_ACT_ID
WSEC_PAGE_MASTER_PAGE_ID
WSEC_PAGE_SESSION_SETTINGS
WSEC_PAGE_DATABASE_SETTINGS
WSEC_PAGE_CAN_OFFLINE

Summary

This chapter covered the basics of database structure of Project Server 2002. The Project server database tables are grouped into the following categories:

- Tables used for global Project Server 2002 Settings
- Tables used for Project Server 2002 only
- Status Tables
- Resources and categories
- Projects, Messages, and Non-Working
- Views
- Assignments and delegations
- Security Tables

Users can add more tables into the database for their organization needs. Understanding the existing database is the foundation for successful customization. For more information, please reference Appendix I: Microsoft Project Server Database Information.

6

Basic Features of Project Server

After you created your project and resources, uploaded the project to Project Server, you can find your project in Project Server immediately. What features are available on Project Server 2002 depend on the type of user logging onto it. Available features expand as users move from a user type of Resource to Manager to Administrator. The basic features of Project Server are available for everybody.

The basic features of Project Server includes: messages, password update, views, timesheet. If the project manager has allowed the resources to delegate tasks, then resources can delegate tasks to others.

Messages

Messages gives you an inbox that shows you the messages received from your manager or other resources (in the case of delegation.)

Whenever you have new messages, you should be able to see the message alert on the front page:

✉ You have 7 new messages.

Go to your Microsoft Project Central Inbox to view them.

When opening the messages page, you will be presented with a page similar to Figure 6-1 that will list all messages in your inbox. You have the option of deleting the message, going to the next or previous message (if available) or replying to the message.

Figure 6-1: Message inbox

From	Subject	Project	Date
Project Manager	Debugging Status	CX VB.NET	04/08/2003 8:42 AM

Once you click on the subject of the message, you will open the message. Doing so will present you with a page that looks similar to Figure 6.1.

There are four sections in the message details view.

The first section contains messages header and function buttons. The message header indicates whether this message requires a response. There are two function buttons: **Send** and **Close**. Once you completed your response, you can send your message by clicking on **Send** button. Or you can close the message and return to the main page by clicking on **Close** button.

The second section contains response header. Project Server already generated this section for you with your user account as sender, the originator as receiver, Subject, and date and time information.

The third section is a scrollable and editable text area. You can add your message here and scroll down to view the complete original message.

The last section is a detailed view of your tasks. On the left pane, you can view the scheduled task, time allocated to each task, remaining time, start date and time, finish date and time, percent work complete, and comment. The left pane is not editable but you have the ability to use active filters to better view tasks in the table.. On the right pane, you can input your actual hours worked for each task. The total hours worked will calculated by Project Server automatically.

Figure 6.1: Message details

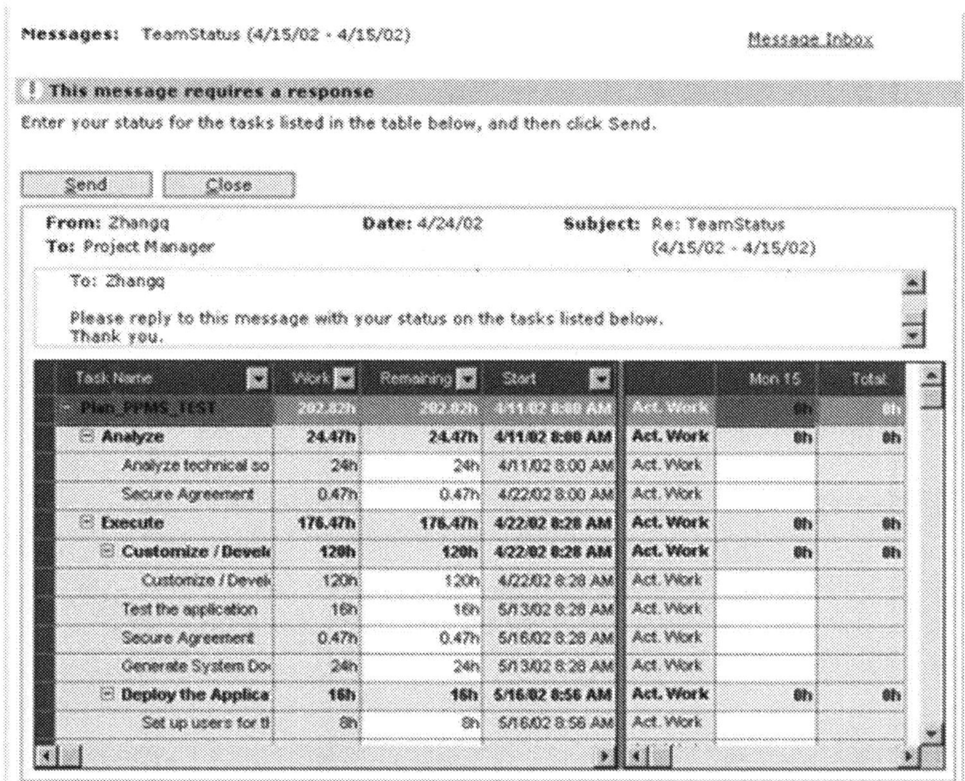

You can either send or close this message after you made some changes.

Password Change

The change password feature is not available to those users that log on to Project Server using a Windows Account. These users are logged onto Project Server automatically and do not need to enter their password.

Only users that use Project Server security to log onto Project Server will have the change password feature.

The change password page is similar to many other change password dialog boxes. It requires that you enter the old password and then type the new password twice to confirm it.

> *Note*
>
> Changing your password here does so only for Project Server and in no way affects you Windows Account password. If your password is forgotten, the administrator can reset it.

The change password screen looks like:

Old Password:

New Password:

Confirm Password:

Timesheet

The Timesheet page displays your tasks from all projects in which you are involved. There are three tabs in the Timesheet section: **View Options, Filter and Grouping,** and **Delegation.** You can simply click on these tabs or use **Alt + I** for View Options, **Alt + R** for Filter and Grouping, **Alt + L** for Delegation.

View Options

The view options section gives you control over how you see your tasks. You can show Scheduled Work, Overtime Work, and Summary Tasks.

Show:
- [x] Scheduled Work
- [x] Overtime Work
- [x] Summary Tasks

You can also choose to show tasks that appear in your Outlook Task List. Note that you must select "Show Outlook Tasks" and click Apply before they will appear in your list. Outlook tasks appear at the bottom of your list under a Summary Task marked Outlook Tasks.

Microsoft Outlook tasks:
- [ ] Show Outlook tasks
  - [ ] Include completed tasks
  - [ ] Always show Outlook tasks

Apply

> **! Caution**
>
> If you log onto Project Server on a computer where another user who is currently logged in has an Outlook session running, your Outlook tasks will not be displayed in Project Server. Instead, the other's user's tasks from Outlook will be displayed in your task list within Project Server. To correct this, the other user must completely exit the current Outlook session. Then when you choose to display Outlook tasks in your Project Server task list, you will have the opportunity to select the profile used.

View Options also give you the ability to choose the timescale and timescale period used to the right of the table.

In the View Options you can also enter and report actual values and add new tasks. Entering actual values on this page is similar to entering actual values in a Usage view inside Project 2000 or Project 2002. Actual values are recorded for the corresponding times that you wish to report on. Note that it is not necessary to record actual values and send them to your manager immediately. Actual values can be saved by clicking on the Save Changes button at the top of the page.

Filter and Grouping

The filter and grouping section of the Timesheet page allows you to view information in ways that help you understand your tasks better. It allows you to apply select filters or group your tasks at eight categories:

- All Tasks
- All Tasks Created by Resource
- All Completed Tasks
- All Incomplete Tasks
- All Tasks Deleted in Microsoft Project

- All Newly Assigned Tasks
- All Overdue Tasks
- All Tasks Changed by a Manager

The Timesheet filter and grouping section looks similar to Figure 6.2.

Figure 6.2 Timesheet – Filter and Grouping

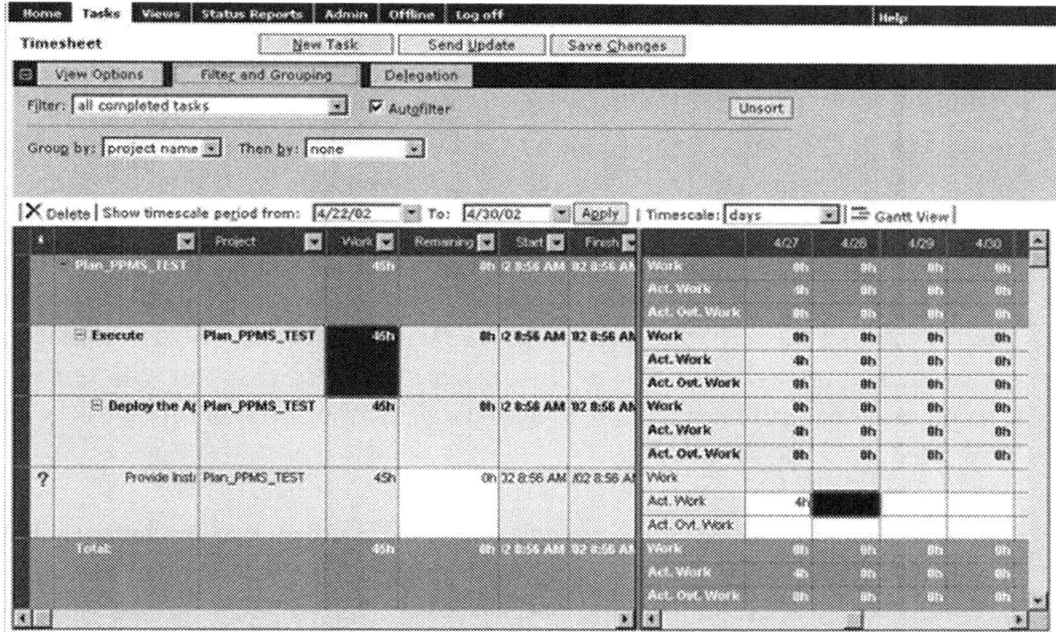

You can also enter and report actual values in the filter and grouping section. Project Server does not have any functionality that allows you to create your own filters. However, you do have the option of using Active Filters. This allows you to filter on any value within any displayed field.

Delegation

Delegation allows you to delegate tasks to other team members from Project Server. This option must be allowed by your manager in order for it to be enabled. Please see the previous chapter for enabling this option in Project.

There are three categories of tasks you can delegate:

- All delegated tasks that I track
- All delegated tasks that I am the lead for
- All delegated tasks that I track but I am not the lead for

Once you found the task you want to delegate, select the task and click the Delegate button. Then you can choose whom you wish to delegate the task to, whether or not you wish to assume a lead role for this task, and whether or not you wish to track this task. Assuming a lead role means that you will receive actuals for the task and must in turn report them to the manager. If you choose to track a delegated task, it simply means that the task will remain in your timesheet and that you will be able to see actuals entered on the task. Once you have made the above choices, you must click the Next button.

You have the options to enter a text message to the person you are delegating the task to and to make any last minute changes to the task. Note that you can also change the options you selected on the previous page. Once you are finished, you must click the **Send** button to finish delegating the task.

If you originally decided to assume a lead role for a task and subsequently decide to relinquish this role to someone else, you can do so by clicking on the Delegate Lead Role button. If your manager has not updated the delegated task, you will receive the following alert:

You can not change the leads for any of the tasks selected.

If your manager has updated the delegated task and you click on the Delegate Lead Role button, you will receive the confirmation page. On this page, you can specify to whom you wish to delegate the lead role and add any comments on that task. Clicking next allows you to make any last minute changes and send a message with the role delegation. To finish the process, click send. You will then be returned to the Timesheet page.

Work Day Change

Sometimes resources need to change their work day. For example, unforeseen sick days that affect work days. Work day change feature gives you a three-step process by which to change your working time.

➢ Step 1: specify the type of work day change and the range of dates for the change

Type of change:

◉ I will be working over a period that was previously scheduled as nonworking time

○ I cannot work over a period that was previously scheduled as working time

- Step 2: who do you want to notify

> You can notify more than one manager. The Project managers list below contains all the managers in the Project Server database. In the list on the left, click the name of each manager you want to send an update to, and then click Add.
>
> Complete the section below, and then click Next above to go to the next page.

- Step 3: Here is a preview of the information that will be sent to your manager

> **From:** Zhangq
>
> **To:** Project Manager
>
> **Date:** 4/25/03
>
> **Subject:** Resource Calendar Update

Once you send the message, the work day change will submit to your manager.

Personal Gantt View

The Personal Gantt allows you the same options as the Timesheet. It simply displays a Gantt Chart to the right of your task list. You can zoom in and zoom out of the Gantt Chart by clicking on the Zoom in and Zoom out tabs. You can also switch to Timesheet view by clicking on the Timesheet tab.

The bars represent the resource's assignment on a task and not the actual task. If, for example, a task is scheduled to from 4/11/03 to 4/15/03, but the resource is scheduled from 4/5/03 to 4/7/03, the bar is drawn from 4/5/03 to 4/7/03.

Figure 6.3: Personal Gantt View

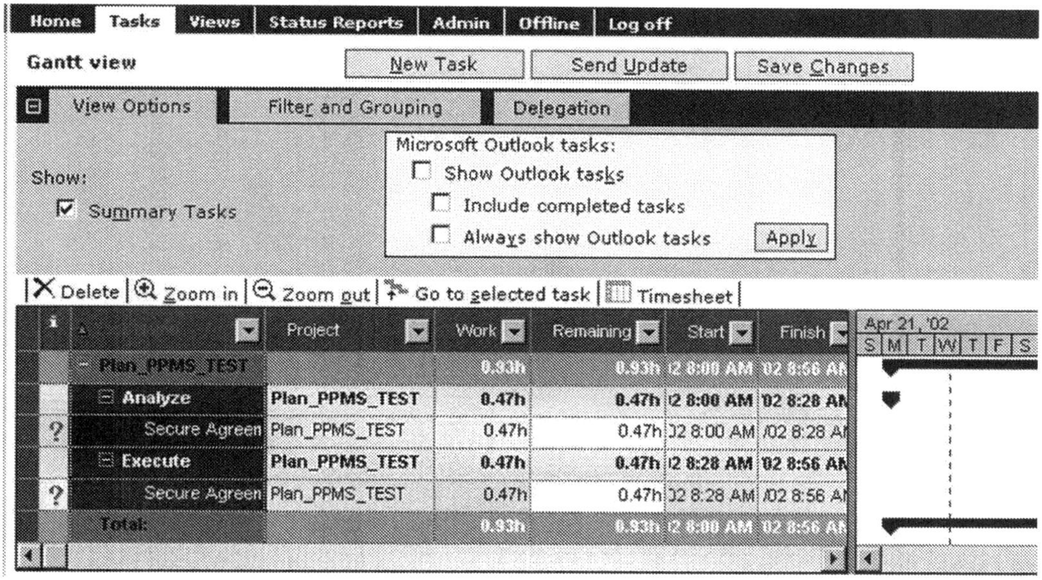

View Portfolio

Portfolios are collection of projects. Your portfolio contains a list of projects that the Project Server administrator has given you permission to see. From the portfolio, you can select a single project to see more details, such as the project's tasks and resources. To view your portfolio, click on **View**, then click on **View Your Portfolio**. You should see your portfolio similar to Figure 6.4.

Figure 6.4: View Your Portfolio

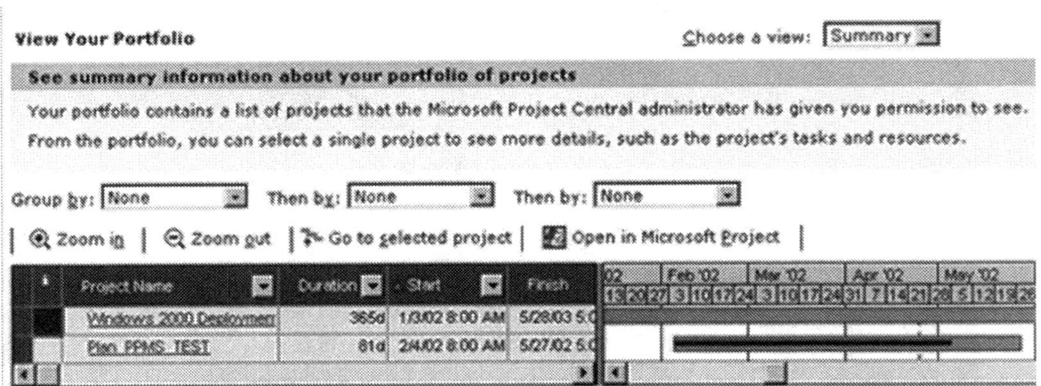

All projects are listed in the left pane, and the corresponding Gantt bar are in the right pane. The project Gantt bars are showing the duration and completed portion of each project.

You can sort your projects by project name, duration, start, finish, % complete, and work. Each category has options of All, Custom, and a list of individual items. All is selected by default when you first load the portfolio view. You can customized the view by clicking on customize. You will see the following customize dialog box as shown in Figure 6.5.

Figure 6.5: Custom AutoFilter

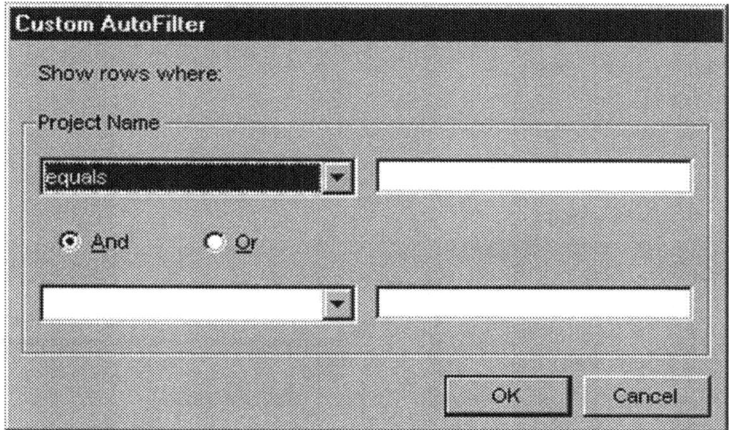

From this dialog box, you can enter your criteria(s) for the portfolio view. Project Server has the same dialog box layout for all categories under the custom option. There are several parameters you can play with: equals, does not equal, is less than, is less than or equal to, is greater than, is greater than or equal to. For example, you can select Project Name equals "Windows XP deployment." This should give you only the "Windows XP deployment" project in your portfolio view.

View Project

If you have Project 2000 or Project 2002 installed on your computer, then you can open a project in Microsoft Project by clicking on the "Open in Microsoft Project" tab. This will launch the Microsoft Project with your selected project.

You can also double click on the project title to view the project in Project Server. From the view drop down list, you can select Summary View to view the project. For project managers, they have more options under the view drop down list. The project Summary View looks similar to Figure 6.6.

Figure 6.6: Project View

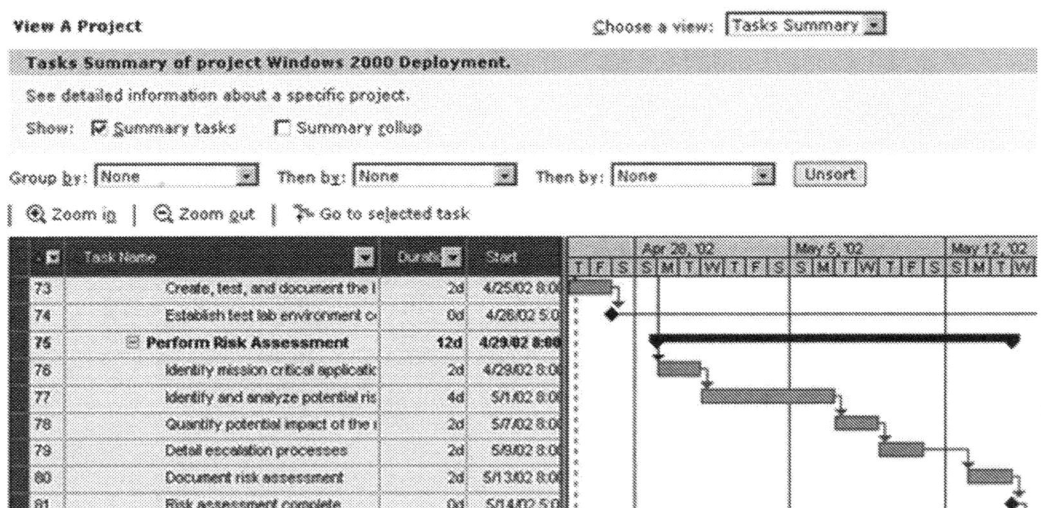

View Assignments

The view assignments page allows you to see assignment information contained within Project Server. You can group your assignment view by resource, project, task name, work, remaining work, start, finish, % complete, comments, resource name. The assignments view is similar to the 6.7.

Figure 6.7: View Assignments

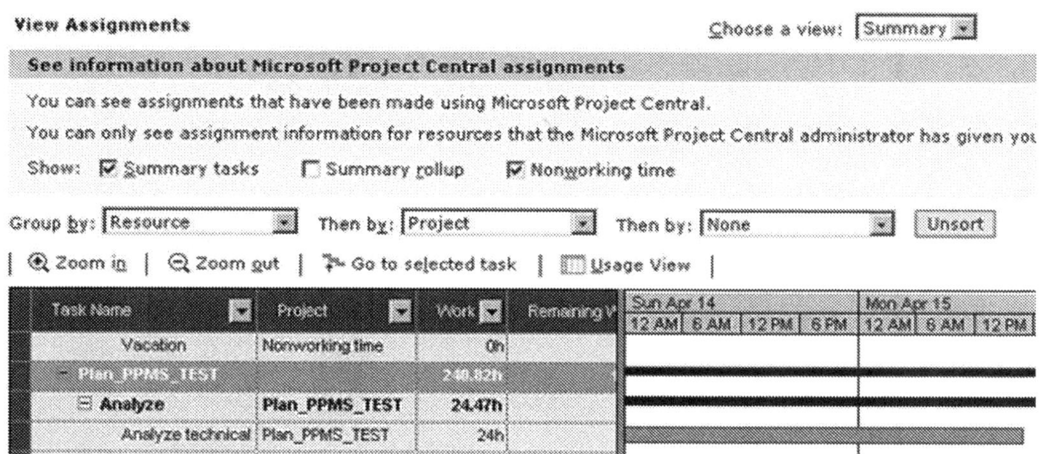

Status Reports

There are two sections under the Status Reports tab. The Overview of status reports page shows all requested status reports and also gives you the option of submitting an un-requested status report. The page looks similar to this:

Upcoming status reports

Report	Due to	Due on
Windows XP Deployment	Project Manager	05/21/2003

My Status Reports

View your previously submitted status reports, saved status reports, and reminders for overdue status reports.

You can respond to upcoming status report requests from your manager, or create and submit an un-requested status report from submit status reports page. You can insert tasks from timesheet into your status report. You can also do some text editing with several editing tools such as bold, italic, underline, cut, copy, paste, and bullet points.

Working offline

To work offline, click **Offline** on the menu bar. On the Go Offline page, click **Go Offline**. The offline page looks like this:

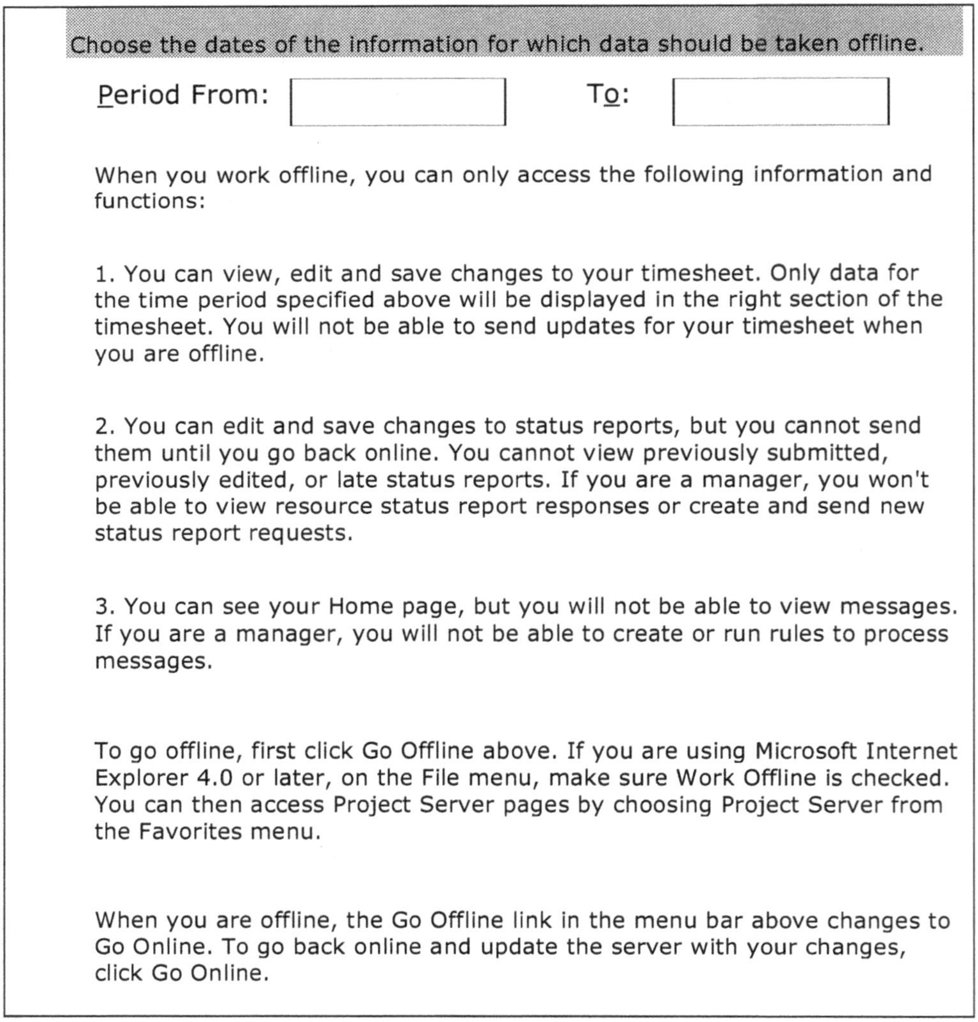

Choose the dates of the information for which data should be taken offline.

Period From: [ ] To: [ ]

When you work offline, you can only access the following information and functions:

1. You can view, edit and save changes to your timesheet. Only data for the time period specified above will be displayed in the right section of the timesheet. You will not be able to send updates for your timesheet when you are offline.

2. You can edit and save changes to status reports, but you cannot send them until you go back online. You cannot view previously submitted, previously edited, or late status reports. If you are a manager, you won't be able to view resource status report responses or create and send new status report requests.

3. You can see your Home page, but you will not be able to view messages. If you are a manager, you will not be able to create or run rules to process messages.

To go offline, first click Go Offline above. If you are using Microsoft Internet Explorer 4.0 or later, on the File menu, make sure Work Offline is checked. You can then access Project Server pages by choosing Project Server from the Favorites menu.

When you are offline, the Go Offline link in the menu bar above changes to Go Online. To go back online and update the server with your changes, click Go Online.

While offline, your work will be saved in a temporary location on your computer, and then it will be automatically copied to the Project Server server when you go back online.

To work online again and update the server with your changes, click Online on the menu bar and then click Go Online (to connect to and update the server with your changes) or Reset (to go online without synchronizing; data you saved offline will be deleted).

Note

In order to work offline, you security settings must be set to allow access of data sources across domains. In the Internet Options dialog box of Microsoft Internet Explorer, click the Security tab, click the Local Intranet icon, click Custom Level, and then in the Miscellaneous section of the Security Settings box, select either Enabled or Prompt for the Access data sources across domains setting.

! Caution

When you work offline, you have access to limited data and functionality:
✗ You cannot send updates for your timesheet when you are offline.
✓ You can edit and save changes to status reports but you cannot send them until you go back online.
✗ You cannot view previously submitted, saved, or late status reports.
✓ You can see your Project Server Home page but you cannot view your messages.
✗ If you are a manager, you cannot create and send new status report requests or view status report responses.
✗ If you are a manager, you cannot create or run rules to process messages.

Summary

The basic features in Project Server are available to everyone in the project team. Therefore, both project manager and resources have rights to utilize these functionalities. Project Server, a powerful collaborative project planning and scheduling tool, provides categorized accessibility to different groups of users. In the next chapter, we will discover the advanced features in Project Server for project managers and administrators.

7

Advanced Features of Project Server

The advanced Features of Project Server are not available to resources. Project managers have all the functionalities that available to resources. Project managers can also set up rules and request status reports. The system administrator has all the functionalities that available to project managers. The system administrator can also manage users, delete record from database, and set up authentication options, etc.

Rules

Rules allow a manager to process messages and update projects automatically. To set up rules, click the **Rules** link on the top of the home page. You should be able to see all the current rules. You can also click on Add New rules to add new rules. The Rules Wizard will kick off when you trying to add new rules. Figure 7.1 through 7.3 shows the process of add new rules.

During the step 1, you can select the types of messages whose information will be used to automatically update Project when rules are processed. Processing rules will always update Project with information from TeamAssign messages.

The options for automatically accept message information are:

1. All of the below message types
2. All new Task Requests
3. All Task Delegation Requests
4. All Task Updates and TeamStatus Replies
5. Only Task Updates and TeamStatus replies that fit the following criteria

You can set criteria parameters to: % complete, % work complete, actual cost, actual duration, actual finish, actual overtime cost, actual overtime work, actual start, actual work, ACWP, assignment delay, etc.

Figure 7.1: Rules Wizard Step 1 of 3

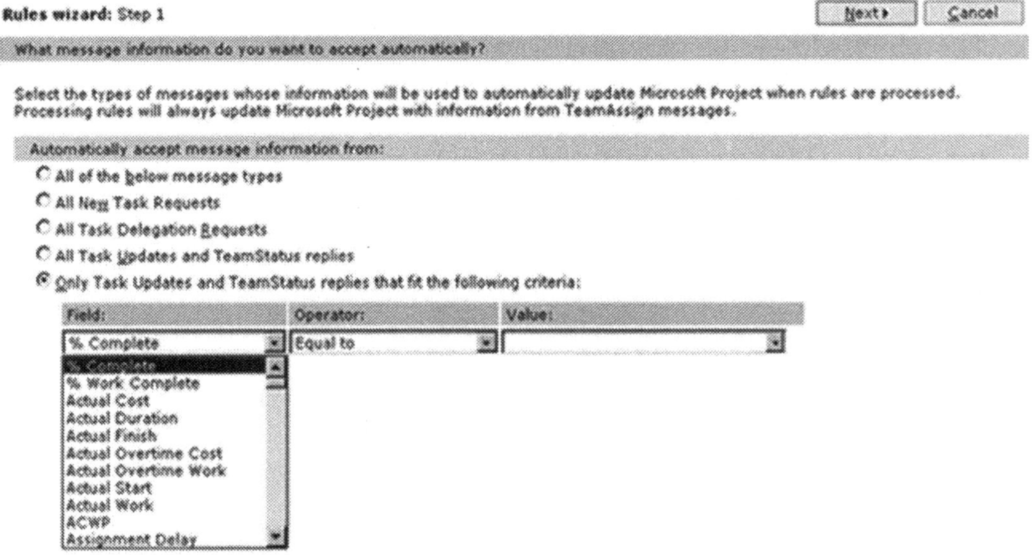

During step 2, you can select either apply the rule to all my current and future projects or specific project(s) along with option of future projects.

Figure 7.2: Rules Wizard Step 2 of 3

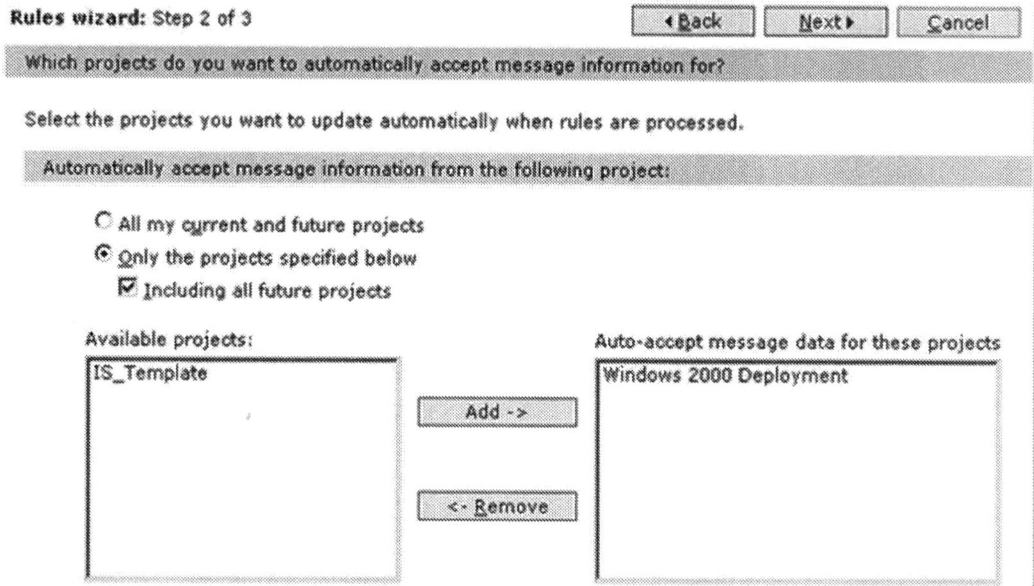

During step 3, you can select either apply the rule to all resources or only some resources.

Figure 7.3: Rules Wizard Step 3 of 3

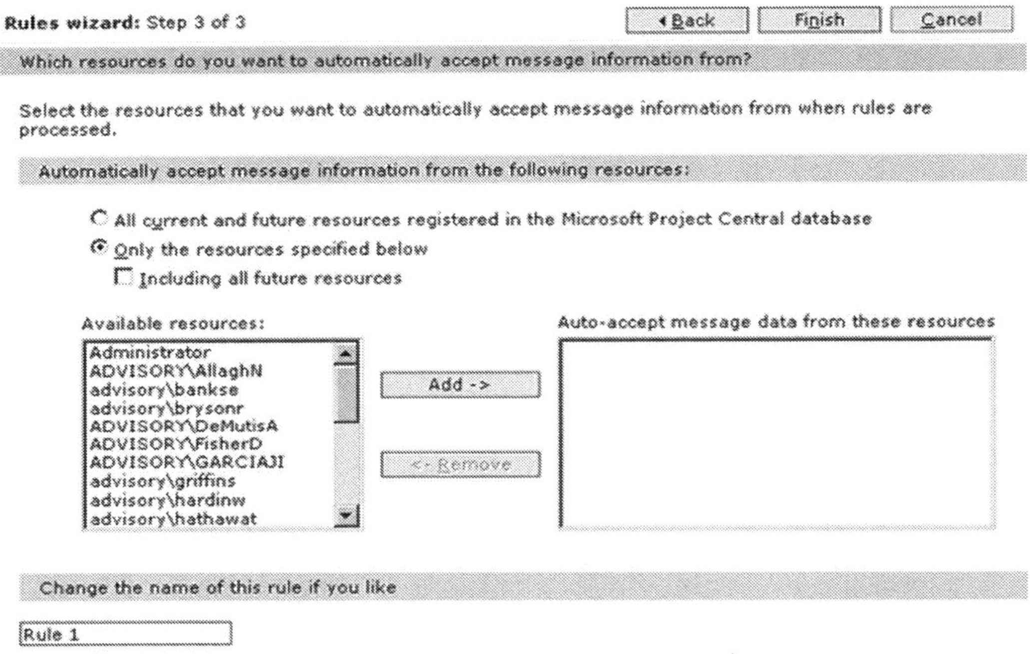

Once you click on Finish, the rule will be save and it will take effect immediately.

To modify a rule, select the rule and click the Modify Rule button. This will lead you the same three pages that you encounter when creating a rule.

! Caution

Rules only apply to messages that are received after the rule has been implemented. If there are currently messages in the inbox, these will not be processed by a newly created rule.

Request a Status Report

You can request, edit or delete existing status reports. These options are shown on the table 7.1:

Table 7.1: Status Report Action Options

Create, edit, or delete a status report.	
What do you want to do:	
◉	Set up a new status report for your team to respond to
○	Edit a status report that you had set up previously for your team
○	Delete a status report so your team members no longer have to respond to it

Once you click on OK, you will be prompted with the selections for status report frequency as shown in table 7.2:

Table 7.2: Status Report Frequency

Title and recurrence of the report

Name the status report, and indicate how often it is due.

What is the name of the report you are requesting?

Name: New Status Report

How often is the report due?

Recurrence: (•) weekly ( ) monthly ( ) yearly

Due [every] week on:

☐ Monday ☐ Tuesday ☐ Wednesday ☐ Thursday

☐ Friday ☐ Saturday ☐ Sunday

When does the first reporting period begin?

Once you selected the status report frequency, you can add the resources who should respond to this status report to the list on the right.

Project Server server can automatically merge individual resources' responses into a group status report for your entire team. If you want a resource's response to be automatically merged into a group report, select the Merge check box next to the resource's name. If you would prefer to review a resource's responses before they are merged into the group report, clear the Merge check box.

The next step is to indicate the topics you want your resources to report on by entering a title and a brief description for each section of the report. There are three default selections: Major Accomplishments, Objectives for the Next Period, and Hot Issues. You can delete these rows and add new row of your own description.

Once you click on Next, you will be prompted with the following message:

You have successfully created a new status report for your team! Click Send to send this status report to your resources. Sending will automatically save a copy of the status report for you. If you do not want to send the report now, click Save to save a copy of the status report so you can send it later.

User Accounts Management

The Users page provides you with a location to add, modify, delete, or merge user accounts. An example of the Users page is provided in Figure 7.4:

Figure 7.4: Users Page

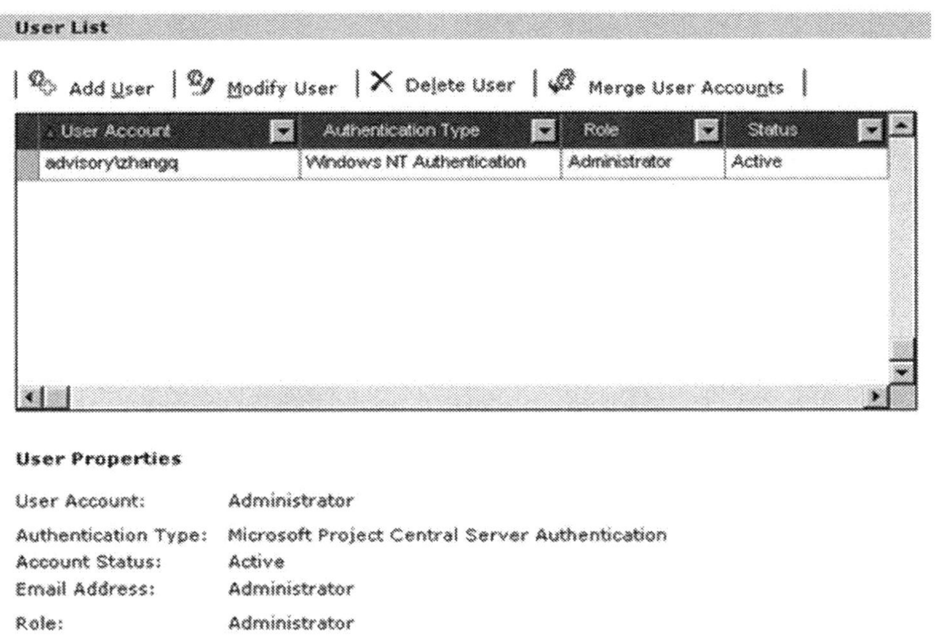

Adding and modifying users is very similar. To add or modify a user, click the corresponding button and edit the information for the user. The available information that needs to be edited is authentication type and the user's role. Depending on the authentication type, you may need to provide additional information such as a password.

Deleting user accounts does not remove the resource from the Project Server database. Instead, it only inactivates the resource and prevents the user from seeing his or her name and logging on. It also prevents a manager from sending further "Team" messages to that user. The account inactivation instead of full deletion is done to prevent historical information such as status reports from being lost.

If you want to permanently delete the user account, you can delete the user account in the MSP_WEB_RESOURCES table from the Project Server database.

Merging user accounts allows you to combine two separate user accounts into one single account. This should be done only in situations where both accounts represent the same person.

In order to merge user accounts, Project Server must be set to single user mode. Once this has been done, simply select the two accounts that you wish to merge. Upon selection, a brief paragraph below the accounts will describe what the result will be based upon your selection. In order to make the selection permanent, click Save Changes.

! Caution

Once you have merged accounts and clicked Save Changes, there is no way to separate the two accounts other than by re-creating it from scratch.

Delete Items From Database

You can delete the following items from the database via the Delete Items from Database page: tasks, messages, status reports, and projects. The administrator has to set server mode to single user prior to any deletion. The Delete Items from Database page looks like Figure 7.5:

Figure 7.5: Delete Items from Database

Delete Items from Database [Delete] [Cancel]

Delete Items from Database

Create more space in the database used by the Microsoft Project Central server by deleting old information:

Specify the items you want to delete:

☑	Tasks:	Delete Only completed task assignments (and their associated timephased work and actuals)	Ever sent Ever sent Older than Sent between
☐	Messages:	Delete all messages	Ever sent
☐	Status Reports:	Delete all status report responses	Ever sent
☐	Project:	Delete the specified project and all its tasks and assignments	IS_Template

Specify the users whose items should be deleted:

◉ Delete the specified task, message and status report items for all users

○ Delete the specified items for only this user: Administrator

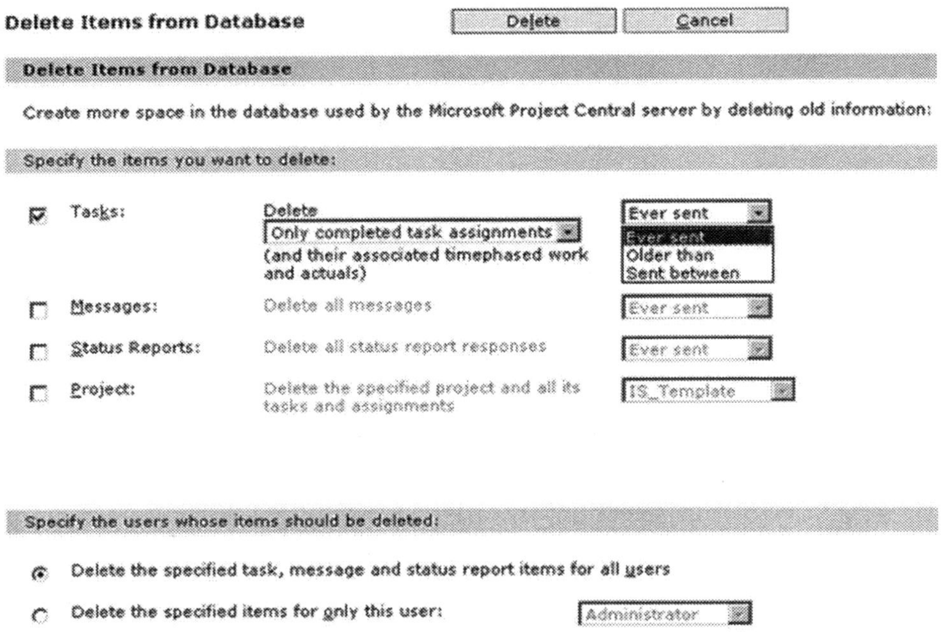

! Caution

Once items are deleted from the database, the information no longer resides in the Project Server database, but does still exist in the original Project file.

Customize

There are several categories you can customize: Nonworking Time Categories, Gantt Bar Styles and Timescale, Task Delegation Settings, Security—Account Creation, Authentication Options, and Add to Home Page. The Customize page is shown as Table 7.3:

Table 7.3: Customize Page

Nonworking Time Categories	Set up categories such as vacation, sick leave and so on, that users can report time against
Gantt Bar Styles and Timescale	Set options to control the formatting and display of Gantt bars and the timescale in Gantt Charts
Task Delegation Settings	Specify whether task delegation should be enabled or not
Security - Account Creation	Set options controlling how user accounts are created
Authentication Options	Specify the authentication methods to be used by Project Server server
Add to Home Page	Add your own links, text or custom content to be displayed on the Home Page

Nonworking Time Categories

Each company has its own nonworking time categories. For example, your company may have a category for jury duties. There are two default nonworking categories: vacation and sick days. You can set up and specify categories of Nonworking or Non-project time in this section. These categories will be displayed in users' timesheets, in a special Nonworking Time section, and users will be able to report time against these categories.

You can change the default nonworking time categories, delete existing categories or create your own. For each category, you can associate a code that can be in numeric, text, or Project outline code format. The Project Server server will not use these codes, and users will not see them, but they will be stored in the Project Server server database, where you can use them for your own reference.

Note that you must click Save Changes at the top of the page for any new categories to be saved. Also, note that there is a column on the left titled Code. This column allows you to enter codes associated with the nonworking time category. These codes do no interact with the functionality of Project Server and are not mandatory. However, they are saved to the Project Server database and can be used in custom solutions that use the Project Server Database.

Gantt Bar Styles and Timescale

The administrator can control the appearance of Gantt bars and the timescale on the Gantt charts for some or all Gantt charts that resources and project managers view in Project Server. Gantt Charts are used not only in the Timesheet's Gantt Chart view, but can also be used in any customized views that you create. Figure 7.6 shows the customize page for Gantt Bar Styles and Timescale.

Figure 7.6: Customize page for Gantt Bar Styles and Timescale

Gantt Bar Styles and Timescale

Save Changes | Cancel

Specify the bar styles and timescale for Gantt Charts

Microsoft Project Central can display a Personal Gantt Chart on the Tasks page and can display up to 19 different types of Gantt Chart views in the Views section.

Gantt Chart: All Gantt Charts | Rename

Bar Name	Display	Middle bar shape	Bar color	Bar pattern	Start shape	Start color
Detail Gantt (Views)						
Normal Task	Yes		Blue			Black
Critical Task	Yes		Red			Black
External Task	Yes		Gray			Black
Milestone	Yes		Black			Black
Summary Task	Yes		Black			Black
Project Summary	Yes		Gray			Gray
Group By Summary	Yes		Black			Black
Progress	Yes		Black			Black
Summary Progress	No		Black			Black
Baseline Task	No		Black			Black
Baseline Summary	No		Black			Black
Baseline Milestone	No		Black			Black
Preleveled Task	No		Black			Black
Preleveled Summary	No		Black			Black

Timescale

Specify the day that you want each week to begin on. This information will be used for the timescale in Gantt Charts.

Week begins on: Sunday

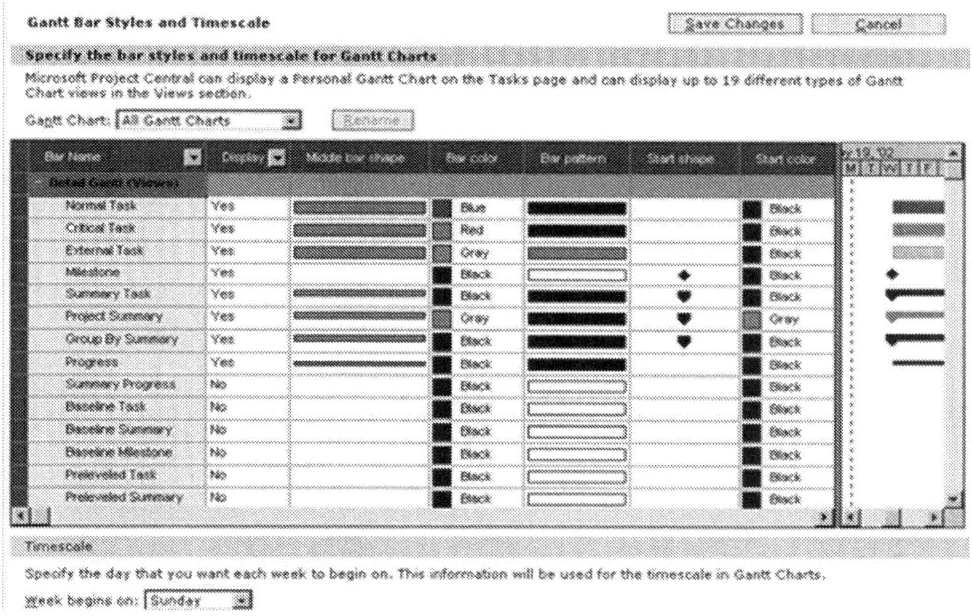

Task Delegation Settings

You can specify here whether you want the Task Delegation feature to be enabled or disabled for Project Server. If the feature is enabled, resources can delegate tasks to other resources. There are only two options: enable task delegation and disable task delegation:

Enable Task Delegation—Users will be able to delegate tasks to other resources.

Disable Task Delegation—Users will not be able to use this feature.

Security—Account Creation

Security—Account Creation page allows you to set options controlling how user accounts are created. There are two options:

- Allow Managers to create accounts for themselves and their resources while sending workgroup messages or requesting status reports
- Allow resources to create accounts for other resources while delegating tasks

Authentication Options

Authentication Options page allows you to specify the authentication methods used by Project Server server. Project Server allows three options for authentication: Mixed, Windows NT Authentication Only, and Project Server Server Authentication Only.

- Mixed. (Users can be authenticated via Windows NT Authentication using the user account logon ID, or by Project Server server authentication, using a logon ID and password entered by the user.)
- Windows NT Authentication only. (Warning: All Project Server server authentication accounts will be disabled immediately. Disabled Windows NT Authentication accounts will remain disabled.)
- Project Server server authentication only. (Warning: All Windows NT Authentication accounts will be disabled immediately. Disabled Project Server server authentication accounts will remain disabled.)

You can also change Password Length for Project Server Server Authentication. For example, you can change the minimum length of password to six digits.

> **! Caution**
>
> Changing the minimum password length will not affect existing passwords; it will only affect password creation when users change their passwords or create new passwords.

Add to Home Page

You to add your own hyperlinks, text or custom content to be displayed on the Home Page from Add to Home Page section as shown in Table 7.4 and Table 7.5.

Table 7.4: Add Links

Link Name	URL

Table 7.5: Add Content

Section Name	URL/Path	Height

Manage Views

A view is composed of a set of fields and filters that allows you to focus on only certain areas of your projects. The Manage Views page allows you to create views that let you to see different aspects of your project information.

You can create and define your own views to see a collection of projects (Portfolio View), to see details of an individual project (Project View), or to look at Project Server assignment information (Assignment View).

Who can see a particular view is dependent on which user category is assigned to a particular view. A user category is a mapping of users to projects and views with which they can see project information.

Project Server includes the following predefined categories:

- Team Member
- Project Manager
- Resource Manager
- Executive

By default, all users defined as resources belong to the Team Member category, and users defined as project managers belong to the Project Manager category.

The Resource Manager and Executive categories do not contain any users by default. You can add users to these categories manually either in the Categories page or in the User Permissions for Views page.

You can also create a new category or modify an existing one. For each category, you can specify the users that belong to that category, the projects those users can see, and the views with which they can look at the collection of projects, individual projects and resource assignment information.

Project Server Resource Center

You can view and edit your resources in the Project Server Resource Center. These are the fields you will be working with:

- Resource Name

- Type
- Material label (for materials only)
- Max Units (up to 100%)
- Checked out (Yes or No)
- Checked out by
- Last Modified
- RBS

Unique ID	Resource Name	Type	Material Label	Max Units	Checked Out	Checked Out by	Last Modified	RBS
1	Sarah Johnson	Work		90%	Yes	Alex Smith	05/07/03	-1
2	Mike Stroud	Work		100%	Yes	Ted Niewald	05/07/03	-1
3	Jim McDermott	Work		100%	Yes	Alex Smith	05/07/03	-1
4	Betty Webster	Work		50%	Yes	Alex Smith	05/07/03	-1
5	Drew Collins	Work		100%	Yes	Ted Niewald	05/07/03	-1
6	Nancy Hunt	Work		100%	No		05/07/03	-1
7	Tim Gore	Work		100%	No		05/07/03	-1

Managing Security Templates

Security template are collections of permissions that may be used by certain permissions that may be used by certain groups of users. Administrators or project managers can either modify default template or create new template.

In the Action pane of the Admin tab, click on the **Manage Security** link. Then click on the **Create and edit templates of security permissions** link.

There are two major categories of selections you can expand in the selection list box: Account Creation and Admin. For example, you can allow or deny users to create accounts when delegating tasks in the Account Creation section. In the Admin section, you can allow or deny users to customize Microsoft Project Web Access.

Modify Template

Template Name and Description

Template Name:	Portfolio Manager
Description:	New template for Portfolio Manager

Permissions: Select the permissions that you want this template to be allowed or denied.

Data Sources for Views

Administrator can establish connections to external databases that contain project information. This page lists all the data source names (DSNs) used by projects in Microsoft Web Access. Make sure that these DSNs also exist on the Microsoft Project Server. You can create DSNs on the Microsoft Project Server by using the ODBC Data Source Administrator in Control Panel.

For each DSN, you must specify a user ID and password that the Microsoft Project Server uses to access projects stored in the database that the DSN points to. Specifying a user ID and password allows users to look at information from Microsoft Project Web Access views without necessarily having direct access to the database itself.

Data Sources for Views

Data Sources

This page lists all the data source names (DSNs) used by projects in Microsoft Web Access. Make sure that these DSNs also exist on the Microsoft Project Server. You can create DSNs on the Microsoft Project Server by using the ODBC Data Source Administrator in Control Panel.

For each DSN, you must specify a user ID and password that the Microsoft Project Server uses to access projects stored in the database that the DSN points to. Specifying a user ID and password allows users to look at information from Microsoft Project Web Access views without necessarily having direct access to the database itself.

| Modify Data Source |

DSN	Description
ExecRpt	Executive report
MgnWeek	Management weekly views

Summary

This chapter covered advanced features of Project Server. Project Managers can do the following:

- Set Rules
- Request a Status Report

In addition to the feature available to project managers, administrators can:

- Manage User Accounts
- Delete Items from Database

- Customize:
  - Nonworking Time Categories
  - Task Delegation Settings
  - Security—Account Creation
  - Authentication Options
  - Add to Home Page
  - Manage Views
  - Edit/View resources in the Resource Center
  - Manage security templates
  - Add/Remove data sources

8

Creating Powerful Projects Analysis

This chapter covers the techniques for an in-depth review of projects to supply a detailed analysis of your project portfolio. Combine the power of Office Web Components and the knowledge from previous chapters, you can extend Project Server data and create additional views, charts, and reports to meet the individual needs of all project stakeholders. A powerful project management system promotes informed resource allocation and better collaboration between executives, senior management, project managers, and team members.

Introducing Chart Component

The Office Web Components are a collection of ActiveX controls designed to let you publish fully interactive worksheets, charts, PivotTable reports, and databases to the Web. When users view a Web page that contains an Office Web Component, they can interact with the data displayed in that document right in Internet Explorer. Users can sort, filter, add, or change data, expand and collapse detail views, work with PivotTable lists, and chart the results of their changes. In addition, the Office Web

Components are fully programmable, which lets you create rich, interactive content for Web-based solutions.

We will use the Chart Component to display a graphical representation of data from Project Server database. When bound to other controls on a page, the Chart control updates instantly in response to changes made to the Project Server database.

For more information about Office Web Components, please reference this book—*Professional ASP Programming Guide for Office Web Component: With Office 2000 and Office XP (ISBN: 0595198465).* This book has complete code samples for all types of charts such as Gantt Chart, Pie Chart, Line Chart, Area Chart, Bar Chart, and Bubble Chart. It is a useful reference for creating powerful, dynamic, visually arresting, and information enriched project management web sites.

Create Charts from Project Server Data

In this section we will step through an example to create a chart from Project Server data on ASP page.

In order to display a chart on your web page, a chart has to be created first. You need to create a folder for storing these charts on your server. Later on, we need to learn how to clean up the out-of-date charts. For example, I created a Temp directory under my customized project portfolio management development folder at "e:\inetpub\ppms_dev-wwwroot\report\temp" on my web server.

The step 1 is to create a chart object:

```
Set oChart = Server.CreateObject("OWC.Chart")
```

The step 2 is to create a constant reference. This step is mostly for convenience — there is a Constants property of the chartspace object that contains the enumerated constants for all of the relevant charting functionality. Typing c instead of objChartSpace.Constants every time is more efficient:

```
Set c = oChart.Constants
```

Then we need to clear the chart object:

```
oChart.Clear
```

The step 3 is to create a chart and declare the chart type:

```
Set cht = oChart.Charts.Add
cht.Type = oChart.Constants.chChartTypeBar
```

In this case we create a bar chart.

The step 4 is to create a database connection to the Project Server database:

```
set objConn = Server.CreateObject("ADODB.Connection")

objConn.Open "provider=sqloledb;data source=myserver;" & _
             "initial catalog=testdb;user id=myuid;pass-
word=mypswd;"

set objRS = Server.CreateObject("ADODB.Recordset")

set objRS.ActiveConnection = objConn

objRS.CursorType = adOpenStatic

objRS.CursorLocation = adUseClient

objRS.Open "select PROJ_NAME as Project, RES_NAME as
Manager, (select count(*) from MSP_WEB_ASSIGNMENTS a
where  a.WPROJ_ID = p.WPROJ_ID) as Assignments from
MSP_WEB_PROJECTS p, MSP_WEB_RESOURCES r where p.WRES_ID =
r.WRES_ID and p.WPROJ_ID <> 1 order by PROJ_NAME,
RES_NAME"
```

The step 5 is to attach the Project Server data to the chart:

```
set objChartSpace.DataSource = objRS
objChart.SetData c.chDimSeriesNames, 0, "Manager"
for each objSeries in objChart.SeriesCollection
   objSeries.SetData c.chDimCategories, 0, "Project"
   objSeries.SetData c.chDimValues, 0, "Assignments"
next
```

The step 6 is to set chart title and captions for X axis and Y axis:

```
Dim strTitle strTitle = "Project Manager Assignment
Overview"
oChart.Charts(0).HasTitle = True
cht.Title.Caption = strTitle

set fnt = oChart.Charts(0).Title.Font
fnt.Bold = True


for each axis in objChart.Axes
   axis.HasTitle = True
   if axis.Type = c.chCategoryAxis then
      axis.Title.Caption = "Number of Assignments"
   else
      axis.Title.Caption = "Project Name"
   end if
next

oChart.Charts(0).HasLegend = True
```

The step 7 is to generate the chart and display it on the web page:

```
Dim sFname
Randomize
sFname = "Temp\" & Timer & Rnd & ".gif"

Dim m_objBinaryFile

Response.Expires = -1
Response.ContentType = "image/gif"
sFullFileName = Server.MapPath(".") & "\" & sFname
oChart.ExportPicture sFullFileName, "gif", 650, 350

on error resume next

set m_objBinaryFile =
server.CreateObject("BinaryFileStream.Object")
Response.BinaryWrite
m_objBinaryFile.GetFileBytes(CStr(sFullFileName))

Response.Write "<p align='center'><img src='" & sFname & "'></p>"

m_objBinaryFile.Close
set m_objBinaryFile = nothing

Response.Flush

oChart.Close
Set oChart = nothing

c.close
set c = nothing
```

The chart looks similar to figure 8.1:

Figure 8.1: Chart sample

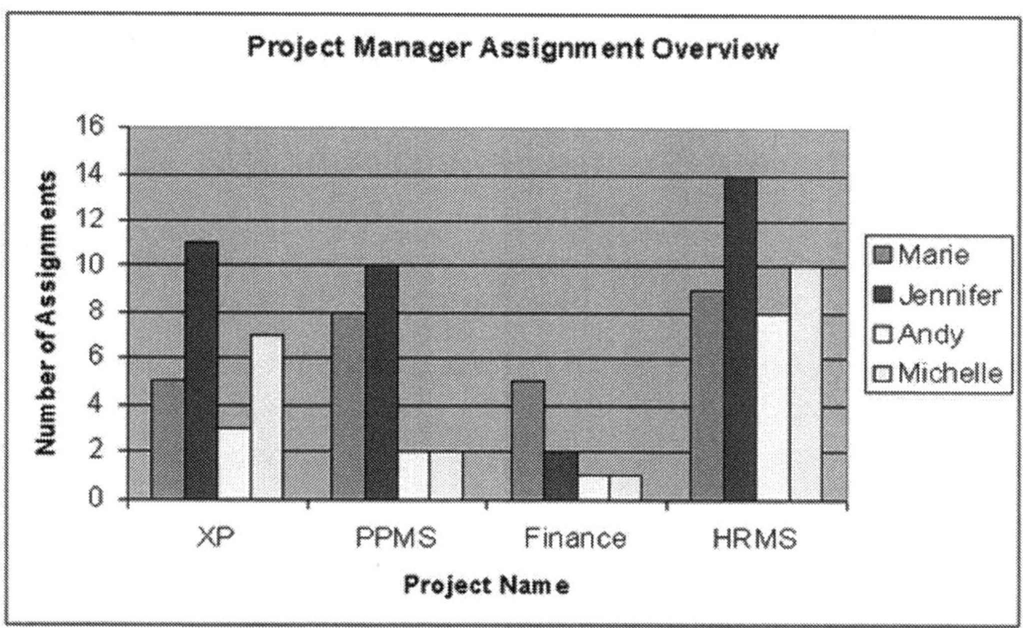

Once we create a temporary chart, we will need to clean it up sometimes later. Because our ASP page will generate a new chart each time you access it or refresh the page to dynamically reflect the data values from Project Server database. Therefore, we need to clean them up from the top of the page. I set the interval for clean up to 10 minutes and put the clean up function on the top of the page:

```
Sub CleanUpGIF(GIFpath)
   Dim objFS
   Dim objFolder
   Dim gif

   set objFS =
Server.CreateObject("Scripting.FileSystemObject")
   set objFolder = objFS.GetFolder(GIFpath)

   'Loop through each file in the GIFpath folder
   for each gif in objFolder.Files
       'Delete GIF files older than 10 minutes
       if instr(gif.Name, ".gif") > 0 and _
         DateDiff("n", gif.DateLastModified, now) > 10
then
           objFS.DeleteFile GIFpath & "\" & gif.Name,
True
       end if
   next
   set objFolder = nothing
   set objFS = nothing
End Sub

call CleanUpGIF("e:\inetpub\ppms_dev-
wwwroot\report\temp")
```

Again, you should reference the book mentioned earlier in this chapter to create charts using Chart Component. The book has complete code samples for all chart types. Creating charts is not an easy programming task. But charts are great elements for high-level views of real-time project information.

Customized Report Samples

Real-time customized reports can enhance the visibility of key project information across the project team. Unlike the default reports provided by Project Server or Project, customized reports extends the scope of those reports and provides organizational, managerial, financial, and performance information. Customized reports allow managers to allocate valuable resources more efficiently. Customized reports can also help decision-makers to ensure all projects stay aligned with core business strategies.

The total project cost report can be generated from aggregate project cost information from Project Server database. The chart can be generated by using Chart Component. This report is used to provide financial glance to all projects:

Figure 8.2: Project Cost Report

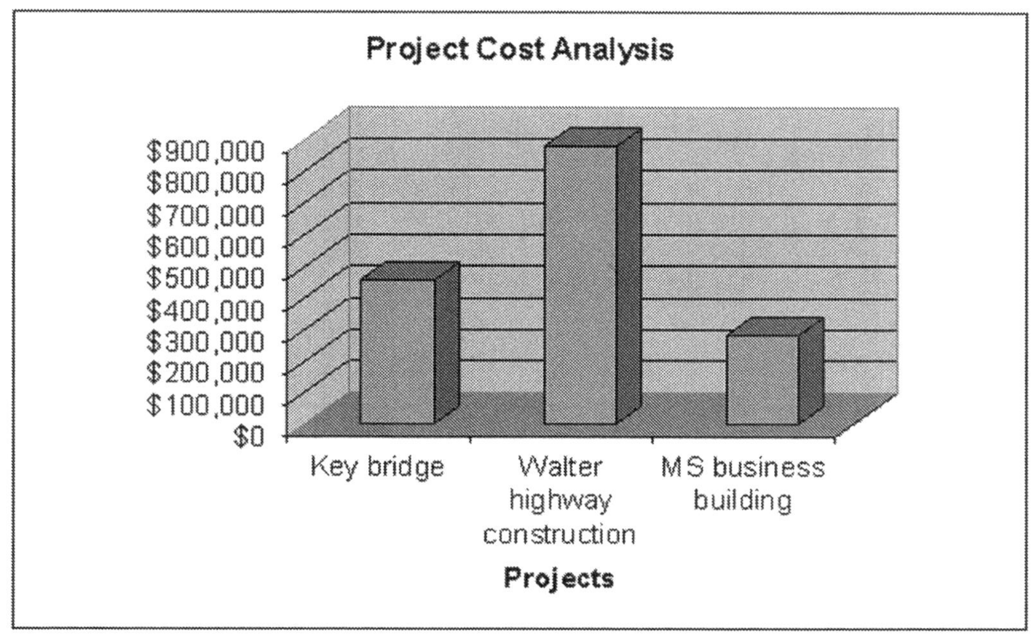

Projects	Cost	Manager
Key bridge	$456,892	James Skinner
Walter highway construction	$876,983	Marie Schafer
MS business building	$283,567	Michelle Zhang

Some organizations need to track project types. For example, an I.T. consulting company needs to analyze how many projects are related to fiber optic network, how many projects are related to network security, and how many projects are related to software development. Therefore, you can add additional information into the Project Server database as we discussed in the previous chapter and generate project type analysis report as shown in figure 8.3:

Figure 8.3: Project Types Analysis

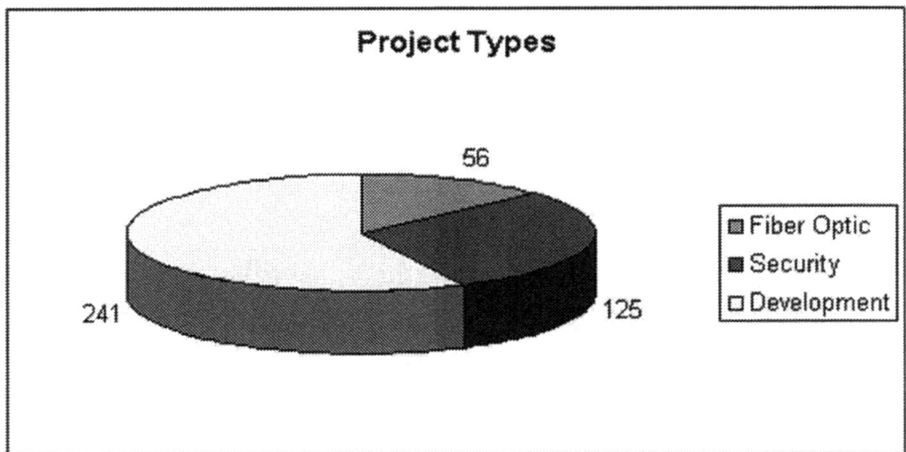

As we discussed in the previous chapter, you can add project risk information into the Project Server database. The risk and value analysis chart displays the detailed information visually as shown in Figure 8.4:

Figure 8.4: Risk and Value Analysis

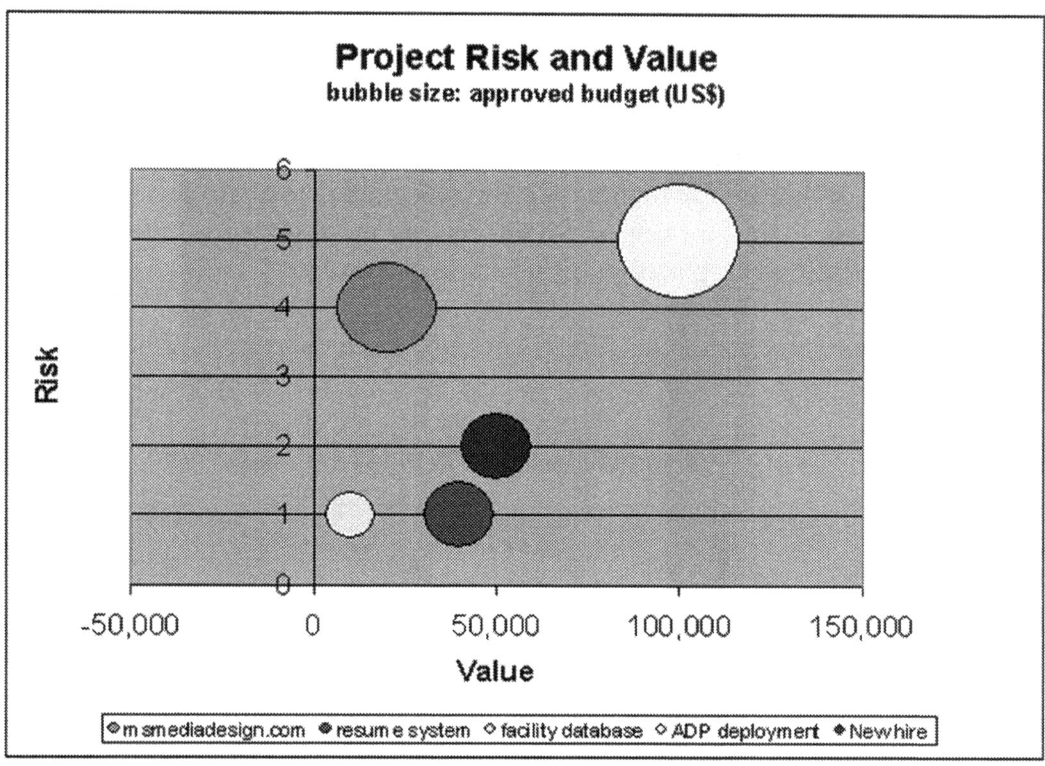

Project managers list composed of all project managers. From MSP_WEB_RESOURCES table you should be able to select all resources with WRES_IS_MANAGER is true. The Project Managers List looks like the following report:

Project Managers

Manager	Email
James Skinner	jskinner@myserver.com
Marie Schafer	mschafer@myserver.com
Michelle Zhang	mzhang@myserver.com

Variance Analysis

When project progress is monitored, variances between projected status and actual status can occur. Project managers should be alert to the cause of these deviations. When the deviations are higher than the acceptable range, project managers should consider take actions for improvement. Project managers must measure each critical project variable to keep project on schedule and budget.

Schedule variance shows the difference between schedule time frame and actual time frame:

Schedule Variance Report (unit: days)

Project	Scheduled Timeframe	Actual Timeframe	Variance	Action Needed
Printing facility database	21	19	2	-
Excel VBA	14	16	-2	-
Time off tracking application	46	70	-24	Yes
J# Programming	37	37	0	-

Budget summary shows the difference between original budget and current budget:

Budget Summary (unit: US $)

Project	Manager	Original Budget	Current Budget	Committed-to-date
Colonial Townhouses	Steve	$2,897,544	$2,789,456	$1,214,890
Mansion restoration	Kim	$155,987	$124,654	$98,247
Single family homes	Joel	$3,563,221	$3,876,910	$3,800,234
Pharmacy Building	Mark	$1,211,604	$1,027,988	$578,925
Loft Ridge Park	Susan	$2,452,889	$2,710,627	$1,238,111

Scope creep can cause significant deviation from original budget. Project managers should not permit any additional expenditure until scope change approval is obtained.

Scope Change Summary (unit: US $)

Project	Date	Requested by	Approved by	Estimated Additional Cost	Paid for by
Single family homes	05/07/03	Joel Greenland	Frank Schafer	$313,689	Sam Properties
Loft Ridge Park	07/24/03	Susan Kennedy	Frank Schafer	$257,738	State Park Authority

Summary

A powerful project management system promotes informed resource allocation and better collaboration between executives, senior management, project managers, and team members. Combine the power of Chart Component and the knowledge from previous chapters, you can extend Project Server data and create additional views, charts, and reports to meet the individual needs of all project stakeholders.

Appendix I

Microsoft Project Server Database Information[1]

General Information

Table naming conventions

The following conventions apply to table names:

- Table names are all uppercase.
- All table names begin with the MSP_WEB_ prefix to identify them as Microsoft Project Server tables, except tables used with Assignment and Resource cubes (MSP_CUBE_n) or Microsoft Project Web Access views (MSP_VIEW_n).
- Underscores separate all words.

Key columns

The following table definitions describe the database structure that is created when you save a whole project to a database. The fields that comprise the primary key for each table are indicated by a **PK** in the left column.

Column naming conventions

The following conventions apply to column names:

- Column names are all uppercase.
- Words are generally separated by underscores.
- Column names are generally prefixed with a unique identifier for their tables.

If a table is not listed in the table shown below, then any of the following may apply:

- Columns in the table do not have a consistent naming convention.
- The table is a view table (MSP_VIEW_n).
- The table is an Assignment or Resource cube table (MSP_CUBE_n).

Table Name	Column Prefix
MSP_WEB_ADMIN	WADMIN_
MSP_WEB_ADMIN_CUBE	WADMIN_CUBE_
MSP_WEB_ADMIN_LINKS	WLINKS_
MSP_WEB_ASSIGNMENTS	WASSN_
MSP_WEB_CALENDAR_TRANSACTIONS	WCTRANS_
MSP_WEB_DELEGATION_ASSIGNMENTS	WDELEG_
MSP_WEB_DELEGATIONS	WDELEG_
MSP_WEB_GANTT_n	WGANTT_
MSP_WEB_GROUP_n	WGROUP_
MSP_WEB_MESSAGES	WMSG_
MSP_WEB_MGR_RULES	WRULE_
MSP_WEB_MODELS	WMOD_
MSP_WEB_NONWORKING	WNONWORK_
MSP_WEB_NONWORKING_CATEGORIES	WNWRK_
MSP_WEB_NOTIFICATION_EVENTS	WNTFY_
MSP_WEB_NOTIFICATIONS	WNTFY_
MSP_WEB_OBJECTn	WOBJn
MSP_WEB_PROJECTS	WPROJ_
MSP_WEB_REMINDER_OPTIONS	WRMND_
MSP_WEB_REMINDERn	WRMND_
MSP_WEB_RESOURCES	WRES_
MSP_WEB_SECURITY_n	WSEC_n_
MSP_WEB_STATUS_FREQUENCIES	WFREQn
MSP_WEB_STATUS_REPORTS	WREPORT_
MSP_WEB_STATUS_REQUESTS	WREQ_
MSP_WEB_STATUS_RESPONSES	WRESP_
MSP_WEB_STS_SERVERS	WSTS_
MSP_WEB_TRANSACTIONS	WTRANS_
MSP_WEB_VIEW_DSNS	WDSN_
MSP_WEB_VIEW_FAVORITES	WVIEW_
MSP_WEB_VIEW_FIELDS	WFIELD_
MSP_WEB_VIEW_REPORTS	WVIEW_
MSP_WEB_WORK	WWORK_

Column name abbreviations

To keep the word components of column names short and consistent, use the following abbreviations when naming columns:

Abbreviation	Word	Abbreviation	Word
ACT	Actual	OVT	Overtime
AVAIL	Available	PCT	Percent
BASE	Baseline	PRED	Predecessor
CAL	Calendar	PROJ	Project
COMP	Complete	REF	Reference
DEF	Default	REG	Regular
DUR	Duration	REM	Remaining
EST	Estimated	RES	Resource
EXT	Externally	SCHED	Schedule
FMT	Format	STD	Standard
LANG	Language	SUCC	Successor
MAX	Maximum	UID	Unique ID
NUM	Number	VAR	Variance

Column data types

The following field types are used in the Microsoft Project Server database structure. The field type for each is indicated in the tables below:

Field Type	Description
char	Character.
datetime	Date, including time.
decimal	Decimal.
float	Floating point number.
image	Binary data greater than 255 bytes.
integer	Integer.
smallint	Small integer; a SQL Server system data type that holds whole numbers from 0 through 255. Its storage size is 1 byte.
tinyint	Single byte integer that stores whole numbers from 0 through 255.
text	Longest text field available; 8000 bytes in SQL Server, 64k in Microsoft Access.
nvarchar(n)	Variable-length character text unless otherwise indicated.
uniqueidentifier	Contains a unique identification number stored as a 16-byte binary string; a globally unique identifier (GUID).

Where Microsoft Project Server needs to store a time value, but not a date value, the time value is stored as a date. When you read the project from the database, the date component in these fields is ignored.

Indicator symbols

The following indicator symbols are available in Microsoft Project:

Value	Indicator symbol	Value	Indicator symbol
0	None	33	Minus, Yellow
1	Sphere, Lime	34	Minus, Red
2	Sphere, Yellow	35	Minus, Black
3	Sphere, Red	36	Minus, White
4	Sphere, Black	37	Diamond, Lime
5	Sphere, White	38	Diamond, Yellow
6	Sphere, Aqua	39	Diamond, Red
7	Sphere, Green	40	Arrow, Left
8	Sphere, Blue	41	Arrow, Right
9	Sphere, Fuschia	42	Arrow, Double
10	Sphere, Purple	43	Arrow, Up
11	Sphere, Maroon	44	Arrow, Down
12	Sphere, Silver	45	Circle, Solid Fill
13	Sphere, Gray	46	Circle, Bottom Fill
14	Flag, Lime	47	Circle, Left Fill
15	Flag, Yellow	48	Circle, Fill
16	Flag, Red	49	Circle, Right Fill
17	Flag, White	50	Circle, Outer Fill
18	Flag, Aqua	51	Circle, No Fill (Hollow)
19	Flag, Blue	52	Light Bulb, Off
20	Flag, Fuschia	53	Light Bulb, On
21	Flag, Gray	54	Check Mark
22	Square, Lime	55	Delete Mark
23	Square, Yellow	56	Question Mark
24	Square, Red	57	Clock
25	Square, Black	58	Push Pin
26	Square, White	59	Happy Face, Yellow
27	Plus, Lime	60	Happy Face, Lime
28	Plus, Yellow	61	Straight Face, Yellow
29	Plus, Red	62	Straight Face, Aqua
30	Plus, Black	63	Sad Face, Yellow
31	Plus, White	64	Sad Face, Red
32	Minus, Lime	65	Dash

Project Server Tables

MSP_WEB_ADMIN

This table stores settings for Microsoft Project Web Access and Microsoft Project Server. You can manage many of the settings in this table through the **Admin** page of Microsoft Project Web Access.

Column Name	Data Type	Description
WADMIN_AUTHENTICATION_TYPE	integer	The type of authentication used by Microsoft Project Web Access when users log on: 1 Windows Authentication only 2 Microsoft Project Server authentication only 3 Mixed (default)
WADMIN_NEW_ACCOUNT_PRIVILEGE	integer	Indicates whether managers and/or resources are allowed to create user accounts: 0 Neither managers or resources are allowed to create user accounts 1 Only managers are allowed to create user accounts 2 Only resources are allowed to create user accounts 3 Both managers and resources are allowed to create user accounts (default) This field is obsolete now with the new security model.
WADMIN_IS_DELEGATION_ALLOWED	tinyint	Indicates whether a resource assigned a task can delegate that task to another resource.
WADMIN_AUTH_REQUIRED_FOR_PUBLISH	tinyint	Indicates whether users are required to authenticate to Microsoft Project Server before publishing projects. **Note** Microsoft Project 2000 clients will only be able to publish to this version of Microsoft Project Server when this option is set to 0.
WADMIN_WEEK_STARTS_ON	integer	The day of the week that a time period begins: 0 Sunday 1 Monday 2 Tuesday 3 Wednesday 4 Thursday 5 Friday 6 Saturday

WADMIN_MIN_PASSWORD_LENGTH	integer	The minimum length for passwords in Microsoft Project Web Access. The default is eight characters; changing this will not affect existing password lengths.
WADMIN_NTFY_FROM_EMAIL	nvarchar(100)	The contents of the From address field as defined on the Notifications and reminders page (Customize Microsoft Project Web Access activity) in the Admin center of Microsoft Project Web Access.
WADMIN_NTFY_EMAIL_TRAILER	nvarchar(255)	The contents of the Company e-mail address field as defined on the Notifications and reminders page (Customize Microsoft Project Web Access activity) in the Admin center of Microsoft Project Web Access.
WADMIN_ORG_EMAIL_ADDRESS	nvarchar(100)	The company's e-mail address as defined on the Notifications and reminders page (Customize Microsoft Project Web Access activity) in the Admin center of Microsoft Project Web Access.
WADMIN_DEFAULT_LANGUAGE	integer	Indicates the default language for e-mail; see MSP_WEB_INSTALLED_LANGUAGES for more information.
WADMIN_DEFAULT_TRACKING_METHOD	integer	Indicates the tracking method used for reporting hours worked on tasks: 1 Hours of work done per day or per week 2 Percent of work complete (default) 3 Actual work done and work remaining
WADMIN_CAN_PUBLISH_CONSOLIDATED _PROJECTS	tinyint	Indicates whether a project plan for a master project can be published.
WADMIN_IS_TRACKING_METHOD_LOCKED	tinyint	Indicates whether project managers are allowed to change the default tracking method; see WADMIN_DEFAULT_TRACKING_METHOD.
WADMIN_TRANS_HISTORY_DAYS	integer	Sets the number of days (1-30) to keep in the transaction history.
WADMIN_TIMESHEET_SPAN	tinyint	Indicates whether a timesheet spans a weekly or monthly time period: 0 Weekly 1 Monthly
WADMIN_WEEKLY_TIMESHEET_NUM_WEEKS	tinyint	Indicates the number of weeks spanned (1-4) for each time period; only available if timesheets span a weekly time as specified in WADMIN_TIMESHEET_SPAN.
WADMIN_MONTHLY_REPORTS_PER_MONTH	tinyint	Indicates the number of time reporting periods (1-3) in a month; only available if timesheets span a monthly time as specified in WADMIN_TIMESHEET_SPAN: 1 One reporting period per month 2 Two reporting periods per month 3 Three reporting periods per month
WADMIN_MONTHLY_1PRD_1ST_START	tinyint	Indicates the day of the month the first reporting period is to begin.

WADMIN_MONTHLY_2PRDS_1ST_START	tinyint	Indicates the day of the month the first reporting period begins and the day of the month the second reporting period ends; only available if there are two reporting periods per month as specified in WADMIN_MONTHLY_REPORTS_PER_MONTH.
WADMIN_MONTHLY_2PRDS_1ST_END	tinyint	Indicates the day of the month the first reporting period ends and the day of the month the second reporting period begins; only available if there are two reporting periods per month as specified in WADMIN_MONTHLY_REPORTS_PER_MONTH.
WADMIN_MONTHLY_3PRDS_1ST_START	tinyint	Indicates the day of the month the first reporting period begins and the day of the month the third reporting period ends; only available if there are three reporting periods per month as specified in WADMIN_MONTHLY_REPORTS_PER_MONTH.
WADMIN_MONTHLY_3PRDS_1ST_END	tinyint	Indicates the day of the month the first reporting period ends and the day of the month the second reporting period begins; only available if there are three reporting periods per month as specified in WADMIN_MONTHLY_REPORTS_PER_MONTH.
WADMIN_MONTHLY_3PRDS_2ND_END	tinyint	Indicates the day of the month the second reporting period ends and the day of the month the third reporting period begins; only available if there are three reporting periods per month as specified in WADMIN_MONTHLY_REPORTS_PER_MONTH.
WADMIN_MAX_HOUR_PER_DAY	decimal	Indicates the maximum number of hours per day (1-24 or unlimited) that resources can enter in their timesheet.
WADMIN_LOOKAHEAD	integer	Indicates the number of days ahead of a task's actual start date that a task will appear in an assigned resource's current task list; default is 10.
WADMIN_TIMEPERIOD_GRANULARITY	tinyint	Indicates the frequency that resources will report hours worked: 0 Resources should report total hours worked for a specified time period 1 Resources should report hours worked every day 2 Resources should report total hours worked for a week
WADMIN_LICENSES	integer	The current number of licensed copies of Microsoft Project Web Access that are available. **Note** For details about licensing for Microsoft Project Server and Microsoft Project Web Access, see the Microsoft end-user license agreements for the products.
WADMIN_AUTO_CREATE_SUBWEBS	tinyint	Indicates whether SharePoint Team Services subwebs are created automatically when a project is first published in Microsoft Project Server (default) or whether they are created manually by the administrator.

WADMIN_AUTO_ADD_USER_TO_SUBWEB	tinyint	Indicates whether Microsoft Project Server users are automatically added to the public subweb when it is created.
WADMIN_AUTO_ADD_USER_AS_ADV_AUTHOR_TO_SUBWEB	tinyint	Indicates whether new Microsoft Project Server users are automatically added into the Advanced Author role on the current server running Microsoft SharePoint Team Services (see WADMIN_CURRENT_STS_SERVER_ID).
WADMIN_CURRENT_STS_SERVER_ID	integer	The path name to the current server running SharePoint Team Services; see MSP_WEB_STS_SERVERS for more information. This field is set to -1 if there is no current server.
WADMIN_PUBDOCS_STS_SERVER_ID	integer	The path name to the pubdocs server running SharePoint Team Services; see MSP_WEB_STS_SERVERS for more information. This field is set to -1 if there is no current server.
WADMIN_ENABLE_ENTERPRISE	tinyint	Indicates whether enterprise features are enabled. If set to 1, users will be granted access to building Assignment and Resource cubes, will be able to check in enterprise projects and enterprise resources, and will be able to manage enterprise versions.
WADMIN_DISPLAY_MASTER_IN_ENTERPRISE	tinyint	Indicates whether master projects are allowed in Microsoft Project Server.
WADMIN_ALLOW_LOCAL_BASE_CALS_IN_ENTERPRISE	tinyint	Indicates whether projects are allowed to use local base calendars.
WADMIN_NPE_LAST_RUN	datetime	The last date and time the NPE was run; the NPE has not been run if this field is NULL.
WADMIN_NPE_NEXT_RUN	datetime	The next date and time the NPE will be run; the date and time has not been set if this field is NULL.
WADMIN_NPE_SCHEDULED_TIME	integer	The scheduled time (in integer, time only, no date). For example: 233030 = 23:30:30.
WADMIN_PUBDOCS_STS_SUBWEB_NAME	nvarchar(128)	The name of the subweb associated with the server running SharePoint Team Services. The default value is (N'MS_ProjectServer_PublicDocuments').
WADMIN_ENFORCE_CURRENCY	tinyint	Indicates whether the user has to use the default currency set in the enterprise global template.
WADMIN_LAST_STS_ADMIN_SYNCH_TIME	nvarchar(50)	The last time the administrators between Microsoft Project Server and servers running SharePoint Team Services were synchronized.
WADMIN_SMTP_SERVER_NAME	nvarchar(256)	The name of the SMTP server.
WADMIN_SMTP_SERVER_PORT	integer	The port used by the SMTP server.
WADMIN_INTRANET_SERVER_URL	nvarchar(255)	The URL for the intranet server.
WADMIN_EXTRANET_SERVER_URL	nvarchar(255)	The URL for the extranet server.
WADMIN_ONLY_PRO_PUBLISH	tinyint	Indicates whether only projects created with Microsoft Project Professional may be published to Microsoft Project Server.

MSP_WEB_ADMIN_CUBE

This table stores information related to setting up the Assignment and Resource cubes, which help provide analysis and reporting functionality in Microsoft Project Web Access. The following tables are generated when building an Assignment or Resource cube. Please see each table's description for more information about the type of data stored in them:

- MSP_CUBE_ASSN_FACT
- MSP_CUBE_ENTERPRISE_ASSIGNMENT_OUTLINE_n
- MSP_CUBE_ENTERPRISE_PROJECT_OUTLINE_n
- MSP_CUBE_ENTERPRISE_RESOURCE_OUTLINE_n
- MSP_CUBE_PROJ_VERSIONS
- MSP_CUBE_PROJECTS
- MSP_CUBE_RESOURCES
- MSP_CUBE_RES_AVAIL_FACT
- MSP_CUBE_TIME_BY_DAY

	Column Name	Data Type	Description
PK	WADMIN_CUBE_ID	integer	The unique ID for the Assignment or Resource cube.
	WADMIN_CUBE_BUILD	tinyint	Indicates whether to build an Assignment or Resource cube of data.
	WADMIN_CUBE_OLAP_SERVER	nvarchar(100)	The name of the OLAP server; required if building an OLAP cube of data.
	WADMIN_CUBE_NAME	nvarchar(100)	The name of the cube.
	WADMIN_CUBE_DESCRIPTION	nvarchar(255)	The description of the cube; optional if building an OLAP cube of data.
	WADMIN_CUBE_DATE_RANGE	integer	Indicates the date range to use when building an OLAP cube: 0 Use the earliest project start date and the latest project finish date (default) 1 Use a rolling date range that begins "x" days before and ends "y" days after the current date 2 Use a date range with fixed start and fixed end dates
	WADMIN_CUBE_DATE_RANGE_NEXT_NUM	integer	Indicates the number of units (days, weeks, or months) to use after the current date when building an OLAP cube; required if you use a rolling date range when building an OLAP cube.

WADMIN_CUBE_DATE_RANGE_ NEXT_UNIT	integer	Indicates the timescale for a rolling date range when building an OLAP cube: 0 Day (default) 1 Week 2 Month
WADMIN_CUBE_DATE_RANGE_ PAST_NUM	integer	Specifies the number of units (days, weeks, or months) to use before the current date when building an OLAP cube; required if you use a rolling date range when building an OLAP cube.
WADMIN_CUBE_DATE_RANGE_ PAST_UNIT	integer	Indicates the timescale for a rolling date range when building an OLAP cube: 0 Day (default) 1 Week 2 Month
WADMIN_CUBE_DATE_ RANGE_FROM	datetime	Specifies the start date to use when building an OLAP cube; required if you use a date range with a fixed start and end date.
WADMIN_CUBE_DATE_ RANGE_TO	datetime	Specifies the end date to use when building an OLAP cube; required if you use a date range with a fixed start and end date.
WADMIN_CUBE_LOG_STATUS_ TIMESTAMP	datetime	The most recent date and time that the admin cube log was accessed.
WADMIN_CUBE_LOG_STATUS	integer	The status of the log timestamp: -1 Warning; the cube was built, but not everything was built correctly 0 The cube was built correctly Any The cube was built incorrectly (failed); refer to WADMIN_CUBE_LOG_STATUS_TEXT for the specific error message
WADMIN_CUBE_LOG_ STATUS_TEXT	nvarchar(255)	The text of the error message.
WADMIN_RES_DATE_RANGE	integer	Indicates the date range to use for resource availability when building a resource cube: 0 Use a rolling date range that begins "x" days before and ends "y" days after the current date 1 Use a date range with a fixed start and end date
WADMIN_RES_DATE_ RANGE_NEXT_NUM	integer	Specifies the number of units (days, weeks, or months) to use after the current date when building a resource cube; required if you use a rolling date range when building a resource cube.
WADMIN_RES_DATE_ RANGE_NEXT_UNIT	integer	Indicates the timescale for a rolling date range when building a resource cube: 0 Day (default) 1 Week 2 Month

WADMIN_RES_DATE_ RANGE_PAST_NUM	integer	Specifies the number of units (days, weeks, or months) to use before the current date when building a resource cube; required if you use a rolling date range when building a resource cube.
WADMIN_RES_DATE_ RANGE_PAST_UNIT	integer	Indicates the timescale for a rolling date range when building a resource cube: 0 Day (default) 1 Week 2 Month
WADMIN_RES_DATE_ RANGE_FROM	datetime	Specifies the availability start date to use when building a Resource cube; required if you use a data range with a fixed start and end date.
WADMIN_RES_DATE_ RANGE_TO	datetime	Specifies the availability end date to use when building a Resource cube; required if you use a data range with a fixed start and end date.
WADMIN_AUTO_LAST_RUN	datetime	The date and time that the OLAP or resource cube was last created automatically by the cube generation process built into Microsoft Project Server and Microsoft Project Web Access. This field is not changed by manual updates.
WADMIN_UPDATE_RECUR	tinyint	Indicates whether updates occur every "x" number of days, weeks, or months (default), or only when specified.
WADMIN_UPDATE_ FREQ_EVERY	integer	Specifies the number of units (days, weeks, or months) that are used when automatically updating an Assignment or Resource cube.
WADMIN_UPDATE_ FREQ_UNIT	integer	Indicates the timescale for the units that are used when automatically updating an Assignment or Resource cube: 0 Day (default) 1 Week 2 Month
WADMIN_UPDATE_ FREQ_START_DATE	datetime	The day of the week that the WADMIN_UPDATE_FREQ_UNIT begins.
WADMIN_UPDATE_ FREQ_START_TIME	integer	The time of day that the WADMIN_UPDATE_FREQ_UNIT begins.
WADMIN_UPDATE_RES	tinyint	Indicates whether a resource cube is being built; this field should be 0 unless you look at the database while building a cube. If this field is set to 1 and you are not building a cube, then an error has occurred.
WADMIN_UPDATE_CUBE	tinyint	Indicates whether an OLAP cube is being built; this field should be 0 unless you look at the database while building a cube. If this field is set to 1 and you are not building a cube, then an error has occurred.

MSP_WEB_ADMIN_LINKS

This table stores information needed to display links and content on the Microsoft Project Web Access Home page. This information can be managed by clicking **Admin**, **Customize Microsoft Project Web Access**, and then **Home page format** in Microsoft Project Web Access.

Note Use caution when adding content from an external Web site to your Microsoft Project Web Access Home page. You should perform a thorough security check on all external content you want to add to Microsoft Project Web Access. If you do not perform this security check, you may leave your Microsoft Project Web Access site open to unnecessary security risks.

	Column Name	Data Type	Description
PK	WLINKS_ID	integer	The unique ID for the link or content
	WLINKS_HREF	nvarchar(500)	The full path for the link or content, including the http:// or full path name
	WLINKS_NAME	nvarchar(255)	The name of the link or content file
	WLINKS_HEIGHT	nvarchar(255)	The height in pixels that a content section occupies on the Microsoft Project Web Access Home page; this field should not be used for links
	WLINKS_TYPE	integer	Indicates whether the row is a link or content: 0 Link 1 Content

MSP_WEB_ASSIGNMENTS

This table contains assignment data plus project summary records.

	Column Name	Data Type	Description
PK	WASSN_ID	integer	The unique ID for the assignment.
	WRES_ID	integer	Refers to a valid WRES_ID in the MSP_WEB_RESOURCES table.
	WASSN_PARENT_ID	integer	Refers to a valid WASSN_ID in the MSP_WEB_ASSIGNMENTS table if this assignment has a parent assignment.
	WPROJ_ID	integer	Refers to a valid WPROJ_ID in the MSP_WEB_PROJECTS table.
	WRES_ID_MGR	integer	The ID of the project manager for this task. Refers to a valid WRES_ID in the MSP_WEB_RESOURCES table.
	ASSN_UID	integer	Refers to a valid ASSN_ID in the MSP_ASSIGNMENTS table.
	TASK_UID	integer	Refers to a valid TASK_UID in the MSP_TASKS table.
	TASK_ID	integer	Refers to a valid TASK_ID in the MSP_TASKS table.

TASK_UID_SUMMARY	integer	Refers to a valid TASK_UID in the MSP_ASSIGNMENTS table if this task is a summary task.
TASK_NAME	nvarchar(255)	Refers to a valid TASK_NAME field in the MSP_TASKS table.
ASSN_START_DATE	datetime	The date and time that an assigned resource is scheduled to begin working on a task.
ASSN_FINISH_DATE	datetime	The date and time that an assigned resource is scheduled to complete work on a task.
ASSN_WORK	decimal	The total amount of work scheduled to be performed by a resource on a task.
ASSN_ACT_WORK	decimal	The amount of work that has already been done by a resource on a task.
ASSN_REM_WORK	decimal	The amount of time required by a resource assigned to a task to complete an assignment.
WASSN_LAST_WORK	decimal	The scheduled work from the last update from Microsoft Project.
WASSN_COMMENTS	ntext	Contains user comments about the assignment; archived to WASSN_HISTORY_NOTES when a manager updates the assignment.
WASSN_HISTORY_NOTES	ntext	Contains history notes about the assignment.
WASSN_NOTE_STATUS	integer	Indicates whether a note has been entered for the assignment: 0 There are no notes for this assignment 1 There are current notes for this assignment 2 There are only history notes for this assignment
TASK_IS_MILESTONE	tinyint	Indicates whether a task is a milestone.
TASK_IS_SUMMARY	tinyint	Indicates whether a task is a summary task.
WASSN_IS_CONFIRMED	tinyint	Indicates whether a resource assigned to a task has accepted or rejected the task assignment.
WASSN_MGR_UPDATED	tinyint	Indicates whether the assignment has been updated by a manager.
WASSN_CREATED_BY_RES	integer	Indicates whether a new task was created by a resource: 0 Not a new task created by a resource 1 A new task created by a resource 2 A new task sent to a Project Manager, but not yet updated
WASSN_REMOVED_BY_RESOURCE	integer	Indicates whether the assignment has been removed from a resource's timesheet by that resource.
WASSN_CURRENT_TRACKING_MODE	integer	Indicates the current method used to track projects: 0 None (default) 1 Timephased actuals 2 Percent complete tracking 3 Total actual work and remaining work tracking

<table>
<tr><td></td><td>WASSN_UPDATE_TRACKING_MODE</td><td>integer</td><td>Indicates the updated method used to track projects:
0 None (default)
1 Timephased actuals
2 Percent complete tracking
3 Total actual work and remaining work tracking</td></tr>
<tr><td></td><td>WASSN_SEND_UPDATE_NEEDED</td><td>tinyint</td><td>Indicates whether an update should be sent to resources for this assignment.</td></tr>
<tr><td></td><td>WASSN_DELETED_IN_PROJ</td><td>tinyint</td><td>Indicates whether an assignment has been deleted by the manager.</td></tr>
<tr><td></td><td>WASSN_RESOURCE_UPDATE</td><td>tinyint</td><td>Indicates whether a team resource has submitted actuals.</td></tr>
<tr><td></td><td>WASSN_REQUEST_UPDATE</td><td>tinyint</td><td>Indicates whether an actuals update was requested.</td></tr>
<tr><td></td><td>WASSN_UPDATES_ACCEPTED</td><td>tinyint</td><td>Indicates whether a task update has been accepted by the resource or manager.</td></tr>
<tr><td></td><td>WASSN_DELEG_ACCEPTED</td><td>tinyint</td><td>Indicates whether task delegation has been accepted by the resource.</td></tr>
<tr><td></td><td>WASSN_DELEG_APPROVED</td><td>tinyint</td><td>Indicates whether task delegation has been approved by the manager.</td></tr>
<tr><td></td><td>WASSN_ACTUALS_PENDING</td><td>tinyint</td><td>Indicates whether actuals have been submitted, but not yet updated by the manager.</td></tr>
<tr><td></td><td>WASSN_DELEG_PENDING</td><td>tinyint</td><td>Indicates whether task delegation is pending manager approval.</td></tr>
<tr><td></td><td>WASSN_IS_DELEGATED</td><td>tinyint</td><td>Indicates whether an assignment has been delegated since the last update.</td></tr>
<tr><td></td><td>WASSN_IS_NEW_ASSN</td><td>tinyint</td><td>Indicates whether the assignment is a new assignment.</td></tr>
<tr><td></td><td>WASSN_UPDATE_STATUS</td><td>integer</td><td>Indicates the status of an assignment:
0 Not edited by resource
1 Edited by resource but not updated to the project manager yet</td></tr>
<tr><td></td><td>WASSN_LAST_DELEG_ID</td><td>integer</td><td>The last delegation performed on this assignment; refers to a valid ID in the MSP_WEB_DELEGATIONS table.</td></tr>
<tr><td></td><td>WASSN_PCT_COMP</td><td>integer</td><td>The percent work complete value of the assignment.</td></tr>
<tr><td></td><td>WASSN_SEND_UPDATE_DATE</td><td>datetime</td><td>The date and time that an assignment update was sent by a resource to a manager.</td></tr>
</table>

	WASSN_SUMMARY_PROGRESS	datetime	Shows progress on a summary task, based on the progress of its subtasks and where these subtasks have been scheduled.
	WRES_ID_TEAM_LEAD	integer	The ID of the team lead; refers to a valid ID in the MSP_WEB_RESOURCES table.
	WNWRK_ID	integer	Refers to a valid WNWRK_ID in the MSP_WEB_NONWORKING_CATEGORIES table.
	WNWRK_ENTRY_ID	nvarchar(300)	The entry ID of the appointment in Microsoft Outlook.
	RESERVED_DATA1	integer	Used to temporarily store editable, calculated values; you should not edit the values in this field.
	RESERVED_DATA2	integer	Used to temporarily store editable, calculated values; you should not edit the values in this field.
	RESERVED_DATA3	integer	Used to temporarily store editable, calculated values; you should not edit the values in this field.

MSP_WEB_CALENDAR_TRANSACTIONS

This table tracks calendar transactions, including the date of each transaction and the WRES_IDs of all senders and receivers.

	Column Name	Data Type	Description
PK	WCTRANS_ID	integer	The unique ID for the calendar transaction.
	WNONWORK_ID	integer	Refers to a valid WNONWORK_ID in the MSP_WEB_NONWORKING table.
	WCTRANS_DATE	datetime	The date of the calendar transaction.
	WCTRANS_ACTION	integer	Indicates the action taken for the transaction: 0 No action taken 1 Accept 2 Reject
	WRES_ID_CTRANS_RECEIVER	integer	Manager who receives the calendar transaction. Refers to a valid WRES_ID in the MSP_WEB_RESOURCES table.
	WRES_ID_CTRANS_SENDER	integer	Resource that submits a calendar transaction. Refers to a valid WRES_ID in the MSP_WEB_RESOURCES table.

MSP_WEB_CONVERSIONS

This table stores the static text in Microsoft Project Server that is represented in different languages, for example Gantt Chart types, or external milestones. CONV_VALUE and LANG_ID together identify a string in a particular language. The contents of some columns are converted to numeric constants.

	Column Name	Data Type	Description
PK	STRING_TYPE_ID	integer	Refers to a valid STRING_TYPE_ID in the MSP_WEB_STRING_TYPES table
PK	CONV_VALUE	integer	The ID value of the string
PK	LANG_ID	integer	The ID of the language in which the conversion text is displayed, for example: 1033 is the language ID for English, the default language for the database
	CONV_STRING	nvarchar(1000)	The text value of the string

MSP_WEB_DELEGATION_ASSIGNMENTS

This table normalizes delegation information for assignments, including whether an assignment has been approved, whether it has been accepted, and whether a copy of the assignment is being kept in order to track progress.

	Column Name	Data Type	Description
PK	WDELEG_ID	integer	The unique ID for the delegation assignment
PK	WASSN_ID	integer	Refers to a valid WASSN_ID in the MSP_WEB_ASSIGNMENTS table
	WDELEG_APPROVE	tinyint	Indicates whether an assignment delegation has been approved by the manager
	WDELEG_ACCEPT	tinyint	Indicates whether an assignment delegation has been accepted by the resource who received the assignment
	WDELEG_KEEP_COPY	tinyint	Indicates whether the delegator chose to keep a copy of the assignment after delegation to track its progress

MSP_WEB_DELEGATIONS

This table stores information about delegations, including who sent the message, who received the message, the data that was sent in the message, whether to keep a copy of the message, and whether the delegation was rejected by the assigned resource.

	Column Name	Data Type	Description
PK	WDELEG_ID	integer	The unique ID for the delegation
	WRES_ID_DELEGATOR	integer	Refers to a valid WRES_ID in the MSP_WEB_RESOURCES table
	WRES_ID_DELEGATEE	integer	Refers to a valid WRES_ID in the MSP_WEB_RESOURCES table
	WDELEG_KEEP_COPY	tinyint	Indicates whether to keep a copy of a delegated assignment in the delegator's timesheet
	WDELEG_DATE	datetime	The date and time the assignment delegation was sent to the resource
	WDELEG_REJECT	tinyint	Indicates whether the resource accepts or rejects the assignment

MSP_WEB_GANTT_SCHEMES

This table contains all of the possible grouping schemes available for use in Microsoft Project Web Access.

	Column Name	Data Type	Description
PK	WGANTT_SCHEME_ID	integer	Refers to a valid WGANTT_SCHEME_ID in the MSP_WEB_GANTT_SETTINGS table
	WGANTT_SCHEME_TYPE	integer	Indicates the type of Gantt scheme: 0 Personal Gantt (default) 1 Assignment or Portfolio views Gantt 2 Project views Gantt
	WGANTT_SCHEME_NAME	nvarchar(50)	The name of the Gantt scheme

MSP_WEB_GANTT_SETTINGS

Microsoft Project Server has nine default Gantt Chart styles and eleven customizable Gantt Chart styles. This information is managed from the **Admin** tab in Microsoft Project Server. Though it is possible to modify this information directly in the database, it is recommended that you use the interface provided in Microsoft Project Server.

	Column Name	Data Type	Description
PK	WGANTT_SCHEME_ID	integer	The unique ID for the Gantt scheme
PK	WGANTT_STYLE_ID	integer	The unique ID for the Gantt bar: 0 Normal task 1 Critical task 2 External task 3 Delegated task 4 Milestone 5 Summary task 6 Project summary (default) 7 Group by summary 8 Progress 9 Summary progress 10 Baseline task 11 Baseline summary 12 Baseline milestone 13 Pre-leveled task 14 Pre-leveled summary 15 Pre-leveled milestone 16 Split 17 Critical split 18 Baseline split 19 Deadline 20 Slack 21 Slippage 22 Delay 23 Custom duration 1 24 Custom duration 2 25 Custom duration 3 26 Custom duration 4 27 Custom duration 5 28 Custom duration 6 29 Custom duration 7 30 Custom duration 8 31 Custom duration 9 32 Custom duration 10 33 Early schedule 34 Late schedule 35 External milestone

WGANTT_SHOW	tinyint	Indicates whether the Gantt bar is shown	
WGANTT_BAR_TYPE	integer	The type of line drawn for the Gantt bar:	
		0	None
		1	Rectangle
		2	Rectangle
		3	Rectangle middle
		4	Rectangle bottom
		5	Line
		6	Line middle
		7	Line bottom
WGANTT_BAR_PATTERN	integer	The fill pattern for the Gantt bar:	
		0	Hollow
		1	Solid fill
		2	Light fill
		3	Medium fill
		4	Dark fill
		5	Diagonal left
		6	Diagonal right
		7	Diagonal cross
		8	Line vertical
		9	Line horizontal
		10	Line cross
WGANTT_BAR_COLOR	integer	The color for the Gantt bar pattern:	
		1	Black
		2	Red
		3	Yellow
		4	Lime
		5	Aqua
		6	Blue
		7	Fuchsia
		8	White
		9	Maroon
		10	Green
		11	Olive
		12	Navy
		13	Purple
		14	Teal
		15	Gray
		16	Silver

WGANTT_START_SHAPE	integer	The start shape of the Gantt bar: 0 No shape 1 House up 2 House down 3 Diamond 4 Triangle up 5 Triangle down 6 Triangle right 7 Triangle left 8 Arrow up 9 Caret down 10 Caret up bottom 11 Line shape 12 Square 13 Circle diamond 14 Arrow down 15 Circle triangle up 16 Circle triangle down 17 Circle arrow up 18 Circle arrow down 19 Circle 20 Star
WGANTT_START_COLOR	integer	The color for the Gantt bar start shape: 1 Black 2 Red 3 Yellow 4 Lime 5 Aqua 6 Blue 7 Fuchsia 8 White 9 Maroon 10 Green 11 Olive 12 Navy 13 Purple 14 Teal 15 Gray 16 Silver

	WGANTT_END_SHAPE	integer	The end shape of the Gantt bar: 0 No shape 1 House up 2 House down 3 Diamond 4 Triangle up 5 Triangle down 6 Triangle right 7 Triangle left 8 Arrow up 9 Caret down 10 Caret up bottom 11 Line shape 12 Square 13 Circle diamond 14 Arrow down 15 Circle triangle up 16 Circle triangle down 17 Circle arrow up 18 Circle arrow down 19 Circle 20 Star
	WGANTT_END_COLOR	integer	The color for the Gantt bar end shape: 1 Black, 8 White 2 Red, 9 Maroon 3 Yellow, 10 Green 4 Lime, 11 Olive 5 Aqua, 12 Navy 6 Blue, 13 Purple 7 Fuchsia, 14 Teal 8 White, 15 Gray 9 Maroon, 16 Silver

MSP_WEB_GANTT_STYLES

This table links the Gantt Chart style identified in the MSP_WEB_GANTT_SCHEMES table to the localized string stored in the MSP_WEB_CONVERSIONS table.

	Column Name	Data Type	Description
PK	WGANTT_STYLE_ID	integer	Refers to a valid WGANTT_STYLE_ID in the MSP_WEB_GANTT_SETTINGS table.
	WGANTT_STYLE_CONV_VALUE	integer	Each Gantt Chart style has an associated text ID. This field references the actual string that is stored in the MSP_WEB_CONVERSIONS table by joining with the CONV_VALUE field in that table.

MSP_WEB_GROUP_SCHEMES

This table contains all of the possible grouping styles available for use in Microsoft Project Server. Timesheet and Views are default styles; there are nine custom grouping styles. See MSP_WEB_GROUP_SETTINGS for more information about how to customize the grouping styles.

	Column Name	Data Type	Description
PK	WGROUP_SCHEME_ID	integer	Refers to a valid WGROUP_SCHEME_ID in the MSP_WEB_GROUP_SETTINGS table
	WGROUP_SCHEME_NAME	nvarchar(50)	The name of the grouping style, for example: "Timesheet" or "Views"

MSP_WEB_GROUP_SETTINGS

Microsoft Project Server can display a personal grouping style on the Tasks page and can display up to 10 different styles of grouping level color schemes in the Views section. This information is managed from the **Admin** tab in Microsoft Project Server. Though it is possible to modify this information directly in the database, it is recommended that you use the interface provided in Microsoft Project Server.

	Column Name	Data Type	Description
PK	WGROUP_SETTING_ID	integer	The unique ID for the Group setting
PK	WGROUP_SCHEME_ID	integer	The unique ID for the Group scheme
	WGROUP_STYLE_ID	integer	The unique ID for the Group style

<table>
<tr><td></td><td>WGROUP_ROW_COLOR</td><td>integer</td><td>Indicates the background color for cells that appear in the grids:
<table>
<tr><td>1</td><td>Black</td></tr>
<tr><td>2</td><td>Red</td></tr>
<tr><td>3</td><td>Yellow</td></tr>
<tr><td>4</td><td>Lime</td></tr>
<tr><td>5</td><td>Aqua</td></tr>
<tr><td>6</td><td>Blue</td></tr>
<tr><td>7</td><td>Fuchsia</td></tr>
<tr><td>8</td><td>White</td></tr>
<tr><td>9</td><td>Maroon</td></tr>
<tr><td>10</td><td>Green</td></tr>
<tr><td>11</td><td>Olive</td></tr>
<tr><td>12</td><td>Navy</td></tr>
<tr><td>13</td><td>Purple</td></tr>
<tr><td>14</td><td>Teal</td></tr>
<tr><td>15</td><td>Gray (default)</td></tr>
<tr><td>16</td><td>Silver</td></tr>
</table></td></tr>
<tr><td></td><td>WGROUP_ROW_PATTERN</td><td>integer</td><td>Indicates the color pattern for cells that appear in the grids:
<table>
<tr><td>0</td><td>Hollow</td></tr>
<tr><td>1</td><td>Solid fill</td></tr>
<tr><td>2</td><td>Light fill</td></tr>
<tr><td>3</td><td>Medium fill</td></tr>
<tr><td>4</td><td>Dark fill (default)</td></tr>
<tr><td>5</td><td>Diagonal left</td></tr>
<tr><td>6</td><td>Diagonal right</td></tr>
<tr><td>7</td><td>Diagonal cross</td></tr>
<tr><td>8</td><td>Line vertical</td></tr>
<tr><td>9</td><td>Line horizontal</td></tr>
<tr><td>10</td><td>Line cross</td></tr>
</table></td></tr>
</table>

	WGROUP_TEXT_COLOR	integer	Indicates the text color for cells that appear in the grids: 1 Black 2 Red 3 Yellow 4 Lime 5 Aqua 6 Blue 7 Fuchsia 8 White (default) 9 Maroon 10 Green 11 Olive 12 Navy 13 Purple 14 Teal 15 Gray 16 Silver
	WGROUP_FONT_STYLE	integer	Indicates the text style color for cells that appear in the grids: 1 Regular (default) 2 Italic 3 Bold 4 Bold italic

MSP_WEB_GROUP_STYLES

This table indicates the level of the grouping style (Level 1, Level 2, Level 3, or Level 4) and maps the grouping style to the MSP_WEB_CONVERSIONS table.

	Column Name	Data Type	Description
PK	WGROUP_STYLE_ID	integer	Refers to a valid WGROUP_STYLE_ID in the MSP_WEB_GROUP_STYLES table
	WGROUP_STYLE_CONV_VALUE	integer	Links the group style to a corresponding value in the CONV_VALUE field in the MSP_WEB_CONVERSIONS table

MSP_WEB_INSTALLED_LANGUAGES

This table stores information for all installed languages for Microsoft Project Server and links the language to the localized strings in the MSP_WEB_CONVERSIONS table.

	Column Name	Data Type	Description
PK	WLANG_LCID	integer	The LCID for the language, for example: 1033 (English)
	CONV_VALUE	integer	Refers to a localized language name string in the MSP_WEB_CONVERSIONS table

MSP_WEB_MESSAGES

This table is no longer used for messaging. Its only remaining purpose is to support calendar transactions to link entries in MSP_WEB_NONWORKING and MSP_CALENDAR_TRANSACTIONS. Most of the fields are obsolete but are kept for backward compatibility.

	Column Name	Data Type	Description
PK	WMSG_ID	integer	The unique ID for the message.
	WMSG_PROJ_TYPE	integer	Indicates the type of message. This value is always 2 for nonworking notification.
	WRES_ID_SENDER	integer	Refers to a valid WRES_ID in the MSP_WEB_RESOURCES table.
	WRES_ID_RECEIVER	integer	Refers to a valid WRES_ID in the MSP_WEB_RESOURCES table.
	WMSG_SUBJECT	nvarchar(255)	*
	WMSG_BODY	nvarchar(3000)	*
	WMSG_TIME	datetime	*
	WPROJ_ID	integer	*
	WMSG_ACTUAL_TYPE	integer	*
	WMSG_PERIOD_START	datetime	*
	WMSG_PERIOD_FINISH	datetime	*
	WMSG_PERIOD_BROKEN_BY	integer	*
	WMSG_PERIOD_WEEK_STARTS_ON	integer	*
	WMSG_WAS_READ	tinyint	*
	WMSG_PROCESS_ST	integer	*
	WMSG_RES_CAN_DECLINE	tinyint	*

* This field is obsolete but kept for backward compatibility.

MSP_WEB_MESSAGES_NONWORKING

This table is used to link a nonworking entry in the MSP_WEB_NONWORKING table to the MSP_WEB_MESSAGES table.

	Column Name	Data Type	Description
PK	WMSGNONWORK_ID	integer	The unique ID for the nonworking message; used by calendar transactions when deleting multiple calendar transactions
	WMSG_ID	integer	Refers to a valid WMSG_ID in the MSP_WEB_MESSAGES table
	WNONWORK_ID	integer	Refers to a valid WNONWORK_ID in the MSP_WEB_NONWORKING table

MSP_WEB_MGR_RULES

This table stores information about message rules for the manager, including the type of message and the specific rules associated with that message.

	Column Name	Data Type	Description
PK	WRULE_ID	integer	The unique ID for the rule
	WRULE_NAME	nvarchar(255)	The name of the rule
	WRES_ID_MGR	integer	Refers to a valid WRES_ID in the MSP_WEB_RESOURCES table
	WRULE_IS_ENABLED	tinyint	Indicates whether the message rule is enabled
	WRULE_TYPE	integer	Indicates the type of rule: 1 — All of the below message types 2 — All New Task Requests 3 — All Task Delegation Requests 4 — All Task Updates and replies to messages requesting status 20 — Only Task Updates and replies to messages requesting status that fit the criteria for the message rule, as defined in WRULE_CONDITION_TYPE
	WRULE_CONDITION_TYPE	integer	The condition for the rule: 0 — Do not check for condition (default) 1 — Field1 operator value (see WRULE_FIELD1_ID, WRULE_VALTYPE, and WRULE_OPERATOR) 2 — Field1 operator Field2 (see WRULE_FIELD1_ID, WRULE_FIELD2_ID, and WRULE_OPERATOR)

WRULE_FIELD1_ID	integer	The field ID used for the first condition type
WRULE_FIELD2_ID	integer	The field ID used for the second condition type
WRULE_OPERATOR	integer	Indicates the type of operator used when determining the condition type for the rule: = Equal to != Not equal to > Greater than < Less than >= Greater than or equal to (default) <= Less than or equal to
WRULE_VALTYPE	integer	Indicates the value type of the data entered: 4 datetime (see WRULE_DATE_VAL) 5 integer (see WRULE_INT_VAL) 6 decimal (see WRULE_DECIMAL_VAL) 21 String (see WRULE_VARCHAR_VAL)
WRULE_INT_VAL	integer	The value if WRULE_VALTYPE = 4
WRULE_DATE_VAL	datetime	The value if WRULE_VALTYPE = 5
WRULE_DECIMAL_VAL	decimal	The value if WRULE_VALTYPE = 6
WRULE_VARCHAR_VAL	nvarchar(255)	The value if WRULE_VALTYPE = 21
WRULE_IS_EXCL_PROJID	tinyint	Indicates whether all current projects are included in the rule (default) or only with current, specified projects
WRULE_IS_EXCL_RES1ID	tinyint	Indicates whether all future resources are included in the rule
WRULE_IS_EXCL_RES2ID	tinyint	Indicates whether all future resources are included in the rule for task delegation requests only
WRULE_DESCRIPTION	nvarchar(255)	The description of the rule

MSP_WEB_MGR_RULES_LISTS

This table links included or excluded rules to resources and projects:

- If this table is empty for a particular WRULE_ID and WRULE_IS_EXCL_PROJID (_RES1ID, _RES2ID) in the MSP_WEB_MGR_RULES table for the same WRULE_ID is 0 then no projects and/or resources are included in that rule.
- If this table is empty for a particular WRULE_ID and WRULE_IS_EXCL_PROJID (_RES1ID, _RES2ID) in the MSP_WEB_MGR_RULES table for the same WRULE_ID is 1 then all current and future projects and/or resources are included in that rule.

	Column Name	Data Type	Description
PK	WRULE_ID	integer	Refers to a valid WRULE_ID in the MSP_WEB_MGR_RULES table.
PK	ITEM_TYPE	integer	Indicates whether the rule is applied to a project or resource: 0 Project 1 Resource 2 Resource delegated to (used for task delegation rules only)
PK	ITEM_ID	integer	Refers to a valid WPROJ_ID in the MSP_WEB_PROJECTS table or a valid WRES_ID in the MSP_WEB_RESOURCES table, depending on the type of rule. The project or resource is either included in the rule or excluded from the rule, depending on the WRULE_IS_EXCL_n fields in the MSP_WEB_MGR_RULES table. For example, if WRULE_IS_EXCL_PROJID for the same WRULE_ID is set to 0, this project is included for that rule. If it is set to 1, this project is excluded from that rule.

MSP_WEB_MODELS

This table is used by the Portfolio Modeling feature.

	Column Name	Data Type	Description
PK	WMOD_MODEL_UID	integer	The unique ID for the web model
	WMOD_MODEL_NAME	nvarchar(255)	The name of the web model
	WMOD_MODEL_DESC	nvarchar(255)	The description of the web model
	WMOD_CREATE_DATE	datetime	The date the web model was created
	WMOD_UPDATE_DATE	datetime	The date the web model was last updated
	WMOD_CREATED_BY	nvarchar(255)	The name of the person who created the model
	WMOD_LAST_UPDATED_BY	nvarchar(255)	The name of the person who last updated the model
	WMOD_LOCKED_BY	nvarchar(255)	The name of the person who locked the model
	WMOD_CREATED_BY_ID	integer	The ID of the resource who created the web model; refers to a valid WRES_ID in the MSP_WEB_RESOURCES table
	WMOD_LAST_UPDATED_BY_ID	integer	The ID of the resource who last updated the web model; refers to a valid WRES_ID in the MSP_WEB_RESOURCES table
	WMOD_LOCKED_BY_ID	integer	The ID of the resource who locked the web model; refers to a valid WRES_ID in the MSP_WEB_RESOURCES table
	WMOD_RESERVED_BINARY_DATA	image	Reserved for use by Microsoft Project Server; do not change the values in this field

MSP_WEB_NONWORKING

This table stores nonworking time data, including the subject, start time, finish time, whether the nonworking time is an all-day event, and whether the nonworking time is an exception.

	Column Name	Data Type	Description
PK	WNONWORK_ID	integer	Refers to a valid WNWRK_ID in the MSP_WEB_NONWORKING_CATEGORIES table
	WNONWORK_SUBJECT	nvarchar(255)	The subject of the nonworking time
	WNONWORK_START	datetime	The date and time that a nonworking time begins
	WNONWORK_END	datetime	The date and time that a nonworking time ends
	WNONWORK_IS_ALL_DAY	tinyint	Indicates whether the nonworking time is an all-day event
	WNONWORK_IS_WORKING	tinyint	Indicates whether the nonworking time is a working time exception

MSP_WEB_NONWORKING_CATEGORIES

This table assigns a unique ID to each nonworking time category. Sick Leave and Vacation are included as standard, default nonworking time categories in Microsoft Project Server. All nonworking time categories contained in this table will appear in a resource's timesheet in the order determined by the WNWRK_ORDER field.

	Column Name	Data Type	Description
PK	WNWRK_ID	integer	The unique ID for the nonworking time category
	WNWRK_NAME	nvarchar(255)	The name of a nonworking time category
	WNWRK_CODE	nvarchar(255)	Used to assign a code to a category that can be in numeric, text, or Microsoft Project outline code format
	WNWRK_ORDER	integer	Determines the order of nonworking time categories appearing in the grid

MSP_WEB_NOTIFICATION_EVENTS

This table stores e-mail notification messages related to new, updated, or cancelled task assignments.

	Column Name	Data Type	Description	
PK	WNTFY_EVENT_ID	integer	The ID for a notification; any notification followed by ** is a notification that is sent automatically and is not available in the user interface:	
			1001	Sent when I receive a new task assignment
			1002	Sent when I receive a task update request **
			1003	Sent when my tasks are updated by my project manager
			1004	Sent when a new issue is assigned to me
			1005	Sent when I receive a new status report
			1006	Sent when I become the lead on a task **
			1007	Sent when my resources submit new tasks
			1008	Sent when my resources delegate their tasks
			1009	Sent when my resources update their tasks
			1010	Sent when my resources submit working and nonworking time changes
			1011	Sent when my resources submit a status report
			1016	Sent when a resource rejects an assignment **
			1017	Sent when a task update has been rejected by a manager **
			1018	Sent when a task request has been rejected by a manager **
			1020	Sent to delegator when a manager rejects a task delegation **
			1021	Sent to delegatee when a manager rejects a task delegation **
			1022	Sent to delegator when a resource rejects a task delegation **
			1023	Sent to manager when a resource rejects a task delegation **
			1024	Sent when a resource declines their assignment and a manager rejects the declined assignment on the Task Changes page **
			1025	Sent when a resource delegates a lead role to another resource **
			1026	Sent when a manager removes a resource from an assignment **
			1027	Sent when a new team lead has been assigned to the task **

			1028 Sent when a status report has been removed ** 1030 Sent when I receive a new to-do list task assignment 1031 Sent when a task on my to-do list has been modified 1032 Sent when a task on my to-do list has been cancelled ** 1033 Sent when my tasks are delegated ** 1034 Sent when an issue created or owned by me is modified 1035 Sent when a new issue is added to the project 1036 Sent when an issue is updated to the project 1038 Sent when new documents are added to my projects 1039 Sent when documents associated with my projects are modified 1040 Sent when documents associated with my projects are deleted
	WNTFY_EVENT_ DEFAULT	tinyint	Indicates whether permission is required for the notification: 0 Do not check security for a resource 1 Check the security for a resource; if a resource does not have permission, then a notification will not be sent or shown in the user interface
	WNTFY_EVENT_ ACTION_ID	integer	Refers to a valid WSEC_FEA_ACT_ID in the MSP_WEB_SECURITY_FEATURES_ACTIONS table
	WNTFY_EVENT_ SHOW_UI	tinyint	Indicates whether this notification is shown in the user interface
	WNTFY_EVENT_ QUERY	nvarchar(1000)	Stores the SQL query statement which is used by this notification
	WNTFY_EMAIL_SUBJECT	integer	Refers to a localized CONV_STRING in the MSP_WEB_CONVERSIONS table
	WNTFY_EMAIL_ TITLE	integer	Refers to a localized CONV_STRING in the MSP_WEB_CONVERSIONS table
	WNTFY_EMAIL_ CONTENT	integer	Refers to a localized CONV_STRING in the MSP_WEB_CONVERSIONS table
	WNTFY_EMAIL_ TAIL1	integer	Refers to a localized CONV_STRING in the MSP_WEB_CONVERSIONS table
	WNTFY_EMAIL_ TAIL2	integer	Refers to a localized CONV_STRING in the MSP_WEB_CONVERSIONS table
	WNTFY_EVENT_ DESC	nvarchar(100)	The description for the notification message

MSP_WEB_NOTIFICATIONS

This table links a resource to a notification stored in the MSP_WEB_NOTIFICATION_EVENTS table.

	Column Name	Data Type	Description
PK	WNTFY_OWNER_ID	integer	Refers to a valid WRES_ID in the MSP_RESOURCES table
PK	WNTFY_EVENT_ID	integer	Refers to a valid WNTFY_EVENT_ID in the MSP_WEB_NOTIFICATIONS_EVENTS table
	WNTFY_IS_ENABLED	tinyint	Indicates whether the notification is enabled

MSP_WEB_OBJECTS

This table stores each object that appears at least once in the MSP_WEB_OBJECT_LINKS table and links external objects to an internal project. External objects include documents and issues stored on servers running SharePoint Team Services, external tasks and projects, and anything else that can be linked together, including third party applications. Objects are first described in this table, then linked to each other in the MSP_WEB_OBJECT_LINKS table.

	Column Name	Data Type	Description
PK	WOBJ_ID	integer	The unique ID for the object
	WOBJ_TYPE	integer	Indicates the type of object: 1 Project 2 Task 3 Document 4 Issue
	WOBJ_PROJ_ID	integer	Refers to a valid WPROJ_ID in the MSP_WEB_PROJECTS table
	WOBJ_TASK_ID	integer	Refers to a valid TASK_UID in the MSP_WEB_ASSIGNMENTS table
	WOBJ_TP_ID	integer	Refers to individual objects, documents, and issues stored on a server running SharePoint Team Services
	WOBJ_LIST_NAME	nvarchar(255)	The name of the document library
	WOBJ_DESC	ntext	Reserved for future use
	WOBJ_DOC_REF_CNT	integer	The number of documents linked to this object
	WOBJ_ISSUE_REF_CNT	integer	The number of issues linked to this object
	WOBJ_OTHER_REF_CNT	integer	The number of projects or tasks linked to this object

MSP_WEB_OBJECT_LINKS

This table links objects to each other; see the MSP_WEB_OBJECTS table for a description of the actual objects. There can only be one link type between any two objects, however any object can be linked to any number of objects.

	Column Name	Data Type	Description
PK	WOBJLINK_ID	integer	The unique ID for the link
	WOBJLINK_OBJECT1	integer	The object ID of the first object; refers to a valid WOBJ_ID in the MSP_WEB_OBJECTS table
	WOBJLINK_OBJECT2	integer	The object ID of the second object; refers to a valid WOBJ_ID in the MSP_WEB_OBJECTS table
	WOBJLINK_TYPE	integer	Indicates the type of link: 1 General (default) 2 Affected task (Issues and Tasks only) 3 Action item (Issues and Tasks only)

MSP_WEB_OBJECT_TYPES

This table stores the IDs and names for all collaboration objects. For reference only.

	Column Name	Data Type	Description
PK	WOBJTYPE_ID	integer	Indicates the type of object: 1 Project 2 Task 3 Document 4 Issue
	WOBJTYPE_NAME	nvarchar(50)	The name of the object type

MSP_WEB_OBJECT_LINK_TYPES

This table stores the link between objects, documents, and issues. For reference only.

	Column Name	Data Type	Description
PK	WLINKTYPE_ID	integer	Indicates the type of object: 1 General (default) 2 Affected task (Issues only) 3 Action item (Issues only)
	WLINKTYPE_DESC	nvarchar(255)	The name of the object link type

MSP_WEB_PROJECT_WORKGROUP_INFO

This table stores the IDs of custom fields the manager sent to the resource for each project.

	Column Name	Data Type	Description
PK	WPROJ_ID	integer	Refers to a valid WPROJ_ID in the MSP_WEB_PROJECTS table
PK	CUSTFIELD_INFO_ID	integer	Links to MSP_WEB_WORKGROUP_FIELDS_INFO
	PICKLIST_INFO	ntext	Reserved for future use

MSP_WEB_PROJECTS

This table stores the list of projects published to Microsoft Project Server.

	Column Name	Data Type	Description
PK	WPROJ_ID	integer	The unique ID for the project.
	PROJ_NAME	nvarchar(255)	The name of the project.
	PROJ_TIMESTAMP	nvarchar(32)	The timestamp identifier for when the project was most recently published.
	WPROJ_DESCRIPTION	nvarchar(255)	Stores a URL, PATH, or XML blob that uniquely describes a document that is not stored on a server running SharePoint Team Services.
	WLOCAL_PATH	nvarchar(260)	The network path to the file on the manager's computer.
	WPATH	nvarchar(260)	The UNC path of the file.
	WRES_ID	integer	Refers to a valid ID in the MSP_WEB_RESOURCES table.

WDSN_ID	integer	The WDSN ID from MSP_WEB_VIEW_DSNS (if the project file is stored in a database).
WPROJ_DELEG_ALLOWED	tinyint	Indicates whether task delegation is allowed for this project.
WPROJ_IS_NONWORKING	tinyint	Indicates whether the project is a nonworking project.
WPROJ_SCOPE	tinyint	Indicates the scope of the project in terms of who gets to view the project. This applies only to to-do lists.
WPROJ_IS_CONSOLIDATED_ PROJECT	tinyint	Indicates whether the project is a consolidated project.
WPROJ_RES_CAN_DECLINE	tinyint	Indicates whether a resource can decline an assigned task.
WPROJ_DEFAULT_WPROJ_ID	integer	Refers to a valid WPROJ_ID in the MSP_WEB_PROJECTS table; this maps a version to a default version.
WPROJ_TRACKING_METHOD	integer	Indicates the tracking method used for reporting hours worked on a specific project: 1 Hours of work done per day or per week 2 Percent of work complete (default) 3 Actual work done and work remaining
WPROJ_LAST_PUB	datetime	The date and time that a project was last published.
PROJ_ID	integer	Refers to a valid PROJ_ID in the MSP_PROJECTS table.
WPROJ_TYPE	integer	Indicates the type of project: 0 Microsoft Project 2000 project 1 Workgroup 2 Enterprise project 3 To-do List project
OPT_DEF_START_TIME	datetime	The default start time for all new tasks.
OPT_DEF_FINISH_TIME	datetime	The default finish time for all new tasks.
WPROJ_STS_SUBWEB_NAME	nvarchar(128)	The name of the subweb that a server running SharePoint Team Services belongs to.
WSTS_SERVER_ID	integer	Refers to a valid ID for a server running SharePoint Team Services in the MSP_WEB_STS_SERVERS table.

MSP_WEB_REMINDER_TYPES

This table links reminders to either status reports or assignments, including whether the reminder is a self-reminder and provides the localized e-mail text that is part of the automatic reminder.

	Column Name	Data Type	Description
PK	WRMND_TYPE_ID	integer	The unique ID for the reminder type
	WRMND_TABLE_ID	integer	Refers to a valid WTABLE_ID in the MSP_WEB_VIEW_TABLES table; only the following WTABLE_IDs are used for this table: 2 Assignments 4 Status reports
	WRMND_IS_SELF	tinyint	Indicates whether a reminder is from a manager (0) or is a self-reminder (1)
	WRMND_QUERY	nvarchar(1000)	Stores the SQL query statement which is used by this reminder
	WRMND_EMAIL_TITLE	integer	Refers to a localized CONV_STRING in the MSP_WEB_CONVERSIONS table
	WRMND_EMAIL_TAIL1	integer	Refers to a localized CONV_STRING in the MSP_WEB_CONVERSIONS table
	WRMND_TYPE_DESC	nvarchar(100)	The description for the reminder

MSP_WEB_REMINDERS

This table contains all the reminders that users create while using Microsoft Project Web Access. WFREQ is a variable with seven possible dependencies based on the initial setting of WFREQ.

	Column Name	Data Type	Description
PK	WRMND_OWNER_ID	integer	Refers to a valid WRES_ID in the MSP_WEB_RESOURCES table.
PK	WRMND_TYPE_ID	integer	Refers to a valid WRMND_TYPE_ID in the MSP_WEB_REMINDER_TYPES table.
	WRMND_IS_ENABLED	tinyint	Indicates whether the reminder is enabled.
	WRMND_SEND_TO	smallint	Indicates who the reminder is sent to: 0 Send to self 1 Send to resource 2 Send to both

WRMND_PARAMETERS	nvarchar (20)	The parameters for the reminder, as described in the user interface; this field contains a numerical representation of the user interface, for example 1,2 is the same as one week.
WRMND_CRITERIA	nvarchar (510)	This field contains SQL used to query the database based on the information set in WRMND_PARAMETERS; you should not modify the values in this field.
WRMND_START_DATE	datetime	The date that a reminder is set to begin.
WFREQ	integer	Indicates how frequently the reminder to be sent: 0 Weekly (default) 1 Monthly 2 Yearly
WFREQPAR1	integer	Variable, depending on the value of WFREQ: 0 1 = Every week 2 = Every other week 3 = Every third week 4 = Every fourth week 5 = Every fifth week 6 = Every sixth week 7 = Every seventh week 8 = Every eighth week 9 = Every ninth week 10 = Every tenth week 11 = Every eleventh week 12 = Every twelfth week 1 0 = First option of yearly 1 = Second option of yearly 2 0 = First option of yearly 1 = Second option of yearly
WFREQPAR2	integer	Variable, depending on the value of WFREQ: 0 Each bit represents a day of the week selected with the lowest bit being Sunday (that is, 9 means Sunday and Wednesday are selected) 1 Day of the month; used by first option: 1 = First day of the month 2 = Second day of the month 3 = Third day of the month and so on up until 28, 29, 30 or 31 (depending on the last day of the month). 2 1 = First, used by first option 2 = Second, used by first option 3 = Third, used by first option 4 = Fourth, used by first option 5 = Last, used by second option

WFREQPAR3	integer	Variable, depending on the value of WFREQ: 0 Not used 1 Every x months; used by second option: 1 = Every month 2 = Every two months 3 = Every three months 4 = Every four months 5 = Every five months 6 = Every six months 7 = Every seven months 8 = Every eight months 9 = Every nine months 10 = Every ten months 11 = Every eleven months 12 = Every twelve months 2 Day of the week; used by second option: 1 = Sunday 2 = Monday 3 = Tuesday 4 = Wednesday 5 = Thursday 6 = Friday 7 = Saturday
WFREQPAR4	integer	Variable, depending on the value of WFREQ: 0 Not used 1 1 = First, used by first option 2 = Second, used by first option 3 = Third, used by first option 4 = Fourth, used by first option 5 = Last, used by second option 2 Month of year; used by second option: 1 = January 2 = February 3 = March 4 = April 5 = May 6 = June 7 = July 8 = August 9 = September 10 = October 11 = November 12 = December

WFREQPAR5	integer	Variable, depending on the value of WFREQ: 0 Not used 1 Day of the week; used by second option: 1 = Sunday 2 = Monday 3 = Tuesday 4 = Wednesday 5 = Thursday 6 = Friday 7 = Saturday 2 Not used
WFREQPAR6	integer	Variable, depending on the value of WFREQ: 0 Not used 1 Every x months; used by second option: 1 = Every month 2 = Every two months 3 = Every three months 4 = Every four months 5 = Every five months 6 = Every six months 7 = Every seven months 8 = Every eight months 9 = Every nine months 10 = Every ten months 11 = Every eleven months 12 = Every twelve months 2 Not used
WFREQPAR_DATE	datetime	Variable frequency date parameter, depending on the value of WFREQ: 0 Not used 1 Not used 2 Date in the first option of yearly; used by first option
WRMND_NEXT_UPDATE	datetime	The date and time that the next notification is to be sent. This is calculated from the WFREQn fields described above and is used by the Notification Processing Engine (NPE) to determine whether the reminder should be processed. This value is calculated from the frequency information shown above. It is used by NPE to check whether this reminder should be processed today. There are two occasions when it will be modified: (1) When a user saves changes to the reminders from the user interface and (2) after NPE processes this reminder, NPE will update this field for the next running time.

MSP_WEB_REMINDERS_TEMP

This table is used as temporary data storage to hold and consolidate e-mail text while the Notification Processing Engine (NPE) works through all of the reminders. This process creates a record for each receiver, then attaches e-mail messages to generate a single, unified e-mail message.

	Column Name	Data Type	Description
PK	WRMND_ID_RECEIVER	integer	Refers to a valid WRES_ID in the MSP_WEB_RESOURCES table
PK	WRMND_TABLE_ID	integer	Refers to a valid WTABLE_ID in the MSP_WEB_VIEW_TABLES table; only the following WTABLE_IDs are used for this table: 2 Assignments 4 Status reports
	WRMND_MSG_SENT	tinyint	Indicates whether the message has been sent
	WRMND_MESSAGE	ntext	The text of the reminder message

MSP_WEB_RESERVED_DATA

This table is reserved for internal use; do not modify the values in this table.

	Column Name	Data Type	Description
PK	RESERVED_DATA1	integer	This field is reserved for internal use; do not modify the values in this field
	RESERVED_DATA2	integer	This field is reserved for internal use; do not modify the values in this field
	RESERVED_DATA3	integer	This field is reserved for internal use; do not modify the values in this field
	RESERVED_DATA4	integer	This field is reserved for internal use; do not modify the values in this field

MSP_WEB_RESOURCE_SETTINGS

This table stores the properties for a resource for a particular page in Microsoft Project Web Access.

	Column Name	Data Type	Description
PK	WSET_ID	integer	The unique ID for the resource setting
	WSEC_PAGE_ID	integer	Refers to a valid ID in the MSP_SEC_SECURITY_PAGES table; -1 for generic or global settings
	WRES_GUID	uniqueidentifier	Refers to a valid WRES_GUID in the MSP_WEB_RESOURCES table
	WSET_VALUE	ntext	Contains an XML blob that contains the resource settings and properties for a particular resource and page in Microsoft Project Web Access

MSP_WEB_RESOURCES

This table stores a record for every unique resource, including material resources, generic resources, local resources subject to being assigned to a task, and project managers assigning a resource to a task.

	Column Name	Data Type	Description
PK	WRES_ID	integer	The unique ID for the resource.
	WRES_GUID	uniqueidentifier	The globally unique ID for the resource; automatically created by Microsoft SQL Server 2000 when a user is created.
	RES_NAME	nvarchar(255)	The friendly name of the resource; this also is the Microsoft Project Web Access user name if WRES_USE_NT_LOGON is set to 0.
	WRES_EUID	integer	The unique enterprise ID for the resource; this maps the resource to the enterprise resource global.
	WRES_USE_NT_LOGON	tinyint	Indicates whether a resource uses a Microsoft Project Web Access user name and password (0) or a Microsoft Windows NT user account name (1).
	WRES_NT_ACCOUNT	nvarchar(255)	The Windows NT user account name; this field is not used unless WRES_USE_NT_LOGON is set to 1.
	WRES_EMAIL	nvarchar(255)	Stores the e-mail address for the resource.
	WRES_EMAIL_LANGUAGE	integer	Indicates which installed language is the default language for e-mail; see MSP_WEB_INSTALLED_LANGUAGES for all available languages
	WRES_LAST_UPDATE_TIME	datetime	Reserved for future use.
	WRES_LAST_CHECKED_TIME	datetime	Reserved for future use.
	WRES_IS_OFFLINE	tinyint	Indicates whether a resource is working offline.

	WRES_LAST_CONNECT	datetime	Stores the last time the user logged on.
	WRES_IS_MANAGER	tinyint	Indicates whether a resource has manager permissions. This field is obsolete now with the new security model.
	WRES_IS_ADMIN	tinyint	Indicates whether a resource has administrator permissions. This field is obsolete now with the new security model.
	WRES_IS_ENABLED	tinyint	Indicates whether the resource is an Active (Enabled) or Inactive user.
	WRES_IS_PC2000	tinyint	Indicates whether the resource has been migrated from a Microsoft Project Central installation or whether the resource was newly created.
	WRES_PASSWORD	nvarchar(255)	The password for the user if WRES_USE_NT_LOGON is set to 0; not used for users of Microsoft Project 2000.
	WRES_DEL_TASKUPDATE_ MSG	tinyint	Obsolete field.
	WRES_DEL_DELEG_MSG	tinyint	Obsolete field.
	WRES_DEL_NEWTASK_MSG	tinyint	Obsolete field.
	WRES_DEL_REASSN_MSG	tinyint	Obsolete field.
	WRES_INCL_TEAMLEAD_ RESOURCES	tinyint	Reserved for future use.
	WRES_INCL_TEAMASSIGN_ RESOURCES	tinyint	Obsolete field.
	WRES_CAN_LOGIN	tinyint	Indicates whether the resource has permission to log on to Microsoft Project Web Access; material resources cannot log on.
	WRES_COUNT_LICENSE	tinyint	Indicates whether the resource counts as a licensed user of Microsoft Project Web Access; material resources do not count as licensed users. **Note** For details about licensing for Microsoft Project Server and Microsoft Project Web Access, see the Microsoft end-user license agreements for the products.
	RES_PHONETICS	nvarchar(255)	Contains phonetic information in either Hiragana or Katakana for resource names; used only in the Japanese version of Microsoft Project.
	RESERVED_DATA1	integer	Reserved for internal use. Do not change this field.
	RESERVED_DATA2	integer	Reserved for internal use. Do not change this field.
	RESERVED_DATA3	integer	Reserved for internal use. Do not change this field.
	RESERVED_DATA4	integer	Reserved for internal use. Do not change this field.

MSP_WEB_SECURITY_CATEGORIES

This table stores the name and description of each security category in Microsoft Project Server, including the following default categories: My Organization, My Projects, and My Tasks. This information can be managed from the Manage Security link in the Admin center of Microsoft Project Web Access. See MSP_WEB_SECURITY_CATEGORY_RULES for more information about specific category types and rules associated with the category.

	Column Name	Data Type	Description
PK	WSEC_CAT_ID	integer	The unique ID for the security category
	WSEC_CAT_NAME	nvarchar(255)	The name of the security category: 1 My Organization 2 My Projects 3 My Tasks
	WSEC_CAT_DESC	nvarchar(255)	The description of the security category, for example: Microsoft Project Web Access pre-defined category

MSP_WEB_SECURITY_CATEGORY_OBJECTS

This table links categories and objects, including the type of object.

	Column Name	Data Type	Description
PK	WSEC_CAT_ID	integer	Refers to a valid project in the MSP_WEB_SECURITY_CATEGORIES table
	WSEC_OBJ_TYPE	tinyint	Indicates the type of object: 1 Project 2 Resource 3 View 4 Model
	WSEC_OBJ_ID	integer	Refers to a valid ID in the MSP_WEB_OBJECT_RULE_TYPES table

MSP_WEB_SECURITY_CATEGORY_RULES

This table provides the information that determines whether a category or permission is allowed or denied.

	Column Name	Data Type	Description
PK	WSEC_CAT_ID	integer	Refers to a valid project in the MSP_WEB_SECURITY_CATEGORIES table
	WSEC_OBJ_TYPE	tinyint	Indicates the type of object: 1 Project 2 Resource 3 View 4 Model
	WSEC_OBJ_RULE_TYPE	tinyint	Depending on the selection in WSEC_OBJ_TYPE, the rule that is associated with the object: 0 All current and future projects 1 All selected projects 2 All current and future projects that I manage 3 All current and future projects for which I am a resource

MSP_WEB_SECURITY_FEATURES_ACTIONS

This table stores information related to security objects in Microsoft Project Server and Microsoft Project Web Access.

If you customize any of the default pages in Microsoft Project Web Access, you may also want to modify the WSEC_FEA_ACT_NAME in the database for the corresponding center or activity.

	Column Name	Data Type	Description	
PK	WSEC_FEA_ACT_ID	integer	The ID for the security feature. See WSEC_FEA_ACT_NAME, left column for a list of all available security feature IDs.	
	WSEC_FEA_ACT_NAME_ID	integer	The name of a security feature. Access to centers and activities is based on allowing or denying access to the security features in Microsoft Project Server and Microsoft Project Web Access for each user, category, group, or organization. The names of available security features are in the right column:	
			100	General
			101	View Home
			102	Log On
			103	Change Password
			104	Set Personal Notifications
			105	Set Resource Notifications
			106	Go Offline
			200	Tasks
			201	View Timesheet
			202	New Project Task
			203	Delegate Task
			204	Hide Task From Timesheet
			205	Transfer Calendar Entries
			206	Change Work Days
			300	To-Do List
			301	Create and Manage To-Do List
			302	Publish To-Do List to All Users
			303	Assign To-Do List Tasks
			400	Transactions
			401	Manage Task Changes
			402	Manage Calendar Changes
			403	Manage Rules
			500	Views
			501	View Project View
			502	View Assignments View
			503	View Project Center
			504	View Resource Center
			505	View Portfolio Analyzer
			506	View Models
			507	View Resource Allocation
			600	Status Reports
			601	View Status Report List
			602	Submit Status Report
			604	Manage Status Report Request

			700	Admin
			710	Manage users and groups
			720	Manage security
			730	Manage views
			740	Manage organization
			750	Customize Microsoft Project Web Access
			760	Manage enterprise features
			770	Manage licenses
			780	Clean up Microsoft Project Server database
			790	Manage SharePoint Team Services
			800	Workgroup
			801	Publish / update / status
			900	Account Creation
			901	Create Accounts from Microsoft Project
			902	Create Manager Accounts from Microsoft Project
			903	Create Accounts when Delegating Tasks
			904	Create Accounts when Requesting Status Reports
			1000	Enterprise Portfolio Management
			1004	New Project
			1005	New Resource
			1006	Read Enterprise Global
			1007	Save Enterprise Global
			1008	Backup Global
			1010	Read Summary Assignments
			1011	Save Project Template
			1016	Open Project Template
			1100	Collaboration
			1101	View Documents
			1102	View Issues
	WSEC_FEA_ACT_PARENT	integer	Refers to a valid ID in the MSP_WEB_SECURITY_FEATURES_ACTIONS table; all activities must have a parent. If the security feature is a parent, the value in this field is 0. Available parent IDs:	
			100	General
			200	Tasks
			300	To-Do List
			400	Transactions
			500	Views
			600	Status Reports
			700	Admin
			800	Workgroup
			900	Account Creation
			1000	Enterprise Portfolio Management
			1100	Collaboration

	WSEC_IS_ACTION	tinyint	Indicates whether a security feature is a level (0) or side pane (1) feature. All side pane security features must belong to a parent.
	WSEC_ON_OBJECT	tinyint	Indicates whether a permission is a global (0) or category (1) level permission.
	WSEC_OBJ_TYPE_ID	integer	The type of object: 1 Project 2 Resource 3 View 4 Model

MSP_WEB_SECURITY_GROUP_MEMBERS

This table stores information that links Microsoft Project Web Access users with the groups they belong to. For each resource, Microsoft Project Server creates a group that contains that resource.

	Column Name	Data Type	Description
PK	WSEC_GRP_GUID	uniqueidentifier	Refers to a valid WSEC_GRP_GUID in the MSP_WEB_SECURITY_GROUPS table
PK	WRES_GUID	uniqueidentifier	Refers to a valid WRES_GUID in the MSP_WEB_RESOURCES table

MSP_WEB_SECURITY_GROUPS

This table stores a name and description for each group in Microsoft Project Server, including the following default groups: Administrators, Executives, Portfolio Managers, Project Managers, Resource Managers, Team Leads, and Team Members.

	Column Name	Data Type	Description
PK	WSEC_GRP_ID	integer	The unique ID for the group
	WSEC_GRP_GUID	uniqueidentifier	The globally unique ID for the group; automatically assigned by Microsoft Project Server
	WSEC_GRP_NAME	nvarchar(100)	The name of the group
	WSEC_GRP_DESC	nvarchar(255)	The description of the group
	WSEC_GRP_DASHBOARD_URL	nvarchar(255)	The Digital Dashboard URL for the group

MSP_WEB_SECURITY_MENUS

This table stores information found in the -level menus in Microsoft Project Web Access, including the name of the menu, its parent, its description, and whether the menu is a custom menu.

	Column Name	Data Type	Description
PK	WSEC_MENU_ID	integer	The unique ID for the security menu
	WSEC_MENU_NAME_ID	integer	Refers to the CONV_VALUE field in the MSP_WEB_CONVERSIONS table and provides the localized string for the menu
	WSEC_MENU_CUSTOM_NAME	nvarchar(100)	The customized name of the link or sub link menu item
	WSEC_MENU_PARENT_ID	integer	Refers to a valid ID in the MSP_WEB_SECURITY_MENUS table: -1: Indicates this menu item is a parent menu item any: Refers to the parent menu; this number must be a valid ID in this table
	WSEC_MENU_SEQ	smallint	The order in which the fields will appear in Microsoft Project Web Access
	WSEC_MENU_DESC_ID	integer	Refers to CONV_VALUE in the MSP_WEB_CONVERSIONS table and provides the localized string for the menu
	WSEC_MENU_CUSTOM_DESC	nvarchar(100)	The description of the custom menu item
	WSEC_MENU_PAGE_ID	integer	Refers to a valid WSEC_PAGE_ID in the MSP_WEB_SECURITY_PAGES table
	WSEC_MENU_IS_CUSTOM	tinyint	Indicates whether the menu item is a custom menu item
	WSEC_MENU_IS__LEVEL	tinyint	Indicates whether the menu item appears across the of the Microsoft Project Web Access browser window
	WSEC_MENU_LINKGROUP_NAME_ID	integer	Refers to a localized string in the MSP_WEB_CONVERSIONS table; displayed as the saved links' type in the actions pane

MSP_WEB_SECURITY_OBJECT_RULES

This table stores information related to security object rules.

	Column Name	Data Type	Description
PK	WSEC_OBJ_TYPE	tinyint	The type of object: 1 Project 2 Resource 3 View 4 Model
PK	WSEC_OBJ_RULE_TYPE	tinyint	Depending on the selection in WSEC_OBJ_TYPE, the rule that is associated with the object: 0 All current and future projects 1 All selected projects 2 All current and future projects that I manage 3 All current and future projects for which I am a resource
	WSEC_OBJ_RULE_DESC	nvarchar(255)	The description of the object rule

MSP_WEB_SECURITY_OBJECT_TYPES

This table is used to associate the object type name with the objects.

	Column Name	Data Type	Description
PK	WSEC_OBJ_TYPE_ID	integer	The unique ID for the object
	WSEC_OBJ_TYPE_NAME	nvarchar(100)	The type of object: 1 Project 2 Resource 3 View 4 Model

MSP_WEB_SECURITY_ORG_PERMISSIONS

This table specifies which Microsoft Project Web Access features are available to an organization.

	Column Name	Data Type	Description
PK	WSEC_FEA_ACT_ID	integer	Refers to a valid ID in the MSP_WEB_SECURITY_FEATURES_ACTIONS table
	WSEC_ALLOW	tinyint	Indicates that the security principle or security object has been granted permission to perform the selected activity
	WSEC_DENY	tinyint	Indicates that the security principle or security object has been denied permission to perform the selected activity; if a user is denied anywhere in Microsoft Project Web Access, a user will be denied everywhere
	WSEC_ACCESS	tinyint	Reserved for future use in Microsoft Project Web Access; you should not modify the values in this field
	WSEC_PAID	tinyint	Reserved for future use in Microsoft Project Web Access; you should not modify the values in this field

MSP_WEB_SECURITY_PAGES

This table links security features with the ASP pages in Microsoft Project Web Access.

	Column Name	Data Type	Description
PK	WSEC_PAGE_ID	integer	The unique ID for the page.
	WSEC_PAGE_MENU_ID	integer	Refers to a valid WSEC_MENU_ID in the MSP_WEB_SECURITY_MENUS table.
	WSEC_PAGE_URL	nvarchar(255)	The URL for the page.
	WSEC_PAGE_CUSTOM_URL	nvarchar(255)	The custom URL for the page.
	WSEC_PAGE_HELP_URL	nvarchar(255)	The URL for the help page associated with a page in Microsoft Project Web Access.
	WSEC_PAGE_ACT_ID	integer	Refers to a valid WSEC_FEA_ACT_ID in the MSP_WEB_SECURITY_FEATURES_ACTION S table.
	WSEC_PAGE_MASTER_PAGE_ID	integer	Refers to a valid WSEC_PAGE_ID in the MSP_WEB_SECURITY_PAGES table.
	WSEC_PAGE_SESSION_SETTINGS	ntext	Contains the initial settings for this page; this information is persisted only within the session.
	WSEC_PAGE_DATABASE_SETTINGS	ntext	Contains the initial settings for this page; this information is persisted across sessions and all changes are stored in the MSP_WEB_RESOURCE_SETTINGS table.
	WSEC_PAGE_CAN_OFFLINE	tinyint	Indicates whether the page can be viewed offline.

MSP_WEB_SECURITY_SP_CAT_PERMISSIONS

This table defines which users and groups have permissions for each category.

	Column Name	Data Type	Description
PK	WSEC_REL_ID	integer	Refers to a valid WSEC_REL_ID in the MSP_WEB_SECURITY_SP_CAT_RELATIONS table.
PK	WSEC_FEA_ACT_ID	integer	Refers to a valid WSEC_FEA_ACT_ID in the MSP_WEB_SECURITY_FEATURES_ACTIONS table.
	WSEC_ALLOW	tinyint	Indicates that a user has been granted permission to perform the selected activity.
	WSEC_DENY	tinyint	Indicates that a user has been denied permission to perform the selected activity; if a user is denied anywhere in Microsoft Project Web Access, a user will be denied everywhere.
	WSEC_ACCESS	tinyint	This field is used internally by Microsoft Project Server; you should not modify the contents of this field.

MSP_WEB_SECURITY_SP_CAT_RELATIONS

This table links the MSP_WEB_SECURITY_GROUPS and MSP_WEB_SECURITY_SP_CAT_PERMISSIONS tables.

	Column Name	Data Type	Description
PK	WSEC_REL_ID	integer	The unique ID for the category relation.
	WSEC_SP_GUID	uniqueidentifier	Refers to a valid WSEC_GRP_GUID in the MSP_WEB_SECURITY_GROUPS table.
	WSEC_CAT_ID	integer	Refers to a valid WSEC_CAT_ID in the MSP_WEB_SECURITY_CATEGORIES table.

MSP_WEB_SECURITY_TEMPLATE_PERMISSIONS

This table stores a list of permissions that are either allowed or denied for each security template.

	Column Name	Data Type	Description
PK	WSEC_TMPL_ID	integer	Refers to a valid WSEC_TMPL_ID in the MSP_WEB_SECURITY_TEMPLATES table.
PK	WSEC_ACT_ID	integer	Refers to a valid WSEC_FEA_ACT_ID in the MSP_WEB_SECURITY_FEATURES_ACTIONS table.
	WSEC_ALLOW	tinyint	Indicates that a user has been granted permission to perform the selected activity.
	WSEC_DENY	tinyint	Indicates that a user has been denied permission to perform the selected activity; if a user is denied anywhere in Microsoft Project Web Access, a user will be denied everywhere.
	WSEC_ACCESS	tinyint	This field is used internally by Microsoft Project Server; you should not modify the contents of this field.

MSP_WEB_SECURITY_TEMPLATES

This table stores the name and description of each security template in Microsoft Project Server. This information is managed on the Admin, Manage Security page in Microsoft Project Web Access.

Microsoft Project Server includes the following default security templates: Administrator, Executive, Portfolio Manager, Project Manager, Resource Manager, Team Lead, and Team Member. See MSP_WEB_SECURITY_TEMPLATE_PERMISSIONS for more information about specific permissions allowed or denied for each security table.

	Column Name	Data Type	Description
PK	WSEC_TMPL_ID	integer	The unique ID for the security template.
	WSEC_TMPL_NAME	nvarchar(100)	The name of the security template, for example: Resources.
	WSEC_TMPL_DESC	nvarchar(255)	Contains a description of the security template, for example: Permissions template for Resources.

MSP_WEB_STATUS_DISTRIBUTION

This table links resources and status reports, including report distribution information and which status report was sent to whom.

	Column Name	Data Type	Description
PK	WRES_ID_DISTR_RECIP	integer	Refers to a valid WRES_ID in the MSP_WEB_RESOURCES table.
PK	WRESP_ID	integer	Status response ID from the MSP_WEB_STATUS_RESPONSES table

MSP_WEB_STATUS_FREQUENCIES

This table stores the recurrence information for status reports. WFREQ is a variable with seven possible dependencies based on the initial setting of WFREQ.

	Column Name	Data Type	Description
PK	WSR_ID	integer	Refers to a valid WSR_ID in the MSP_WEB_STATUS_REPORTS table.
PK	WREPORT_START_DATE	datetime	The date that status reporting is to begin.
	WFREQ	integer	Indicates how often the status report is to be submitted by resources: 0 Weekly (default) 1 Monthly 2 Yearly
	WFREQPAR1	integer	Variable, depending on the value of WFREQ: 0 1 = Every week 2 = Every other week 3 = Every third week 4 = Every fourth week 5 = Every fifth week 6 = Every sixth week 7 = Every seventh week 8 = Every eighth week 9 = Every ninth week 10 = Every tenth week 11 = Every eleventh week 12 = Every twelfth week 1 0 = First option of yearly 1 = Second option of yearly 2 0 = First option of yearly 1 = Second option of yearly

WFREQPAR2	integer	Variable, depending on the value of WFREQ:	
		0	Each bit represents a day of the week selected with the lowest bit being Sunday (that is, 9 means Sunday and Wednesday are selected)
		1	Day of the month; used by first option: 1 = First day of the month 2 = Second day of the month 3 = Third day of the month and so on up until 28, 29, 30 or 31 (depending on the last day of the month).
		2	1 = First, used by first option 2 = Second, used by first option 3 = Third, used by first option 4 = Fourth, used by first option 5 = Last, used by second option
WFREQPAR3	integer	Variable, depending on the value of WFREQ:	
		0	Not used
		1	Every x months; used by second option: 1 = Every month 2 = Every two months 3 = Every three months 4 = Every four months 5 = Every five months 6 = Every six months 7 = Every seven months 8 = Every eight months 9 = Every nine months 10 = Every ten months 11 = Every eleven months 12 = Every twelve months
		2	Day of the week; used by second option: 1 = Sunday 2 = Monday 3 = Tuesday 4 = Wednesday 5 = Thursday 6 = Friday 7 = Saturday

<table>
<tr><td>WFREQPAR4</td><td>integer</td><td>Variable, depending on the value of WFREQ:
<table>
<tr><td>0</td><td>Not used</td></tr>
<tr><td>1</td><td>1 = First, used by first option
2 = Second, used by first option
3 = Third, used by first option
4 = Fourth, used by first option
5 = Last, used by second option</td></tr>
<tr><td>2</td><td>Month of year; used by second option:

1 = January
2 = February
3 = March
4 = April
5 = May
6 = June
7 = July
8 = August
9 = September
10 = October
11 = November
12 = December</td></tr>
</table></td></tr>
<tr><td>WFREQPAR5</td><td>integer</td><td>Variable, depending on the value of WFREQ:
<table>
<tr><td>0</td><td>Not used</td></tr>
<tr><td>1</td><td>Day of the week; used by second option:

1 = Sunday
2 = Monday
3 = Tuesday
4 = Wednesday
5 = Thursday
6 = Friday
7 = Saturday</td></tr>
<tr><td>2</td><td>Not used</td></tr>
</table></td></tr>
<tr><td>WFREQPAR6</td><td>integer</td><td>Variable, depending on the value of WFREQ:
<table>
<tr><td>0</td><td>Not used</td></tr>
<tr><td>1</td><td>Every x months; used by second option:

1 = Every month
2 = Every two months
3 = Every three months
4 = Every four months
5 = Every five months
6 = Every six months
7 = Every seven months
8 = Every eight months
9 = Every nine months
10 = Every ten months
11 = Every eleven months
12 = Every twelve months</td></tr>
<tr><td>2</td><td>Not used</td></tr>
</table></td></tr>
</table>

	WFREQPAR_DATE	datetime	Variable frequency date parameter, depending on the value of WFREQ: 0 Not used 1 Not used 2 Date in the first option of yearly; used by first option

MSP_WEB_STATUS_REPORTS

This table stores general information about status reports.

	Column Name	Data Type	Description
PK	WSR_ID	integer	The unique ID for the status report.
	WRES_ID_MGR	integer	The resource ID of the manager who created the status report; refers to a valid ID in the MSP_WEB_RESOURCES table.
	WREPORT_NAME	nvarchar(255)	The name of the status report.
	WREPORT_UNREQUESTED	tinyint	Indicates whether the status report is an unrequested status report.
	WREPORT_IS_ENABLED	tinyint	Indicates whether the status report is enabled (0); the status report becomes disabled (1) if a manager deletes the report.
	WREPORT_FORMAT	ntext	The status report contained within XML.

MSP_WEB_STATUS_REQUESTS

This table stores detailed information about status requests and links each request with resources.

	Column Name	Data Type	Description
PK	WRES_ID_RECEIVER	integer	Refers to a valid WRES_ID in the MSP_WEB_RESOURCES table.
PK	WSR_ID	integer	The unique ID for a status request.
	WDUE_ON	datetime	The next date the report is due for this request.
	WREQ_IS_AUTOMERGE	tinyint	Indicates whether the status request is an auto-merge response.
	WREQ_IS_NEW_REQUEST	tinyint	Indicates whether the status request is a new status request.
	WREQ_IS_SENT	tinyint	Indicates whether the status request has been sent.
	WREQ_IS_ENABLED	tinyint	Indicates whether a status request is enabled; a status request becomes unenabled if a manager deletes a resource from that status request.

MSP_WEB_STATUS_RESPONSES

This table stores the responses for status reports.

	Column Name	Data Type	Description
PK	WRESP_ID	integer	The unique ID for a status response.
	WRES_ID	integer	Refers to a valid WRES_ID in the MSP_WEB_RESOURCES table.
	WSR_ID	integer	Refers to a valid WSR_ID in the MSP_WEB_STATUS_REPORTS table.
	WSRESP_PERIOD_START	datetime	The start date for the date range covering the status report.
	WSRESP_PERIOD_FINISH	datetime	The end date for the date range covering the status report.
	WSUBMIT_STATUS	integer	Indicates whether the status report has been submitted or saved: 0 Not submitted 1 Saved 2 Submitted
	WSUBMIT_DATE	datetime	The date a status report was submitted.
	WUPDATE_STATUS	integer	Indicates whether the status report has been updated or if it is an original: 0 No updates 1 Original 2 Update
	WNUM_SECTIONS	integer	The number of sections that can't be removed.
	WRESP_IS_MATCHING	tinyint	Indicates whether the time period for a status response matches the time period for the status request.
	WRESP_IS_NEW_RESPONSE	tinyint	Indicates whether a manager has seen the status response.
	WRESP_IS_MERGED	tinyint	Indicates whether a status report has been merged into a manager's compiled report.
	WRESP_TEXT	ntext	The text of the status response message.

MSP_WEB_STRING_TYPES

This table maps certain strings used in Microsoft Project Server to their language locale IDs. This is used only for Gantt bar styles and field names in Microsoft Project views.

	Column Name	Data Type	Description
PK	STRING_TYPE_ID	integer	The unique ID for the string type.
PK	STRING_LANG_ID	integer	The language locale ID for the string, for example: 1033 is the language ID for English, the default language for the database.
	STRING_TYPE	nvarchar(200)	The localized name of the string type, for example: Gantt Bar Styles for the English version.

MSP_WEB_STS_SERVERS

This table contains all the information related to servers running SharePoint Team Services. This information is automatically populated to this table (along with WADMIN_PUBDOCS_STS_SERVER_ID and WADMIN_CURRENT_STS_SERVER_ID in the MSP_WEB_ADMIN table) during the installation of Microsoft Project Server and SharePoint Team Services. This information is entered and maintained on the Admin page in Microsoft Project Web Access.

	Column Name	Data Type	Description
PK	WSTS_SERVER_ID	integer	The unique ID for the server running SharePoint Team Services.
	WSTS_SERVER_NAME	nvarchar(255)	The name of the server running SharePoint Team Services.
	WSTS_SERVER_WEB_PORT	integer	The web port number required to access the server running SharePoint Team Services; default is 80.
	WSTS_SERVER_ADMIN_PORT	integer	The admin port number required to access the administration pages on the server running SharePoint Team Services; default is None.
	WSTS_WEB_PORT_IS_SSL	tinyint	Indicates whether the web port for the server running SharePoint Team Services is an SSL port. If this is true, then all connections to WSTS_SERVER_WEB_PORT will be HTTPS.
	WSTS_ADMIN_PORT_IS_SSL	tinyint	Indicates whether the admin port for the server running SharePoint Team Services is an SSL port. If this is true, then all connections to WSTS_SERVER_ADMIN_PORT will be HTTPS.
	WSTS_DB_SERVER_NAME	nvarchar(255)	The name of the database server; relates to the SharePoint Team Services database.
	WSTS_DB_NAME	nvarchar(255)	The name of the database; relates to the SharePoint Team Services database.
	WSTS_SERVER_WEB_SSL_PORT	integer	The SSL port number used by a server running SharePoint Team Services; used only if WSTS_WEB_PORT_IS_SSL is set to 1.

MSP_WEB_TRANSACTIONS

This table stores resource task updates, including details such as whether they have been reviewed by a project manager or updated to Microsoft Project Server.

	Column Name	Data Type	Description
PK	WTRANS_ID	integer	The unique ID for the transaction.
	WASSN_ID	integer	Refers to a valid WASSN_ID in the MSP_WEB_ASSIGNMENTS table.
	WTRANS_DATE	datetime	The date the resource task update was sent.
	WTRANS_PROJ_UPDATE_DATE	datetime	The date the resource task update was updated to Microsoft Project Server by a project manager.
	WTRANS_STATE	integer	Indicates the state of the transaction: 0 Pending 1 Processed, but not yet updated 2 Updated, but not yet sent to history 3 Sent to history
	WTRANS_TYPE	integer	Indicates the type of transaction: 0 Task update 1 Declined tasks 2 New tasks 3 Task delegation
	WTRANS_ACTION	integer	Indicates the action taken for the transaction: 0 No action taken 1 Accept 2 Reject
	WRES_ID_TRANS_SENDER	integer	Refers to a valid WRES_ID in the MSP_WEB_RESOURCES table.
	WDELEG_ID	integer	Refers to a valid WDELEG_ID in the MSP_WEB_DELEGATIONS table.
	WTRANS_DESC	nvarchar(100)	Depending on the type of transaction selected in WTRANS_TYPE, the user will see the following messages: 0 Task update by [resource] 1 New task created by [resource] 2 Task declined by [resource] 3 Task delegated from [delegator] to [delegatee]

MSP_WEB_VIEW_DSNS

This table is used by Microsoft Project Server to maintain backward compatibility with Microsoft Project 2000.

This table stores data source names (DSNs) used by projects in Microsoft Project Server. Any DSN listed in this table must also exist in Microsoft Project Server. You can create DSNs in Microsoft Project Server using the ODBC Data Source Administrator in Control Panel. For each DSN, you must specify a user ID and password for Microsoft Project Server to use when accessing projects stored in the database that each DSN points to. Specifying a user ID and password allows users to look at information from Microsoft Project Server views without necessarily having direct access to the database itself.

	Column Name	Data Type	Description
PK	WDSN_ID	integer	The unique ID for the DSN.
	WDSN_NAME	nvarchar(255)	The name of the DSN.
	WDSN_DESCRIPTION	nvarchar(255)	The description of the DSN.
	WDSN_LOGIN_ID	nvarchar(255)	The user ID Microsoft Project Server uses to access projects stored in the database that the DSN points to.
	WDSN_PASSWORD	nvarchar(255)	The password Microsoft Project Server uses to access projects stored in the database that the DSN points to.

MSP_WEB_VIEW_FAVORITES

This table stores favorite views.

	Column Name	Data Type	Description
PK	WVIEW_FAV_ID	integer	The unique ID for the view favorite.
	WRES_ID	integer	Refers to a valid ID in the MSP_WEB_RESOURCES table.
	WVIEW_TYPE	integer	Indicates the type of view: 0 Project view 1 Portfolio view 2 Assignment view 3 Resource view 4 Portfolio Analyzer view
	WPROJ_ID	integer	Refers to a valid ID in the MSP_WEB_PROJECTS table.

	WVIEW_OWC_PIVOT_XML	ntext	Contains an XML blob that stores the default settings for a PivotTable or chart in Microsoft Project Web Access; used only for Portfolio Analyzer views.
	WVIEW_OWC_CHART_XML	ntext	Contains the settings of the chart; used only for Portfolio Analyzer views.
	WVIEW_FAV_NAME	nvarchar(100)	The name of the favorite view.
	WVIEW_FAV_URL	ntext	The URL parameter for the view.
	WVIEW_FAV_COLUMN_ORDER	ntext	The grid column order for that particular view; only used if the view is a grid.
	WVIEW_FAV_AUTOFILTER	ntext	The autofilter clause; used only if the autofilter is applied to the view.
	WSEC_MENU_ID	integer	Refers to a valid WSEC_MENU_ID in the MSP_WEB_SECURITY_MENUS table.
	WVIEW_DEFAULT_SETTINGS	ntext	Contains an XML blob that carries the default view settings for Show Field List and Show Toolbar in Microsoft Project Web Access.
	WVIEW_TIMESTAMP	uniqueidentifier	The timestamp from the MSP_WEB_VIEW_REPORTS table; if this is not the same value as WVIEW_TIMESTAMP in MSP_WEB_VIEW_REPORTS, this view is out of date.

MSP_WEB_VIEW_FIELDS

This table stores information about the fields displayed for each view.

	Column Name	Data Type	Description
PK	WFIELD_ID	integer	The unique ID for the field.
	WFIELD_NAME_OLEDB	nvarchar(255)	The name of the field used in the Microsoft Project OLE DB provider.
	WFIELD_NAME_SQL	nvarchar(255)	The name of the field in the Microsoft Project Server database.
	WFIELD_NAME_CONV_VALUE	integer	Refers to the CONV_VALUE field in the MSP_WEB_CONVERSIONS table, and provides the localized description of the field.

WFIELD_TEXTCONV_TYPE	integer	The type of field: 0 Invalid type 2 Priority (enumeration index into priority table) 3 Constraint type (index into constraint table) 4 Date 5 Percent (for example, 5%) 6 Duration (for example, 5 days) 8 Work (for example, 5h) 9 Cost (for example, $5.00) 11 Cost rate (for example, $5/hr) 12 Units 13 Accrual type (index into accrual table) 14 Contour type (index into contour table) 15 Plain number 16 Boolean (index into Boolean string table) 17 Yes/No (index into yesno string table) 18 Double (a double value) 21 String 23 Time (minutes since 12:00 midnight) 24 Long 25 Link type (SS, FF, FS, or SF) 28 Elapsed duration (for example, 5ed) 29 Task type (for example, fixed units, fixed work, fixed duration) 30 Hyperlink (friendly name) 31 Hyperlink (target) 32 Hyperlink (location) 33 Hyperlink (HREF)
WTABLE_ID	integer	Indicates the type of view: 0 Project view 1 Tasks 2 Assignments 3 Resources 4 Portfolio Analyzer view
WFIELD_IN_PROJECT_VIEW	tinyint	Indicates whether the field is in a Project view.
WFIELD_IN_PORTFOLIO_VIEW	tinyint	Indicates whether the field is in a Portfolio view.
WFIELD_IN_WEBCLIENT_VIEW	tinyint	Indicates whether the field is in an Assignment view.
WFIELD_IS_CUSTOM_FIELD	tinyint	Indicates whether the field is a custom field in the Microsoft Project Server database.
WFIELD_IS_GANTT_DEFAULT	tinyint	Indicates whether the field is required to draw a Gantt bar (such as Start, Finish, Baselines).
WFIELD_IS_ENTRES_FIELD	tinyint	Indicates whether the field is an enterprise resource field.

MSP_WEB_VIEW_REPORTS

This table stores information about views, including the type of view and how that view will be seen by end users in Microsoft Project Web Access.

	Column Name	Data Type	Description
PK	WVIEW_ID	integer	The unique ID of the view report.
	WVIEW_NAME	nvarchar(255)	The name of the report.
	WVIEW_DESCRIPTION	nvarchar(255)	The description of the report.
	WVIEW_TYPE	integer	Indicates the type of view: 0 Project view 1 Portfolio view 2 Assignment view 3 Resource view 4 Portfolio Analyzer view
	WVIEW_DISPLAY_TYPE	integer	Specifies the type of chart used to display the information in the report: 0 PivotTable only (default) 1 Chart only 2 Both PivotTable and Chart
	WVIEW_WORK_TYPE	integer	Reserved for future use; not used for Portfolio Analyzer views.
	WGANTT_SCHEME_ID	integer	Refers to a valid ID in the MSP_WEB_GANTT_SCHEMES table; not used for Portfolio Analyzer views.
	WTABLE_ID	integer	Refers to a valid ID in the MSP_WEB_VIEW_TABLES table; not used for Portfolio Analyzer views.
	WVIEW_FILTER_PARAM1	nvarchar(255)	SQL clause for the first filter of the project view; not used for Portfolio Analyzer views.
	WVIEW_FILTER_PARAM2	nvarchar(255)	SQL clause for the second filter of the project view; not used for Portfolio Analyzer views.
	WVIEW_FILTER_PARAM3	nvarchar(255)	SQL clause for the third filter of the project view; not used for Portfolio Analyzer views.
	WVIEW_REPORT_KIND	integer	Specifies the method used to display the report: 0 Normal (default) 1 Active Server Page 2 HTML 3 Data Access Page
	WVIEW_PATH	nvarchar(1024)	URL defined in the Get Additional Views section on the Specify Views page; not used for Portfolio Analyzer views.

	WVIEW_OWC_PIVOT_XML	ntext	Office Web Components (OWC); the XML blob that stores the settings of the Pivot control.
	WVIEW_OWC_CHART_XML	ntext	Office Web Components (OWC); the XML blob that stores the settings of the Chart control.
	WGROUP_SCHEME_ID	integer	Refers to a valid ID in the MSP_WEB_GROUP_SCHEMES table; not used for Portfolio Analyzer views.
	WVIEW_DEFAULT_SETTINGS	ntext	Contains an XML blob that carries the default view settings for Show Field List and Show Toolbar in Microsoft Project Web Access.
	WVIEW_TIMESTAMP	uniqueidentifier	The timestamp of the view; stored as a GUID.

MSP_WEB_VIEW_REPORTS_FIELDS

This table specifies the fields displayed for each view, links the fields with their associated view, and determines the order in which the fields appear.

	Column Name	Data Type	Description
PK	WVIEW_ID	integer	Refers to a valid WVIEW_ID in the MSP_WEB_VIEW_REPORTS table.
PK	WFIELD_ID	integer	Refers to the CONV_VALUE field in the MSP_WEB_WORKGROUP_FIELDS_INFO table.
	WVIEW_FIELD_ORDER	integer	The order in which the fields will appear; for each unique WVIEW_ID.

MSP_WEB_VIEW_TABLES

This table specifies which table to view. This table is currently not used in any specific query in Microsoft Project Server.

	Column Name	Data Type	Description
PK	WTABLE_ID	integer	Indicates which table (1, 2, 3, 4, or 5) to use.
	WTABLE_NAME	nvarchar(255)	The name of the table selected in WTABLE_ID: 1 Tasks 2 Assignments 3 Resources 4 Status Report

MSP_WEB_WORK

This table stores all of the hours worked by a resource on an assignment, including actual work, scheduled work, and overtime actual work.

	Column Name	Data Type	Description
	WRES_ID	integer	Refers to a valid ID in the MSP_WEB_RESOURCES table.
PK	WASSN_ID	integer	Refers to a valid ID in the MSP_WEB_ASSIGNMENTS table.
PK	WWORK_START	datetime	The start date for the work.
PK	WWORK_FINISH	datetime	The finish date for the work.
PK	WWORK_TYPE	integer	Indicates the type of work performed: 0 Scheduled work 1 Actual work 2 Overtime actual work
	WWORK_VALUE	decimal	The number of hours worked, measured as minutes * 1000; for example: 8 hours worked is stored as 480000.
	WWORK_UPDATE_STATUS	integer	Indicates whether the work entry has been edited by the resource. 0 Not edited by resource 1 Edited by resource but not updated to the project manager yet
	RESERVED_DATA1	integer	Reserved for use by Microsoft Project Server; do not change the values in this field.
	WWORK_READONLY	tinyint	Indicates whether the work entry is editable or read-only.

MSP_WEB_WORKGROUP_FIELDS

This table stores the values for the workgroup (custom) fields in the timesheet.

	Column Name	Data Type	Description
PK	WASSN_ID	integer	Refers to a valid assignment in the MSP_WEB_ASSIGNMENTS table
PK	FIELD_ID	integer	The unique ID for the workgroup field.

CUSTFIELD_TYPE	integer	Indicates the type of field; same as WFIELD_TEXTCONV_TYPE in the MSP_WEB_VIEW_FIELDS table: 0 Invalid type 2 Priority (enumeration index into priority table) 3 Constraint type (index into constraint table) 4 Date 5 Percent (for example, 5%) 6 Duration (for example, 5 days) 8 Work (for example, 5h) 9 Cost (for example, $5.00) 11 Cost rate (for example, $5/hr) 12 Units 13 Accrual type (index into accrual table) 14 Contour type (index into contour table) 15 Plain number 16 Boolean (index into Boolean string table) 17 Yes/No (index into yesno string table) 18 Double (a double value) 21 String 23 Time (minutes since 12:00 midnight) 24 Long 25 Link type (SS, FF, FS, or SF) 28 Elapsed duration (for example, 5ed) 29 Task type (for example, fixed units, fixed work, fixed duration) 30 Hyperlink (friendly name) 31 Hyperlink (target) 32 Hyperlink (location) 33 Hyperlink (HREF)
INT_VAL	integer	The value of CUSTFIELD_TYPE if the value is an integer.
DATE_VAL	datetime	The value of CUSTFIELD_TYPE if the value is an date.
DECIMAL_VAL	decimal	The value of CUSTFIELD_TYPE if the value is an decimal.
VARCHAR_VAL	nvarchar(255)	The value of CUSTFIELD_TYPE if the value is an string.
INDICATOR_VAL	integer	The enumerated value of CUSTFIELD_TYPE if the value is an indicator.
DURATION_UNIT	integer	The value of CUSTFIELD_TYPE if the value is a duration.

	WWORKGRP_UPDATE_STATUS	integer	Indicates whether the custom field entry has been edited by the resource. 0 Not edited by resource 1 Edited by resource but not updated to the project manager yet
	WWORKGRP_INFO_IS_READONLY	tinyint	Indicates whether workgroup information is read-only.

MSP_WEB_WORKGROUP_FIELDS_INFO

This table stores the names and other information about workgroup (custom) fields in the timesheet.

	Column Name	Data Type	Description
PK	CUSTFIELD_INFO_ID	integer	The unique ID for the custom workgroup field.
	FIELD_ID	integer	The field ID for the custom workgroup field. Refers to a valid ID in the MSP_WEB_WORKGROUP_FIELDS table.
	CUSTFIELD_NAME	nvarchar(255)	The name of the custom workgroup field.
	CONV_VALUE	integer	Refers to a valid CONV_VALUE in the MSP_WEB_CONVERSIONS table.

Project and Resource View Tables

View tables contain all the information for all projects and resources needed to generate project drill down and resource availability views in Microsoft Project Web Access and are also used as the starting point for OLAP Cube generation. The following OLE DB tables will be written out to the project view tables for non-enterprise projects (OLE DB table name listed first, Microsoft Project Server view table name second)

- Assignments: MSP_VIEW_PROJ_ASSN_STD, MSP_VIEW_PROJ_ASSN_CF, and MSP_VIEW_PROJ_ASSN_ENT (enterprise-only)
- AssignmentTimephasedByDay: MSP_VIEW_PROJ_ASSN_TP_BY_DAY (enterprise-only)
- Calendars: MSP_VIEW_PROJ_CAL, MSP_VIEW_PROJ_CAL_DATA, and MSP_VIEW_PROJ_CAL_EXCEPTIONS.
- Predecessors: MSP_VIEW_PROJ_PRED

- Project: MSP_VIEW_PROJ_PROJECTS_STD and MSP_VIEW_PROJ_PROJECTS_ENT (enterprise-only)
- Resources: MSP_VIEW_PROJ_RES_STD, MSP_VIEW_PROJ_RES_CF, and MSP_VIEW_PROJ_RES_ENT (enterprise-only)
- Successors: MSP_VIEW_PROJ_SUCC
- Tasks: MSP_VIEW_PROJ_TASKS_STD, MSP_VIEW_PROJ_TASKS_CF, and MSP_VIEW_PROJ_TASKS_ENT (enterprise-only)
- TaskTimephasedByDay: MSP_VIEW_PROJ_TASK_TP_BY_DAY (enterprise-only)
- TaskSplits: MSP_VIEW_PROJ_TASKSPLITS

Note

When the project view tables are written out, they will have an additional column for the Microsoft Project Server Project ID, and the OLE DB tables will expose the enterprise project UID.

Resource view tables contain the latest information and the availability of each resource. These tables are created only for enterprise resources.

- Resources: MSP_VIEW_RES_STD, MSP_VIEW_RES_CF, and MSP_VIEW_RES_ENT
- AssignmentTimephasedByDay: MSP_VIEW_RES_TP_BY_DAY

Unique aspects of the Microsoft Project Server View tables

Some aspects of the Microsoft Project Server View tables are unique:

- Duration fields return minutes * 10 (for example, 8 hours is 4800) and Work fields return minutes * 1000 (for example, 8 hours is 480000).
- Dates that would be be displayed as NA in the interface are returned as 0.
- A formula in a custom field that would be displayed as #ERROR in the interface returns the default value for the field.
- Custom fields where no value has been set return the default value.

- Custom field indicator fields where no indicator has been set return "-1".
- Work values for material resources are returned in the units defined in the interface, rather than minutes * 1000.

MSP_VIEW_PROJ_ASSN_CF

This table contains custom field information for assignments. Information in this table is obtained from the Assignments table in the Microsoft Project OLE DB provider.

Column Name	Data Type	Description
WPROJ_ID	integer	Refers to a valid WPROJ_ID in the MSP_WEB_PROJECTS table.
CF_ProjectUniqueID	integer	Refers to a valid ProjectUniqueID in the MSP_VIEW_PROJ_PROJECTS_STD table.
CF_AssignmentUniqueID	integer	Refers to a valid AssignmentUniqueID in the MSP_VIEW_PROJ_ASSN_STD table.
CF_ResourceEnterpriseUniqueID	integer	Refers to a valid ResourceEnterpriseUniqueID in the MSP_VIEW_PROJ_RES_STD table.
AssignmentCost1-10	decimal	Custom cost information.
AssignmentDate1-10	datetime	Custom date information.
AssignmentDuration1-10	integer	Custom duration information.
AssignmentFinish1-10	datetime	Custom finish information.
AssignmentFlag1-20	tinyint	Custom flag information.
AssignmentNumber1-20	decimal	Custom number information.
AssignmentStart1-10	datetime	Custom start information.
Assignmentntext1-30	ntext	Custom text information.

MSP_VIEW_PROJ_ASSN_ENT

This table contains enterprise information for assignments. Information in this table is obtained from the Assignments table in the Microsoft Project OLE DB provider.

Column Name	Data Type	Description
WPROJ_ID	integer	Refers to a valid WPROJ_ID in the MSP_WEB_PROJECTS table.
ENT_ProjectUniqueID	integer	Refers to a valid ProjectUniqueID in the MSP_VIEW_PROJ_PROJECTS_STD table.
ENT_AssignmentUniqueID	integer	Refers to a valid AssignmentUniqueID in the MSP_VIEW_PROJ_ASSN_STD table.
ENT_ResourceEnterpriseUniqueID	integer	Refers to a valid ResourceEnterpriseUniqueID in the MSP_VIEW_PROJ_RES_STD table.
AssignmentEnterpriseCost1-10	decimal	Custom enterprise-level cost information.
AssignmentEnterpriseDate1-30	datetime	Custom enterprise-level date information.
AssignmentEnterpriseDuration1-10	integer	Custom enterprise-level duration information.
AssignmentEnterpriseFlag1-20	tinyint	Custom enterprise-level flag information.
AssignmentEnterpriseNumber1-40	decimal	Custom enterprise-level number information.
AssignmentOutlineCode1-30ID	integer	Custom enterprise-level outline code information.
AssignmentEnterprisentext1-40	ntext	Custom enterprise-level text information.

MSP_VIEW_PROJ_ASSN_STD

This table contains standard information for assignments. Information in this table is obtained from the Assignments table in the Microsoft Project OLE DB provider.

Column Name	Data Type	Description
WPROJ_ID	integer	Refers to a valid WPROJ_ID in the MSP_WEB_PROJECTS table.
ProjectUniqueID	integer	Refers to a valid ProjectUniqueID in the MSP_VIEW_PROJ_PROJECTS_STD table.
AssignmentUniqueID	integer	The unique ID for the assignment.
ResourceEnterpriseUniqueID	integer	Refers to a valid ResourceEnterpriseUniqueID in the MSP_VIEW_PROJ_RES_STD table.
ResourceUniqueID	integer	Refers to a valid ResourceUniqueID in the MSP_VIEW_PROJ_RES_STD table.
TaskUniqueID	integer	Refers to a valid TaskUniqueID in the MSP_VIEW_PROJ_TASKS_STD table.
AssignmentPercentWorkComplete	smallint	The current status of an assignment, expressed as the percentage of the assignment's work that has been completed.
AssignmentActualCost	decimal	The cost incurred for work already performed by a resource on a task.

AssignmentActualFinish	datetime	The date and time when an assignment was actually completed.
AssignmentActualOvertimeCost	decimal	The cost incurred for overtime work already performed by a resource on a task.
AssignmentActualOvertimeWork	decimal	The actual amount of overtime work already performed by a resource on an assigned task.
AssignmentActualStart	datetime	The date and time that an assignment actually began.
AssignmentActualWork	decimal	The amount of work that has already been done by a resource on a task.
AssignmentACWP	decimal	The costs incurred for work already performed by a resource on a task up to the project status date or today's date; also called Actual Cost of Work Performed.
AssignmentBaselineCost	decimal	The total planned cost for work to be performed by a resource on a task.
AssignmentBaselineFinish	datetime	The planned completion date for an assignment at the time a baseline is saved.
AssignmentBaselineStart	datetime	The planned beginning date for an assignment at the time a baseline is saved.
AssignmentBaselineWork	decimal	The originally planned amount of work to be performed by a resource on a task.
AssignmentBCWP	decimal	The cumulative value of the assignment's timephased percentage of work complete multiplied by the assignment's timephased baseline cost up to the status date or today's date; also known as Earned Value.
AssignmentBCWS	decimal	The cumulative timephased baseline costs up to the status date or today's date.
AssignmentConfirmed	tinyint	Indicates whether a resource assigned to a task has accepted or rejected the task assignment in response to a message notifying a resource of an assignment.
AssignmentCost	decimal	The total scheduled (or projected) cost for an assignment based on costs already incurred for work performed by the resource on a task, in addition to the costs planned for the remaining work for the assignment.
CostRateTable	smallint	Indicates which cost rate table to use for a resource on an assignment: 0 A (default) 1 B 2 C 3 D 4 E

AssignmentCostVariance	decimal	The difference between the baseline cost and total cost for an assignment.
AssignmentCV	decimal	The difference between how much it should have cost to achieve the current level of completion on the assignment and how much it has actually cost to achieve the current level of completion up to the status date or today's date.
AssignmentDelay	integer	The amount of time a resource is to wait after the task start date before starting work on an assignment.
AssignmentFinish	datetime	The date and time that an assigned resource is scheduled to complete work on a task.
AssignmentFinishVariance	integer	The difference between an assignment's baseline finish date and its scheduled finish date.
AssignmentFixedMaterial	tinyint	Indicates whether the consumption of the assigned material resource occurs in a single, fixed amount.
AssignmentHasFixedRateUnits	tinyint	Indicates whether an assignment has fixed rate units.
AssignmentHyperlink	ntext	The title or explanatory text for a hyperlink associated with an assignment.
AssignmentHyperlinkAddress	ntext	The address for a hyperlink associated with an assignment.
AssignmentHyperlinkHref	ntext	The combination, or concatenation, of the hyperlink address and hyperlink sub-address fields associated with an assignment.
AssignmentHyperlinkScreenTip	ntext	The text contained in a ScreenTip associated with a hyperlink.
AssignmentHyperlinkSubAddress	ntext	The specific location in a document within a hyperlink associated with an assignment.
AssignmentLevelingDelay	integer	The amount of time that an assignment is to be delayed from the scheduled start date as a result of resource leveling.
AssignmentLinkedFields	tinyint	Indicates whether there are OLE links to the assignment.
AssignmentMilestone	tinyint	Indicates whether the assignment task is a milestone.
AssignmentNotes	ntext	Contains notes about an assignment.
AssignmentOtherType	smallint	Indicates the type of assignment: 0 Regular 1 Task-only work 2 Fixed cost 3 Fixed cost and task-only work
AssignmentOverallocated	tinyint	Indicates whether a resource is assigned to more work on a specific task than can be done within the resource's normal working capacity.

AssignmentOvertimeCost	decimal	The total overtime cost for a resource assignment.
AssignmentOvertimeWork	decimal	The amount of overtime to be performed by a resource on a task; charged at the resource's overtime rate.
AssignmentPeakUnits	decimal	The maximum percentage of units for which a resource is assigned to a task for a given period of time.
AssignmentRegularWork	decimal	The total amount of non-overtime work scheduled to be performed by a resource assigned to a task.
AssignmentRemainingCost	decimal	The costs associated with completing all remaining scheduled work by any resources on a specific task.
AssignmentRemainingOvertimeCost	decimal	The remaining scheduled overtime expense for an assignment.
AssignmentRemainingOvertimeWork	decimal	The amount of overtime work that remains on an assignment.
AssignmentRemainingWork	decimal	The amount of time required by a resource assigned to a task to complete an assignment.
AssignmentResourceID	integer	Refers to a valid ResourceID in the MSP_VIEW_PROJ_RES_STD table.
AssignmentResourceName	nvarchar(255)	The name of the resource associated with the assignment.
AssignmentResourceRequestType	smallint	The type of request: 0 None (default) 1 Request 2 Demand
AssignmentResourceType	smallint	The resource type: 0 Work (default); people and equipment 1 Material; consumable supplies like steel, concrete, or soil
AssignmentResponsePending	tinyint	Indicates whether an answer has been received from a message notifying a resource of an assignment sent to a resource assigned to a task.
AssignmentStart	datetime	The date and time that an assigned resource is scheduled to begin working on a task.
AssignmentStartVariance	integer	The difference between an assignment's baseline start date and its currently scheduled start date.
AssignmentSummary	tinyint	Indicates whether the assignment is part of a summary task.
AssignmentSV	decimal	The difference in cost terms between the current progress and the baseline plan of the assignment up to the status date or today's date.
AssignmentTaskID	integer	Refers to a valid TaskID in the MSP_VIEW_PROJ_TASKS_STD table.
AssignmentTaskName	nvarchar(255)	The name of the task associated with the assignment.

AssignmentTaskSummaryName	nvarchar(255)	The name of the summary task for the task associated with the assignment.
AssignmentTeamStatusPending	tinyint	Indicates whether a status message has been received in response to a message requesting status that was sent to a resource assigned to a task.
AssignmentUnits	decimal	The number of units for which a resource is assigned to a task, expressed as a percentage of 100%, assuming a resource's MaxUnits value is 100%.
AssignmentUpdateNeeded	tinyint	Indicates whether a message notifying a resource of changes that affect tasks should be sent to the resource assigned to a task because of changes to the start date, finish date, or resource reassignments.
AssignmentVAC	decimal	The variance at completion (VAC) between the baseline cost and the total cost for an assignment on a task.
AssignmentWork	decimal	The total amount of work scheduled to be performed by a resource on a task.
AssignmentWorkContour	smallint	Indicates how work for an assignment is to be distributed across the duration of the assignment: 0 Flat (default) 1 Back Loaded 2 Front Loaded 3 Double Peak 4 Early Peak 5 Late Peak 6 Bell 7 Turtle 8 Contoured
AssignmentWorkVariance	decimal	The difference between an assignment's baseline work and the currently scheduled work.

MSP_VIEW_PROJ_ASSN_TP_BY_DAY

This table contains timephased information for assignments. Information in this table is obtained from the AssignmentsTimephasedByDay table in the Microsoft Project OLE DB provider.

Column Name	Data Type	Description
WPROJ_ID	integer	Refers to a valid WPROJ_ID in the MSP_WEB_PROJECTS table.
ProjectUniqueID	integer	Refers to a valid ProjectUniqueID in the MSP_VIEW_PROJ_PROJECTS_STD table.
AssignmentUniqueID	integer	Refers to a valid AssignmentUniqueID in the MSP_VIEW_PROJ_ASSN_STD table.
AssignmentTimeStart	datetime	The date and time that an assigned resource is scheduled to begin working on a task.
AssignmentTimeFinish	datetime	The date and time that an assigned resource is scheduled to complete work on a task.
AssignmentTimeActualCost	decimal	Shows costs incurred for work already performed by a resource on a task.
AssignmentTimeActualOvertimeWork	decimal	The actual amount of overtime work already performed by a resource on an assigned task.
AssignmentTimeActualWork	decimal	The amount of work that has already been done by a resource on a task.
AssignmentTimeBaselineCost	decimal	Specifies the total planned cost for work to be performed by a resource on a task.
AssignmentTimeBaselineWork	decimal	The originally planned amount of work to be performed by a resource on a task.
AssignmentTimeCost	decimal	The total scheduled (or projected) cost for a resource assignment based on costs already incurred for work performed by the resource on a task, in addition to the costs planned for the remaining work for the assignment.
AssignmentTimeCumulativeCost	decimal	The scheduled cumulative timephased cost for a resource assignment to date, based on costs already incurred for work performed by the resource on the task, in addition to the costs planned for the remaining work for the assignment.
AssignmentTimeCumulativeWork	decimal	The total amount of work scheduled to be performed by a resource on a task.
AssignmentTimeOvertimeWork	decimal	The amount of overtime to be performed by a resource on a task; charged at the resource's overtime rate.
AssignmentTimePeakUnits	decimal	The maximum percentage of units for which a resource is assigned to a task for a given period of time.
AssignmentTimeRegularWork	decimal	The total amount of non-overtime work scheduled to be performed by a resource assigned to a task.
AssignmentTimeWork	decimal	The total amount of time for work scheduled to be performed by a resource on a task.

MSP_VIEW_PROJ_CAL

This table contains information about calendars. Information in this table is obtained from the Calendars table in the Microsoft Project OLE DB provider.

Column Name	Data Type	Description
WPROJ_ID	integer	Refers to a valid WPROJ_ID in the MSP_WEB_PROJECTS table.
ProjectUniqueID	integer	Refers to a valid ProjectUniqueID in the MSP_VIEW_PROJ_PROJECTS_STD table.
CalendarUniqueID	integer	The unique ID for the calendar.
ResourceUniqueID	integer	Refers to a valid ResourceUniqueID in the MSP_VIEW_PROJ_RES_STD table.
ResourceEnterpriseUniqueID	integer	Refers to a valid ResourceEnterpriseUniqueID in the MSP_VIEW_PROJ_RES_STD table.
CalendarName	nvarchar(255)	The name of the calendar; empty if this calendar is a resource calendar.
CalendarIsBaseCalendar	tinyint	Indicates whether this calendar is a base calendar; a resource calendar cannot be a base calendar.
CalendarBaseCalendarUniqueID	integer	Refers a calendar to its parent base calendar (required for all resource calendars).

MSP_VIEW_PROJ_CAL_DATA

This table contains calendar data. Information in this table is obtained from the CalendarData table in the Microsoft Project OLE DB provider.

Column Name	Data Type	Description
WPROJ_ID	integer	Refers to a valid WPROJ_ID in the MSP_WEB_PROJECTS table.
ProjectUniqueID	integer	Refers to a valid ProjectUniqueID in the MSP_VIEW_PROJ_PROJECTS_STD table.
CalendarUniqueID	integer	Refers to a valid CalendarUniqueID in the MSP_VIEW_PROJ_CAL table.
CalendarWeekly	integer	Indicates the defined working day for the calendar: 0 Exception 1 Sunday 2 Monday 3 Tuesday 4 Wednesday 5 Thursday 6 Friday 7 Saturday

CalendarWorking	integer	Indicates whether the selected days are working or nonworking days.
CalendarFromDate	datetime	The date the exception begins.
CalendarToDate	datetime	The date the exception ends.
CalendarFromTime1-5	datetime	The time the first, second, third, fourth, or fifth shift begins.
CalendarToTime1-5	datetime	The time the first, second, third, fourth, or fifth shift ends.

MSP_VIEW_PROJ_CAL_EXCEPTIONS

This table contains calendar data. Information in this table is obtained from the CalendarExceptions table in the Microsoft Project OLE DB provider.

Column Name	Data Type	Description
WPROJ_ID	integer	Refers to a valid WPROJ_ID in the MSP_WEB_PROJECTS table.
ProjectUniqueID	integer	Refers to a valid ProjectUniqueID in the MSP_VIEW_PROJ_PROJECTS_STD table.
CalendarUniqueID	integer	Refers to a valid CalendarUniqueID in the MSP_VIEW_PROJ_CAL table.
CalendarExceptionFromDate	datetime	The date the calendar exception begins.
CalendarExceptionToDate	datetime	The date the calendar exception ends.
CalendarExceptionWorking	integer	Indicates whether the days contained in the calendar exception date range are working or nonworking days.
CalendarExceptionFromTime1-3	datetime	The time the first, second, or third time period begins.
CaldnearExceptionToTime1-3	datetime	The time the first, second, or third time period ends.

MSP_VIEW_PROJ_PRED

This table contains information about predecessor projects. Information in this table is obtained from the Predecessors table in the Microsoft Project OLE DB provider.

Column Name	Data Type	Description
WPROJ_ID	integer	Refers to a valid WPROJ_ID in the MSP_WEB_PROJECTS table.
ProjectUniqueID	integer	Refers to a valid ProjectUniqueID in the MSP_VIEW_PROJ_PROJECTS_STD table.

TaskUniqueID	integer	Refers to a valid TaskUniqueID in the MSP_VIEW_PROJ_TASKS_STD table.
PredecessorTaskUniqueID	integer	Refers to a valid TaskUniqueID in the MSP_VIEW_PROJ_TASKS_STD table.
PredecessorLag	integer	The amount of lead (negative number) or lag (positive number) time for the predecessor task; for example: -3d or +4d.
PredecessorPath	nvarchar(260)	The path to the predecessor task (even if the successor task is contained in another project); for example: C:\My Documents\Bldg E Construction.mpp\3FF.
PredecessorType	smallint	The type of predecessor task: 0 FF (finish-to-finish) 1 FS (finish-to-start) 2 SF (start-to-finish) 3 SS (start-to-start)
PredecessorLagType	smallint	Indicates the format for the amount of lag specified in PredecessorLag: 3 m 4 em 5 h 6 eh 7 d 8 ed 9 w 10 ew 11 mo 12 emo 19 % 20 e% 35 m? 36 em? 37 h? 38 eh? 39 d? 40 ed? 41 w? 42 ew? 43 mo? 44 emo? 51 %? 52 e%?

MSP_VIEW_PROJ_PROJECTS_ENT

This table contains enterprise information for projects. Information in this table is obtained from the Project table in the Microsoft Project OLE DB provider.

Column Name	Data Type	Description
WPROJ_ID	integer	Refers to a valid WPROJ_ID in the MSP_WEB_PROJECTS table.
ENT_ProjectUniqueID	integer	Refers to a valid ProjectUniqueID in the MSP_VIEW_PROJ_PROJECTS_STD table.
ProjectEnterpriseName	nvarchar(255)	The name of the project within the enterprise.
ProjectEnterpriseVersion	nvarchar(255)	The version of the project within the enterprise.
ProjectEnterpriseCost1-10	decimal	Custom project-level enterprise cost information.
ProjectEnterpriseCost1-10Indicator	smallint	The indicator symbol for the corresponding custom field. See Indicator symbols for more information.
ProjectEnterpriseDate1-30	datetime	Custom project-level enterprise date information.
ProjectEnterpriseDate1-30Indicator	smallint	The indicator symbol for the corresponding custom field. See Indicator symbols for more information.
ProjectEnterpriseDuration1-10	integer	Custom project-level enterprise duration information.
ProjectEnterpriseDuration1-10Indicator	smallint	The indicator symbol for the corresponding custom field. See Indicator symbols for more information.
ProjectEnterpriseFlag1-20	tinyint	Custom project-level enterprise flag information.
ProjectEnterpriseFlag1-20Indicator	smallint	The indicator symbol for the corresponding custom field. See Indicator symbols for more information.
ProjectEnterpriseNumber1-40	integer	Custom project-level enterprise number information.
ProjectEnterpriseNumber1-40Indicator	smallint	The indicator symbol for the corresponding custom field. See Indicator symbols for more information.
ProjectEnterpriseOutlineCode1-30ID	integer	Custom project-level enterprise outline code information.
ProjectEnterprisentext1-40	ntext	Custom project-level enterprise text information.
ProjectEnterprisentext1-40Indicator	smallint	The indicator symbol for the corresponding custom field. See Indicator symbols for more information.

MSP_VIEW_PROJ_PROJECTS_STD

This table contains standard information for projects. Information in this table is obtained from the Project table in the Microsoft Project OLE DB provider.

Column Name	Data Type	Description
WPROJ_ID	integer	Refers to a valid WPROJ_ID in the MSP_WEB_PROJECTS table.
ProjectUniqueID	integer	The unique ID for the project.
ProjectCurrencyDigits	smallint	The number of digits that are to appear after the decimal when currency values are shown in Microsoft Project: 0 No digits after the decimal; $0 1 One digit after the decimal; $0.0 2 Two digits after the decimal (default); $0.00
ProjectCurrencyPosition	smallint	Indicates the placement of the currency symbol in relation to the currency value: 0 Before, no space (default); $0 1 After, no space; 0$ 2 Before, with space; $ 0 3 After, with space; 0 $
ProjectCurrencySymbol	nvarchar(10)	The currency symbol used to represent the type of currency used in the project.
ProjectDefaultFinishTime	smallint	The default finish time for all new tasks.
ProjectDefaultStartTime	smallint	The default start time for all new tasks.
ProjectTitle	nvarchar(255)	The title of the project; used to group similar projects together.
ProjectCalendarName	nvarchar(255)	The name of the calendar associated with the project.
ProjectFinishDate	datetime	The date and time that a project is scheduled for completion.
ProjectStartDate	datetime	The date and time that a project is scheduled to begin.
ProjectStatusDate	datetime	The project status date.

MSP_VIEW_PROJ_RES_CF

This table contains custom field information for resources. Information in this table is obtained from the Resources table in the Microsoft Project OLE DB provider.

Column Name	Data Type	Description
WPROJ_ID	integer	Refers to a valid WPROJ_ID in the MSP_WEB_PROJECTS table.
CF_ProjectUniqueID	integer	Refers to a valid ProjectUniqueID in the MSP_VIEW_PROJ_PROJECTS_STD table.
CF_ResourceUniqueID	integer	Refers to a valid ResourceUniqueID in the MSP_VIEW_PROJ_RES_STD table.
CF_ResourceEnterpriseUniqueID	integer	Refers to a valid ResourceEnterpriseUniqueID in the MSP_VIEW_PROJ_RES_STD table.
ResourceCost1-10	decimal	Custom cost information.
ResourceCost1-10Indicator	smallint	The indicator symbol for the corresponding custom field. See Indicator symbols for more information.
ResourceDate1-10	datetime	Custom date information.
ResourceDate1-10Indicator	smallint	The indicator symbol for the corresponding custom field. See Indicator symbols for more information.
ResourceDuration1-10	integer	Custom duration information.
ResourceDuration1-10Indicator	smallint	The indicator symbol for the corresponding custom field. See Indicator symbols for more information.
ResourceFinish1-10	datetime	Custom finish date information.
ResourceFinish1-10Indicator	smallint	The indicator symbol for the corresponding custom field. See Indicator symbols for more information.
ResourceFlag1-20	tinyint	Indicates whether a resource is marked for further action or identification of some kind.
ResourceFlag1-20Indicator	smallint	The indicator symbol for the corresponding custom field. See Indicator symbols for more information.
ResourceNumber1-20	decimal	Custom numeric information.
ResourceNumber1-20Indicator	smallint	The indicator symbol for the corresponding custom field. See Indicator symbols for more information.
ResourceOutlineCode1-10	ntext	An alphanumeric code defined to represent a hierarchical structure of resources.
ResourceStart1-10	datetime	Custom start date information.
ResourceStart1-10Indicator	smallint	The indicator symbol for the corresponding custom field. See Indicator symbols for more information.
ResourceText1-30	ntext	Custom text information.
ResourceText1-30Indicator	smallint	The indicator symbol for the corresponding custom field. See Indicator symbols for more information.

MSP_VIEW_PROJ_RES_ENT

This table contains enterprise information for resources. Information in this table is obtained from the Resources table in the Microsoft Project OLE DB provider.

Column Name	Data Type	Description
WPROJ_ID	integer	Refers to a valid WPROJ_ID in the MSP_WEB_PROJECTS table.
ENT_ProjectUniqueID	integer	Refers to a valid ProjectUniqueID in the MSP_VIEW_PROJ_PROJECTS_STD table.
ENT_ResourceUniqueID	integer	Refers to a valid ResourceUniqueID in the MSP_VIEW_PROJ_RES_STD table.
ENT_ResourceEnterpriseUniqueID	integer	Refers to a valid ResourceEnterpriseUniqueID in the MSP_VIEW_PROJ_RES_STD table.
ResourceEnterpriseCost1-10	decimal	Custom enterprise-level cost information.
ResourceEnterpriseCost1-10Indicator	smallint	The indicator symbol for the corresponding custom field. See Indicator symbols for more information.
ResourceEnterpriseDate1-30	datetime	Custom enterprise-level date information.
ResourceEnterpriseDate1-30Indicator	smallint	The indicator symbol for the corresponding custom field. See Indicator symbols for more information.
ResourceEnterpriseDuration1-10	integer	Custom enterprise-level duration information.
ResourceEnterpriseDuration1-10Indicator	smallint	The indicator symbol for the corresponding custom field. See Indicator symbols for more information.
ResourceEnterpriseFlag1-20	tinyint	Custom enterprise-level flag information.
ResourceEnterpriseFlag1-20Indicator	smallint	The indicator symbol for the corresponding custom field. See Indicator symbols for more information.
ResourceEnterpriseGeneric	smallint	Indicates whether the resource is an enterprise-level generic resource.
ResourceEnterpriseNumber1-40	decimal	Custom enterprise-level number information.
ResourceEnterpriseNumber1-40Indicator	smallint	The indicator symbol for the corresponding custom field. See Indicator symbols for more information.
ResourceEnterpriseOutlineCode1-30ID	integer	Custom enterprise-level outline code information.
ResourceEnterpriseText1-40	ntext	Custom enterprise-level text information.
ResourceEnterpriseText1-40Indicator	smallint	The indicator symbol for the corresponding custom field. See Indicator symbols for more information.

MSP_VIEW_PROJ_RES_STD

This table contains standard information for resources. Information in this table is obtained from the Resources table in the Microsoft Project OLE DB provider.

Column Name	Data Type	Description
WPROJ_ID	integer	Refers to a valid WPROJ_ID in the MSP_WEB_PROJECTS table.
ProjectUniqueID	integer	Refers to a valid ProjectUniqueID in the MSP_VIEW_PROJ_PROJECTS_STD table.
ResourceUniqueID	integer	The unique ID for the resource.
ResourceEnterpriseUniqueID	integer	The unique enterprise ID for the resource.
ResourcePercentWorkComplete	smallint	The current status of all tasks assigned to a resource, expressed as the total percentage of the resource's work that has been completed.
ResourceAccrueAt	smallint	Indicates how and when resource standard and overtime costs are to be charged, or accrued, to the cost of a task: 1 Start; costs are accrued as soon as the task starts, as indicated by a date entered in the ActualStart field. 2 End; costs are not incurred until remaining work is zero. 3 Pro-rated (default); costs accrue as work is scheduled to occur and as actual work is reported.
ResourceActualCost	decimal	The sum of costs incurred for the work already performed by a resource for all assigned tasks.
ResourceActualOvertimeCost	decimal	The cost incurred for overtime work already performed by a resource for all assigned tasks.
ResourceActualOvertimeWork	decimal	The actual amount of overtime work already performed for all assignments assigned to a resource.
ResourceActualWork	decimal	The actual amount of work that has already been done for all assignments assigned to a resource.
ResourceACWP	decimal	The sum of Actual Cost of Work Performed (ACWP) values for all of a resource's assignments, up to the status date or today's date.
ResourceAvailableFrom	datetime	The starting date that a resource is available for work at the units specified for the current time period.
ResourceAvailableTo	datetime	The ending date in which a resource will be available for work at the units specified for the current time period.

ResourceBaseCalendar	ntext	Lists all calendars available to be applied to a resource, including the standard calendar and any custom calendars: 0 Standard (default) 1+ Custom calendar
ResourceBaselineCost	decimal	The total planned cost for a resource for all assigned tasks; also called Budget At Completion (BAC).
ResourceBaselineCost1-10	decimal	Custom baseline cost information.
ResourceBaselineFinish	datetime	The planned finish date for assignments.
ResourceBaselineFinish1-10	datetime	Custom baseline finish information.
ResourceBaselineStart	datetime	The planned beginning date for assignments.
ResourceBaselineStart1-10	datetime	Custom baseline start information.
ResourceBaselineWork	decimal	The originally planned amount of work to be performed for all assignments assigned to a resource.
ResourceBaselineWork1-10	decimal	Custom baseline work information.
ResourceBCWP	decimal	The rolled-up summary of a resource's BCWP values for all assigned tasks, calculated up to the status date or today's date; also called Budgeted Cost of Work Performed.
ResourceBCWS	decimal	The rolled-up summary of a resource's BCWS values for all assigned tasks; also called Budgeted Cost of Work Scheduled.
ResourceCanLevel	tinyint	Indicates whether resource leveling can be done with a resource.
ResourceCode	ntext	A code, initials, or number entered as part of a resource's information.
ResourceConfirmed	tinyint	Indicates whether a resource has accepted or rejected all task assignments in response to a message notifying a resource of an assignment.
ResourceCost	decimal	The total scheduled cost for a resource for all assigned tasks, based on costs already incurred for work performed by the resource on all assigned tasks in addition to the costs planned for all remaining work.
ResourceCostPerUse	decimal	The cost that accrues each time a resource is used.
ResourceCostVariance	decimal	The difference between the baseline cost and total cost for a resource.
ResourceCV	decimal	The difference between how much it should have cost for the resource to achieve the current level of completion, and how much it has actually cost to achieve the current level of completion, up to the status date or today's date.

ResourceEmailAddress	ntext	The e-mail address of a resource; if this field is left blank, Microsoft Project will use the name in the ResourceName field as the e-mail address.
ResourceFinish	datetime	The date and time that a resource is scheduled to complete work on all assigned tasks.
ResourceGroup	ntext	The name of the group associated with the resource.
ResourceHyperlink	ntext	The title or explanatory text for a hyperlink associated with a resource.
ResourceHyperlinkAddress	ntext	The address for a hyperlink associated with a resource.
ResourceHyperlinkHref	ntext	The combination, or concatenation, of the Hyperlink Address and Hyperlink SubAddress fields associated with a resource.
ResourceHyperlinkScreenTip	ntext	The text contained in a ScreenTip associated with a hyperlink.
ResourceHyperlinkSubAddress	ntext	The specific location in a document within a hyperlink associated with a resource.
ResourceID	integer	Indicates the position of a resource in relation to other resources.
ResourceInitials	ntext	The initials for a resource name.
ResourceIsNull	tinyint	Indicates whether the resource is a null resource.
ResourceLinkedFields	tinyint	Indicates whether there are OLE links to the resource, either from elsewhere in the active project, another Microsoft Project file, or from another program.
ResourceMaterialLabel	ntext	The unit of measurement entered for a material resource, for example: tons, boxes, or cubic yards. This is used in conjunction with the material resource's Assignment Units and is only available if ResourceType is set to Material.
ResourceMaxUnits	decimal	The maximum percentage, or number of units, that represents the maximum capacity for which a resource is available to accomplish any tasks during the current time period: 0-99: Resource is 0%-99% available for the specified task 100: Resource is 100% available for the specified task (default)
ResourceName	nvarchar(255)	The name of the resource; must be unique within the enterprise whether or not the resource is active.
ResourceNotes	ntext	Notes about a resource.
ResourceNTAccount	ntext	The Windows NT Account name for a resource; for example: *domain name\user name.*

ResourceObjects	integer	The number of objects associated with a resource, not including those in notes.
ResourceOverallocated	tinyint	Indicates whether a resource is assigned to do more work on all assigned tasks than can be done within the resource's normal work capacity.
ResourceOvertimeCost	decimal	The total overtime cost for a resource on all assigned tasks.
ResourceOvertimeRate	decimal	The rate of pay for overtime work performed by a resource.
ResourceOvertimeWork	decimal	The amount of overtime to be performed for all tasks assigned to a resource and charged at the resource's overtime rate.
ResourcePeakUnits	decimal	The maximum percentage, or number of units, for which a resource is assigned at any one time for all tasks assigned to the resource.
ResourcePhonetics	ntext	Contains phonetic information in either Hiragana or Katakana for resource names; used only in the Japanese version of Microsoft Project.
ResourceRegularWork	decimal	The total amount of non-overtime work scheduled to be performed for all assignments assigned to a resource.
ResourceRemainingCost	decimal	The remaining scheduled expense that will be incurred in completing the remaining work assigned to a resource.
ResourceRemainingOvertimeCost	decimal	The remaining scheduled overtime expense of a resource that will be incurred in completing the remaining planned overtime work by a resource on all assigned tasks.
ResourceRemainingOvertimeWork	decimal	The remaining amount of overtime required by a resource to complete all tasks.
ResourceRemainingWork	decimal	The amount of time, or person-hours, still required by a resource to complete all assigned tasks.
ResourceResponsePending	tinyint	Indicates whether an answer has been received from all messages notifying a resource of an assignment sent to a resource about assigned tasks.
ResourceStandardRate	decimal	The rate of pay for regular, non-overtime work performed by a resource.
ResourceStart	datetime	The date and time that an assigned resource is scheduled to begin working on all assigned tasks.
ResourceSV	decimal	The difference in cost terms between the current progress and the baseline plan of all the resource's assigned tasks up to the status date or today's date; also called Earned Value Schedule Variance.

<table>
<tr><td>ResourceTeamStatusPending</td><td>tinyint</td><td>Indicates whether an answer has been received in response to a message requesting status that was sent to a resource about an assigned task.</td></tr>
<tr><td>ResourceType</td><td>smallint</td><td>The resource type (Work or Material):
0 Work (default); people and equipment
1 Material; consumable supplies like steel, concrete, or soil</td></tr>
<tr><td>ResourceUpdateNeeded</td><td>tinyint</td><td>Indicates whether a message notifying a resource of changes that affect tasks should be sent to a resource because of changes to any of the resource's assigned tasks.</td></tr>
<tr><td>ResourceVAC</td><td>decimal</td><td>The difference between the baseline cost and the total cost for a resource.</td></tr>
<tr><td>ResourceWork</td><td>decimal</td><td>The total amount of work scheduled to be performed by a resource on all assigned tasks.</td></tr>
<tr><td>ResourceWorkgroup</td><td>smallint</td><td>The messaging method used to communicate with a project workgroup:
0 Default
1 Web (Microsoft Project Web Access)
2 E-mail only
3 None; Workgroup messaging is not used on this project</td></tr>
<tr><td>ResourceWorkVariance</td><td>decimal</td><td>The difference between a resource's total baseline work and the currently scheduled work.</td></tr>
</table>

MSP_VIEW_PROJ_SUCC

This table contains information about successor projects. Information in this table is obtained from the Successors table in the Microsoft Project OLE DB provider.

Column Name	Data Type	Description
WPROJ_ID	integer	Refers to a valid WPROJ_ID in the MSP_WEB_PROJECTS table.
ProjectUniqueID	integer	Refers to a valid ProjectUniqueID in the MSP_VIEW_PROJ_PROJECTS_STD table.
TaskUniqueID	integer	Refers to a valid TaskUniqueID in the MSP_VIEW_PROJ_TASKS_STD table.
SuccessorTaskUniqueID	integer	Refers to a valid TaskUniqueID in the MSP_VIEW_PROJ_TASKS_STD table.

SuccessorLag	integer	The amount of lead (negative number) or lag (positive number) time for the successor task; for example: -3d or +4d.
SuccessorPath	nvarchar(260)	The path to the successor task (even if the successor task is contained in another project); for example: C:\My Documents\Bldg E Construction.mpp\3FF.
SuccessorType	smallint	The type of successor task: 0 FF (finish-to-finish) 1 FS (finish-to-start) 2 SF (start-to-finish) 3 SS (start-to-start)

MSP_VIEW_PROJ_TASKS_CF

This table contains custom field information for tasks. Information in this table is obtained from the Tasks table in the Microsoft Project OLE DB provider.

Column Name	Data Type	Description
WPROJ_ID	integer	Refers to a valid WPROJ_ID in the MSP_WEB_PROJECTS table.
CF_ProjectUniqueID	integer	Refers to a valid ProjectUniqueID in the MSP_VIEW_PROJ_PROJECTS_STD table.
CF_TaskUniqueID	integer	Refers to a valid TaskUniqueID in the MSP_VIEW_PROJ_TASKS_STD table.
TaskCost1-10	decimal	Custom cost information.
TaskCost1-10Indicator	smallint	The indicator symbol for the corresponding custom field. See Indicator symbols for more information.
TaskDate1-10	datetime	Custom date information.
TaskDate1-10Indicator	smallint	The indicator symbol for the corresponding custom field. See Indicator symbols for more information.
TaskDuration1-10	integer	Custom duration information.
TaskDuration1-10Estimated	tinyint	Indicates whether the corresponding TaskDuration1-10 field is estimated.
TaskDuration1-10Indicator	smallint	The indicator symbol for the corresponding custom field. See Indicator symbols for more information.
TaskFinish1-10	datetime	Custom finish date information.
TaskFinish1-10Indicator	smallint	The indicator symbol for the corresponding custom field. See Indicator symbols for more information.
TaskFlag1-20	tinyint	Custom flag information.
TaskFlag1-20Indicator	smallint	The indicator symbol for the corresponding custom field. See Indicator symbols for more information.
TaskNumber1-20	decimal	Custom numeric information.
TaskNumber1-20Indicator	smallint	The indicator symbol for the corresponding custom field. See Indicator symbols for more information.

TaskNumber1-20	decimal	Custom numeric information.
TaskNumber1-20Indicator	smallint	The indicator symbol for the corresponding custom field. See Indicator symbols for more information.
TaskOutlineCode1-10	ntext	An alphanumeric code that represents a hierarchical structure of tasks.
TaskStart1-10	datetime	Custom start date information.
TaskStart1-10Indicator	smallint	The indicator symbol for the corresponding custom field. See Indicator symbols for more information.
Taskntext1-30	ntext	Custom text information.
Taskntext1-30Indicator	smallint	The indicator symbol for the corresponding custom field. See Indicator symbols for more information.

MSP_VIEW_PROJ_TASKS_ENT

This table contains enterprise information for tasks. Information in this table is obtained from the Tasks table in the Microsoft Project OLE DB provider.

Column Name	Data Type	Description
WPROJ_ID	integer	Refers to a valid WPROJ_ID in the MSP_WEB_PROJECTS table.
ENT_ProjectUniqueID	integer	Refers to a valid ProjectUniqueID in the MSP_VIEW_PROJ_PROJECTS_STD table.
ENT_TaskUniqueID	integer	Refers to a valid TaskUniqueID in the MSP_VIEW_PROJ_TASKS_STD table.
TaskEnterpriseCost1-10	decimal	Custom enterprise-level cost information.
TaskEnterpriseCost1-10Indicator	smallint	The indicator symbol for the corresponding custom field. See Indicator symbols for more information.
TaskEnterpriseDate1-30	datetime	Custom enterprise-level date information.
TaskEnterpriseDate1-30Indicator	smallint	The indicator symbol for the corresponding custom field. See Indicator symbols for more information.
TaskEnterpriseDuration1-10	integer	Custom enterprise-level duration information.
TaskEnterpriseDuration1-10Indicator	smallint	The indicator symbol for the corresponding custom field. See Indicator symbols for more information.
TaskEnterpriseFlag1-20	tinyint	Custom enterprise-level flag information.
TaskEnterpriseFlag1-20Indicator	smallint	The indicator symbol for the corresponding custom field. See Indicator symbols for more information.
TaskEnterpriseNumber1-40	decimal	Custom enterprise-level number information.
TaskEnterpriseNumber1-40Indicator	smallint	The indicator symbol for the corresponding custom field. See Indicator symbols for more information.
TaskEnterpriseOutlineCode1-30ID	integer	Custom enterprise-level outline code information.
TaskEnterprisentext1-40	ntext	Custom enterprise-level text information.
TaskEnterprisentext1-40Indicator	smallint	The indicator symbol for the corresponding custom field. See Indicator symbols for more information.

MSP_VIEW_PROJ_TASKS_STD

This table contains standard information for tasks. Information in this table is obtained from the Tasks table in the Microsoft Project OLE DB provider.

Column Name	Data Type	Description
WPROJ_ID	integer	Refers to a valid WPROJ_ID in the MSP_WEB_PROJECTS table.
ProjectUniqueID	integer	Refers to a valid ProjectUniqueID in the MSP_VIEW_PROJ_PROJECTS_STD table.
TaskUniqueID	integer	The unique ID for the task.
TaskPercentComplete	smallint	The current status of a task, expressed as the percentage of the task's duration that has been completed.
TaskPercentWorkComplete	smallint	The current status of a task, expressed as the percentage of the task's work that has been completed.
TaskActualCost	decimal	The costs incurred for work already performed by all resources on a task, along with any other recorded costs associated with the task.
TaskActualDuration	integer	The span of actual working time for a task so far, based on the scheduled duration and current remaining work or completion percentage.
TaskActualFinish	datetime	The date and time that a task actually finished.
TaskActualOvertimeCost	decimal	The costs incurred for overtime work already performed on a task by all assigned resources.
TaskActualOvertimeWork	decimal	The actual amount of overtime work already performed by all resources assigned to a task.
TaskActualStart	datetime	The date and time that a task actually began.
TaskActualWork	decimal	The amount of work that has already been done by the resources assigned to a task.
TaskACWP	decimal	The costs incurred for work already done on a task up to the project status date or today's date.
TaskBaselineCost	decimal	The total planned cost for a task; also referred to as Budget At Completion (BAC).
TaskBaselineCost1-10	decimal	Custom baseline cost information.
TaskBaselineDuration	integer	The original span of time planned to complete a task.
TaskBaselineDuration1-10	integer	Custom baseline duration information.
TaskBaselineDurationEstimated	tinyint	Indicates whether the baseline duration is estimated.
TaskBaselineDurationEstimated1-10	tinyint	Custom baseline estimated duration information.
TaskBaselineFinish	datetime	The planned completion date for a task at the time a baseline is saved.

TaskBaselineFinish1-10	datetime	Custom baseline finish information.
TaskBaselineStart	datetime	The planned beginning date for a task at the time a baseline is saved.
TaskBaselineStart1-10	datetime	Custom baseline start information.
TaskBaselineWork	decimal	The originally planned amount of work to be performed by all resources assigned to a task.
TaskBaselineWork1-10	decimal	Custom baseline work information.
TaskBCWP	decimal	The cumulative value of the task's timephased percent complete multiplied by the task's timephased baseline cost, up to the status date or today's date; also known as Earned Value.
TaskBCWS	decimal	The cumulative timephased baseline costs up to the status date or today's date.
TaskCalendar	ntext	Lists all calendars available to be applied to a task, including the standard calendar and any custom calendars: 0 Standard (default) 1+ Custom calendar
TaskCompleteThrough	datetime	The progress of a task on the Gantt Chart, up to the point that actuals have been reported for the task.
TaskConfirmed	tinyint	Indicates whether all resources assigned to a task have accepted or rejected the task assignment in response to a message notifying a resource of an assignment.
TaskConstraintDate	datetime	Indicates the constrained start or finish date as defined in TaskConstraintType. Required unless TaskContstraintType is set to As late as possible or As soon as possible.
TaskConstraintType	smallint	The constraint on a scheduled task: 0 As soon as possible 1 As late as possible 2 Must start on; TaskConstraintDate is required 3 Must finish on; TaskConstraintDate is required 4 Start no earlier than; TaskConstraintDate is required 5 Start no later than; TaskConstraintDate is required 6 Finish no earlier than; TaskConstraintDate is required 7 Finish no later than; TaskConstraintDate is required
TaskContact	ntext	The name of the individual who is responsible for a task.

TaskCost	decimal	The total scheduled, or projected, cost for a task, based on costs already incurred for work performed by all resources assigned to the task, in addition to the costs planned for the remaining work for the assignment.
TaskCostVariance	decimal	The difference between the baseline cost and the total cost for a task.
TaskCPI	decimal	The cost performance index, or the ratio of budget to actual cost.
TaskCreated	datetime	The date and time that a task was added to a project.
TaskCritical	tinyint	Indicates whether a task has room in the schedule to slip, or if it is on the critical path.
TaskCV	decimal	The difference between how much it should have cost to achieve the current level of completion on the task and how much it has actually cost to achieve the current level of completion up to the status date or today's date; also called cost variance.
TaskCVP	smallint	The cost variance percentage for a task.
TaskDeadline	datetime	The date entered as a deadline for the task.
TaskDuration	integer	The total span of active working time for a task.
TaskDurationElapsed	integer	Indicates which field is used to base BCWP values on.
TaskDurationVariance	integer	The difference between the baseline duration of a task and the total duration (current estimate) of a task.
TaskEarlyFinish	datetime	The earliest date that a task could possibly finish, based on early finish dates of predecessor and successor tasks, other constraints, and any leveling delay.
TaskEarlyStart	datetime	The earliest date that a task could possibly begin, based on the early start dates of predecessor and successor tasks, and other constraints.
TaskEffortDriven	tinyint	Indicates whether scheduling for a task is effort-driven.
TaskEstimated	tinyint	Indicates whether the task's duration is flagged as an estimate.
TaskExternalTask	tinyint	Indicates whether the task is linked from another project or whether it originated in the current project.
TaskEAC	decimal	The total scheduled or projected cost for a task, resource, or assignment based on costs already incurred, in addition to the costs planned for remaining work.
TaskFinish	datetime	The date and time that a task is scheduled to be completed.

TaskFinishSlack	integer	The duration between the Early Finish and Late Finish dates.
TaskFinishVariance	integer	The amount of time that represents the difference between a task's baseline finish date and its current finish date.
TaskFixedCost	decimal	A task expense that is not associated with a resource cost.
TaskFixedCostAccrual	smallint	Indicates how fixed costs are to be charged, or accrued, to the cost of a task: 1 Start; costs are accrued as soon as the task starts, as indicated by a date entered in the ActualStart field. 2 End; costs are not incurred until remaining work is zero. 3 Pro-rated (default); costs accrue as work is scheduled to occur and as actual work is reported.
TaskFreeSlack	integer	The amount of time that a task can be delayed without delaying any successor tasks; if a task has zero successor tasks, then free slack is the amount of time a task can be delayed without delaying the entire project.
TaskHideBar	tinyint	Indicates whether the Gantt bars and Calendar bars for a task are hidden.
TaskHyperlink	ntext	The title or explanatory text for a hyperlink associated with a task.
TaskHyperlinkAddress	ntext	The address for a hyperlink associated with a task.
TaskHyperlinkHref	ntext	The combination, or concatenation, of the hyperlink address and hyperlink sub-address fields associated with a task.
TaskHyperlinkScreenTip	ntext	The text contained in a ScreenTip associated with a hyperlink.
TaskHyperlinkSubAddress	ntext	The specific location in a document within a hyperlink associated with a task.
TaskID	integer	Indicates the position of a task in relation to other tasks.
TaskIgnoreResourceCalendar	tinyint	Indicates whether the scheduling of the task takes into account the calendars of the resources assigned to the task.
TaskIsNull	tinyint	Indicates whether a task is a null task.
TaskLateFinish	datetime	The latest date that a task can finish without delaying the finish of the project.
TaskLateStart	datetime	The latest date that a task can start without delaying the finish of the project.

TaskLevelAssignments	tinyint	Indicates whether the leveling function can delay and split individual assignments (rather than the entire task) in order to resolve overallocations.
TaskLevelingCanSplit	tinyint	Indicates whether the resource leveling function can cause splits on remaining work on a task.
TaskLevelingDelay	integer	The amount of time that a task is to be delayed from its early start date as a result of resource leveling.
TaskLinkedFields	tinyint	Indicates whether there are OLE links to a task, either from elsewhere in the active project, another Microsoft Project file, or from another program.
TaskMarked	tinyint	Indicates whether a task is marked for further action or identification of some kind.
TaskMilestone	tinyint	Indicates whether a task is a milestone.
TaskName	nvarchar(255)	The name of a task.
TaskNotes	ntext	Notes entered about a task.
TaskObjects	integer	The number of objects attached to a task.
TaskOutlineLevel	smallint	The number that indicates the level of a task in the project outline hierarchy.
TaskOutlineNumber	ntext	Indicates the exact position of a task in the outline. For example, 7.2 indicates that a task is the 2nd subtask under the 7th -level summary task.
TaskOverallocated	tinyint	Indicates whether an assigned resource on a task has been assigned to more work on the task than can be done within the normal working capacity.
TaskOvertimeCost	decimal	The actual overtime cost for a task.
TaskOvertimeWork	decimal	The amount of overtime scheduled to be performed by all resources assigned to a task and charged at overtime rates.
TaskPredecessors	ntext	The task ID numbers for the predecessor tasks to this task.
TaskPreleveledFinish	datetime	The finish date of a task as it was before resource leveling was done.
TaskPreleveledStart	datetime	The start date of a task as it was before resource leveling was done.
TaskPriority	smallint	Indicates the level of importance assigned to a task; the higher the number, the higher the priority: 0 Lowest priority; task will always be leveled 500 Default value 1000 Highest priority; task will never be leveled
TaskRecurring	tinyint	Indicates whether a task is a recurring task.
TaskRegularWork	decimal	The total amount of non-overtime work scheduled to be performed by all resources assigned to a task.

TaskRemainingCost	decimal	The remaining scheduled expense of a task that will be incurred in completing the remaining scheduled work by all resources assigned to a task.
TaskRemainingDuration	integer	The amount of time required to complete the unfinished portion of a task. Remaining duration can be calculated in two ways (either based off of Percent (%) Complete or Actual Duration).
TaskRemainingOvertimeCost	decimal	The remaining scheduled overtime expense for a task.
TaskRemainingOvertimeWork	decimal	The amount of remaining overtime scheduled by all assigned resources to complete a task.
TaskRemainingWork	decimal	The amount of time still required by all assigned resources to complete a task.
TaskResourceGroup	ntext	The list of resource groups to which the resources assigned to a task belong.
TaskResourceInitials	ntext	Lists the initials for the names of resources assigned to a task.
TaskResourceNames	ntext	Lists the names of all resources assigned to a task.
TaskResourcePhonetics	ntext	Contains information in either Hiragana or Katakana for the names of resources assigned to a task; used only in the Japanese version of Microsoft Project.
TaskResponsePending	tinyint	Indicates whether an answer has been received from all messages notifying a resource of an assignment sent to the resources assigned to a task.
TaskResume	datetime	The date the remaining portion of a task is scheduled to resume after you enter a new value for the Percent (%) Complete field.
TaskRollup	tinyint	Indicates whether the summary task bar displays rolled-up bars or whether information on the sub-task Gantt bars will be rolled up to the summary task bar; must be set to True for sub-tasks to be rolled up to summary tasks.
TaskStart	datetime	The date and time that a task is scheduled to begin; this value is automatically calculated if a task has a predecessor.
TaskStartSlack	integer	The amount of time a task can be delayed without affecting the start date of a successor task or the project finish date.
TaskStartVariance	integer	The difference between a task's baseline start date and its currently scheduled start date.
TaskS	datetime	The date that represents the end of the actual portion of a task; contains NA until you enter actual work or a completion percentage.
TaskStatus	smallint	The current status of a task.

TaskSubprojectFile	ntext	The name of a project inserted into the active project file including the sub-project's path and file name.
TaskSubprojectReadOnly	tinyint	Indicates whether the sub-project of this task is a read-only project.
TaskSuccessors	ntext	The task ID numbers for the successor tasks to this task.
TaskSummary	tinyint	Indicates whether a task is a summary task.
TaskSummaryProgress	datetime	The progress on a summary task, based on the progress of its sub-tasks.
TaskSV	decimal	The difference between the current progress and the baseline plan of the task up to the status date or today's date; also known as Earned Value Schedule Variance.
TaskSVP	smallint	The Schedule Variance Percentage (SVP) for a task.
TaskTCPI	decimal	The To Complete Performance Index (TCPI) for a task.
TaskTeamStatusPending	tinyint	Indicates whether an answer has been received in response to a message requesting status that was sent to the resources assigned to a task.
TaskTotalSlack	integer	The amount of time a task can be delayed without delaying a project's finish date.
TaskType	smallint	Indicates the effect that editing work, assignment units, or duration has on the calculations of the other two fields: 0 Fixed work; the amount of work remains constant, regardless of any change in duration or the number of resources (Assignment Units) assigned to the task 1 Fixed units (default); the number of Assignment Units remains constant, regardless of the amount of work or duration on the task 2 Fixed duration; the duration of the task remains constant, regardless of the number of resources (Assignment Units) assigned or the amount of work
TaskUniqueIDPredecessors	ntext	The unique IDs for predecessor tasks. For example, 15FS+3d means that this task's predecessor is task ID 15, with a finish-to-start dependency, and 3 days lag time.
TaskUniqueIDSuccessors	ntext	The unique IDs for successor tasks. For example, 15FS+3d means that this task's successor is task ID 15, with a finish-to-start dependency, and 3 days lag time.

TaskUpdateNeeded	tinyint	Indicates whether a message notifying a resource of changes that affect tasks should be sent to the assigned resources because of changes to the start date, finish date, or resource reassignments of the task.
TaskVAC	decimal	The difference between the baseline cost and the total cost for a task; also called Variance At Completion (VAC).
TaskWBS	ntext	A unique code (WBS) used to represent a task's position within the hierarchical structure of the project.
TaskWBSPredecessors	ntext	The WBS codes associated with a predecessor task on which the task depends before it can start or finish.
TaskWBSSuccessors	ntext	Lists the WBS codes associated with the successor tasks.
TaskWork	decimal	The total amount of work scheduled to be performed on a task by all assigned resources.
TaskWorkVariance	decimal	The difference between a task's baseline work and the currently scheduled work.

MSP_VIEW_PROJ_TASK_TP_BY_DAY

This table contains timephased information for tasks. Information in this table is obtained from the TaskTimephasedByDay table in the Microsoft Project OLE DB provider.

Column Name	Data Type	Description
WPROJ_ID	integer	Refers to a valid WPROJ_ID in the MSP_WEB_PROJECTS table.
ProjectUniqueID	integer	Refers to a valid ProjectUniqueID in the MSP_VIEW_PROJ_PROJECTS_STD table.
TaskUniqueID	integer	Refers to a valid TaskUniqueID in the MSP_VIEW_PROJ_TASK_STD table.
TaskTimeStart	datetime	The date and time that a task is scheduled to begin.
TaskTimeFinish	datetime	The date and time that a task is scheduled to be completed.
TaskTimeFixedCost	decimal	A task expense that is not associated with a resource cost.
TaskTimeActualFixedCost	decimal	The actual timephased non-resource task expenses, charged over time according to the selected cost accrual method.

MSP_VIEW_PROJ_TASKSPLITS

This table contains information for split tasks. Information in this table is obtained from the TaskSplits table in the Microsoft Project OLE DB provider.

Column Name	Data Type	Description
WPROJ_ID	integer	Refers to a valid WPROJ_ID in the MSP_WEB_PROJECTS table.
ProjectUniqueID	integer	Refers to a valid ProjectUniqueID in the MSP_VIEW_PROJ_PROJECTS_STD table.
TaskUniqueID	integer	Refers to a valid TaskUniqueID in the MSP_VIEW_PROJ_TASKS_STD table.
SplitStart	datetime	The date the task split begins.
SplitFinish	datetime	The date the task split ends.

MSP_VIEW_RES_CF

This table contains custom field information for resources and is used to determine resource availability for Assignment and Resource cube generation. Information in this table is obtained from the Resources table in the Microsoft Project OLE DB provider.

Column Name	Data Type	Description
CF_ResourceUniqueID	integer	Refers to a valid ResourceUniqueID in the MSP_VIEW_RES_STD table.
ResourceCost1-10	decimal	Custom cost information.
ResourceCost1-10Indicator	smallint	The indicator symbol for the corresponding custom field. See Indicator symbols for more information.
ResourceDate1-10	datetime	Custom date information.
ResourceDate1-10Indicator	smallint	The indicator symbol for the corresponding custom field. See Indicator symbols for more information.
ResourceDuration1-10	integer	Custom duration information.
ResourceDuration1-10Indicator	smallint	The indicator symbol for the corresponding custom field. See Indicator symbols for more information.
ResourceFinish1-10	datetime	Custom finish date information.
ResourceFinish1-10Indicator	smallint	The indicator symbol for the corresponding custom field. See Indicator symbols for more information.
ResourceFlag1-20	tinyint	Indicates whether a resource is marked for further action or identification of some kind.
ResourceFlag1-20Indicator	smallint	The indicator symbol for the corresponding custom field. See Indicator symbols for more information.

ResourceNumber1-20	decimal	Custom numeric information.
ResourceNumber1-20Indicator	smallint	The indicator symbol for the corresponding custom field. See Indicator symbols for more information.
ResourceOutlineCode1-10	ntext	An alphanumeric code defined to represent a hierarchical structure of resources.
ResourceStart1-10	datetime	Custom start date information.
ResourceStart1-10Indicator	smallint	The indicator symbol for the corresponding custom field. See Indicator symbols for more information.
Resourcentext1-30	ntext	Custom text information.
Resourcentext1-30Indicator	smallint	The indicator symbol for the corresponding custom field. See Indicator symbols for more information.

MSP_VIEW_RES_ENT

This table contains enterprise information for resources and is used to determine resource availability for Assignment and Resource cube generation. Information in this table is obtained from the Resources table in the Microsoft Project OLE DB provider.

Column Name	Data Type	Description
ENT_ResourceUniqueID	integer	Refers to a valid ResourceUniqueID in the MSP_VIEW_RES_STD table.
ResourceEnterpriseCost1-10	decimal	Custom enterprise-level cost information.
ResourceEnterpriseCost1-10Indicator	smallint	The indicator symbol for the corresponding custom field. See Indicator symbols for more information.
ResourceEnterpriseDate1-30	datetime	Custom enterprise-level date information.
ResourceEnterpriseDate1-30Indicator	smallint	The indicator symbol for the corresponding custom field. See Indicator symbols for more information.
ResourceDuration1-10	integer	Custom duration information.
ResourceDuration1-10Indicator	smallint	The indicator symbol for the corresponding custom field. See Indicator symbols for more information.
ResourceEnterpriseFlag1-20	tinyint	Custom enterprise-level flag information.
ResourceEnterpriseFlag1-20Indicator	smallint	The indicator symbol for the corresponding custom field. See Indicator symbols for more information.
ResourceEnterpriseGeneric	smallint	Indicates whether the resource is an enterprise-level generic resource.
ResourceEnterpriseNumber1-40	decimal	Custom enterprise-level number information.
ResourceEnterpriseNumber1-40Indicator	smallint	The indicator symbol for the corresponding custom field. See Indicator symbols for more information.
ResourceEnterpriseOutlineCode1-30ID	integer	Custom enterprise-level outline code information.
ResourceEnterprisentext1-40	ntext	Custom enterprise-level text information.
ResourceEnterprisentext1-40Indicator	smallint	The indicator symbol for the corresponding custom field. See Indicator symbols for more information.

MSP_VIEW_RES_STD

This table contains standard information for resources and is used to determine resource availability for Assignment and Resource cube generation. Information in this table is obtained from the Resources table in the Microsoft Project OLE DB provider.

Column Name	Data Type	Description
ResourceUniqueID	integer	The unique ID for the resource.
ResourcePercentWorkComplete	smallint	The current status of all tasks assigned to a resource, expressed as the total percentage of the resource's work that has been completed.
ResourceAccrueAt	smallint	Indicates how and when resource standard and overtime costs are to be charged, or accrued, to the cost of a task: 1 Start; costs are accrued as soon as the task starts, as indicated by a date entered in the ActualStart field. 2 End; costs are not incurred until remaining work is zero. 3 Pro-rated (default); costs accrue as work is scheduled to occur and as actual work is reported.
ResourceActualCost	decimal	The sum of costs incurred for the work already performed by a resource for all assigned tasks.
ResourceActualOvertimeCost	decimal	The cost incurred for overtime work already performed by a resource for all assigned tasks.
ResourceActualOvertimeWork	decimal	The actual amount of overtime work already performed for all assignments assigned to a resource.
ResourceActualWork	decimal	The actual amount of work that has already been done for all assignments assigned to a resource.
ResourceACWP	decimal	The sum of Actual Cost of Work Performed (ACWP) values for all of a resource's assignments, up to the status date or today's date.
ResourceAvailableFrom	datetime	The starting date that a resource is available for work at the units specified for the current time period.
ResourceAvailableTo	datetime	The ending date in which a resource will be available for work at the units specified for the current time period.
ResourceBaseCalendar	ntext	Lists all calendars available to be applied to a resource, including the standard calendar and any custom calendars: 0 Standard (default) 1+ Custom calendar

ResourceBaselineCost	decimal	The total planned cost for a resource for all assigned tasks; also called Budget At Completion (BAC).
ResourceBaselineCost1-10	decimal	Custom baseline cost information.
ResourceBaselineFinish	datetime	The planned finish date for assignments.
ResourceBaselineFinish1-10	datetime	Custom baseline finish information.
ResourceBaselineStart	datetime	The planned beginning date for assignments.
ResourceBaselineStart1-10	datetime	Custom baseline start information.
ResourceBaselineWork	decimal	The originally planned amount of work to be performed for all assignments assigned to a resource.
ResourceBaselineWork1-10	decimal	Custom baseline work information.
ResourceBCWP	decimal	The rolled-up summary of a resource's BCWP values for all assigned tasks, calculated up to the status date or today's date; also called Budgeted Cost of Work Performed.
ResourceBCWS	decimal	The rolled-up summary of a resource's BCWS values for all assigned tasks; also called Budgeted Cost of Work Scheduled.
ResourceCanLevel	tinyint	Indicates whether resource leveling can be done with a resource.
ResourceCode	ntext	A code, initials, or number entered as part of a resource's information.
ResourceConfirmed	tinyint	Indicates whether a resource has accepted or rejected all task assignments in response to a message notifying a resource of an assignment.
ResourceCost	decimal	The total scheduled cost for a resource for all assigned tasks, based on costs already incurred for work performed by the resource on all assigned tasks in addition to the costs planned for all remaining work.
ResourceCostPerUse	decimal	The cost that accrues each time a resource is used.
ResourceCostVariance	decimal	The difference between the baseline cost and total cost for a resource.
ResourceCV	decimal	The difference between how much it should have cost for the resource to achieve the current level of completion, and how much it has actually cost to achieve the current level of completion, up to the status date or today's date.
ResourceEmailAddress	ntext	The e-mail address of a resource; if this field is left blank, Microsoft Project will use the name in the ResourceName field as the e-mail address.
ResourceFinish	datetime	The date and time that a resource is scheduled to complete work on all assigned tasks.
ResourceGroup	ntext	The name of the group associated with the resource.
ResourceHyperlink	ntext	The title or explanatory text for a hyperlink associated with a resource.

ResourceHyperlinkAddress	ntext	The address for a hyperlink associated with a resource.
ResourceHyperlinkHref	ntext	The combination, or concatenation, of the Hyperlink Address and Hyperlink SubAddress fields associated with a resource.
ResourceHyperlinkScreenTip	ntext	The text contained in a ScreenTip associated with a hyperlink.
ResourceHyperlinkSubAddress	ntext	The specific location in a document within a hyperlink associated with a resource.
ResourceID	integer	Indicates the position of a resource in relation to other resources.
ResourceInitials	ntext	The initials for a resource name.
ResourceIsNull	tinyint	Indicates whether the resource is a null resource.
ResourceLastPublished	datetime	The date and time that a resource was last published.
ResourceLinkedFields	tinyint	Indicates whether there are OLE links to the resource, either from elsewhere in the active project, another Microsoft Project file, or from another program.
ResourceMaterialLabel	ntext	The unit of measurement entered for a material resource, for example: tons, boxes, or cubic yards. This is used in conjunction with the material resource's Assignment Units and is only available if ResourceType is set to Material.
ResourceMaxUnits	decimal	The maximum percentage, or number of units, that represents the maximum capacity for which a resource is available to accomplish any tasks during the current time period: 0-99: Resource is 0%-99% available for the specified task 100: Resource is 100% available for the specified task (default)
ResourceName	nvarchar(255)	The name of the resource; must be unique within the enterprise whether or not the resource is active.
ResourceNotes	ntext	Notes about a resource.
ResourceNTAccount	ntext	The Windows NT Account name for a resource; for example: *domain name\user name.*
ResourceObjects	integer	The number of objects associated with a resource, not including those in notes.
ResourceOverallocated	tinyint	Indicates whether a resource is assigned to do more work on all assigned tasks than can be done within the resource's normal work capacity.
ResourceOvertimeCost	decimal	The total overtime cost for a resource on all assigned tasks.

ResourceOvertimeRate	decimal	The rate of pay for overtime work performed by a resource.
ResourceOvertimeWork	decimal	The amount of overtime to be performed for all tasks assigned to a resource and charged at the resource's overtime rate.
ResourcePeakUnits	decimal	The maximum percentage, or number of units, for which a resource is assigned at any one time for all tasks assigned to the resource.
ResourcePhonetics	ntext	Contains phonetic information in either Hiragana or Katakana for resource names; used only in the Japanese version of Microsoft Project.
ResourceRegularWork	decimal	The total amount of non-overtime work scheduled to be performed for all assignments assigned to a resource.
ResourceRemainingCost	decimal	The remaining scheduled expense that will be incurred in completing the remaining work assigned to a resource.
ResourceRemainingOvertimeCost	decimal	The remaining scheduled overtime expense of a resource that will be incurred in completing the remaining planned overtime work by a resource on all assigned tasks.
ResourceRemainingOvertimeWork	decimal	The remaining amount of overtime required by a resource to complete all tasks.
ResourceRemainingWork	decimal	The amount of time, or person-hours, still required by a resource to complete all assigned tasks.
ResourceResponsePending	tinyint	Indicates whether an answer has been received from all messages notifying a resource of an assignment sent to a resource about assigned tasks.
ResourceStandardRate	decimal	The rate of pay for regular, non-overtime work performed by a resource.
ResourceStart	datetime	The date and time that an assigned resource is scheduled to begin working on all assigned tasks.
ResourceSV	decimal	The difference in cost terms between the current progress and the baseline plan of all the resource's assigned tasks up to the status date or today's date; also called Earned Value Schedule Variance.
ResourceTeamStatusPending	tinyint	Indicates whether an answer has been received in response to a message requesting status that was sent to a resource about an assigned task.
ResourceType	smallint	The resource type (Work or Material): 0 Work (default); people and equipment 1 Material; consumable supplies like steel, concrete, or soil

ResourceUpdateNeeded	tinyint	Indicates whether a message notifying a resource of changes that affect tasks should be sent to a resource because of changes to any of the resource's assigned tasks.
ResourceVAC	decimal	The difference between the baseline cost and the total cost for a resource.
ResourceWork	decimal	The total amount of work scheduled to be performed by a resource on all assigned tasks.
ResourceWorkgroup	smallint	The messaging method used to communicate with a project workgroup: 0 Default 1 Web (Microsoft Project Web Access) 2 E-mail only 3 None; Workgroup messaging is not used on this project
ResourceWorkVariance	decimal	The difference between a resource's total baseline work and the currently scheduled work.

MSP_VIEW_RES_TP_BY_DAY

This table contains timephased information for resources and is used to determine resource availability for Assignment and Resource cube generation. Information in this table is obtained from the ResourcesTimephasedByDay table in the Microsoft Project OLE DB provider.

Column Name	Data Type	Description
ResourceUniqueID	integer	Refers to a valid ResourceUniqueID in the MSP_VIEW_RES_STD table.
ResourceTimeStart	datetime	The date and time that an assigned resource is scheduled to begin working on all assigned tasks.
ResourceTimeFinish	datetime	The date and time that an assigned resource is scheduled to finish working on all assigned tasks.
ResourceTimeWorkAvailability	decimal	The maximum amount of time a work resource is available to be scheduled for work during any selected time period.

Assignment and Resource Cube Tables

Assignment and Resource cubes are used to provide project and resource drill down views in Microsoft Project Web Access. Assignment and Resource cubes pull data from the project, assignment, and resource view tables (see Project and Resource View Tables for more information).

MSP_CUBE_ASSN_FACT

The Assignments Cube is made up of this table and all of its associated dimension tables:

- MSP_CUBE_TIME_BY_DAY
- MSP_CUBE_ENTERPRISE_ASSIGNMENT_OUTLINE_n
- MSP_CUBE_PROJECTS
- MSP_CUBE_RESOURCES
- MSP_CUBE_PROJ_VERSIONS

Column Name	Data Type	Description
PROJ_UID	integer	Refers to a valid PROJ_UID in the MSP_CUBE_PROJECTS table.
RES_ENTUID	integer	Refers to a valid RES_ENTRUID in the MSP_CUBE_RESOURCES table.
TIME_ID	integer	Refers to a valid TIME_ID in the MSP_CUBE_TIME_BY_DAY table.
TIME_DATE	datetime	Refers to the TIME_DATE field for the same TIME_ID row in the MSP_CUBE_TIME_BY_DAY table.
ENT_ASSIGNMENT_CODEn	integer	Refers to a valid ASSN_OUTLINECODE_ID in the MSP_CUBE_ENTERPRISE_ASSIGNMENT_OUTLINE_n table; n is represented by a number ranging from 1-30.
ASSN_ACTUALCOST	float	Refers to the AssignmentActualCost field in the MSP_VIEW_PROJ_ASSN_STD table.
ASSN_ACTUALOVERTIMEWORK	float	Refers to the AssignmentActualOvertimeWork field in the MSP_VIEW_PROJ_ASSN_STD table.
ASSN_ACTUALWORK	float	Refers to the AssignmentActualWork field in the MSP_VIEW_PROJ_ASSN_STD table.
ASSN_BASELINECOST	float	Refers to the AssignmentBaselineCost field in the MSP_VIEW_PROJ_ASSN_STD table.
ASSN_BASELINEWORK	float	Refers to the AssignmentBaselineWork field in the MSP_VIEW_PROJ_ASSN_STD table.

ASSN_COST	float	Refers to the AssignmentCost field in the MSP_VIEW_PROJ_ASSN_STD table.
ASSN_OVTERTIMEWORK	float	Refers to the AssignmentOvertimeWork field in the MSP_VIEW_PROJ_ASSN_STD table.
ASSN_REGULARWORK	float	Refers to the AssignmentRegularWork field in the MSP_VIEW_PROJ_ASSN_STD table.
ASSN_WORK	float	Refers to the AssignmentWork field in the MSP_VIEW_PROJ_ASSN_STD table.
ASSN_MATERIAL_ACTUALWORK	float	Refers to the AssignmentActualWork field in the MSP_VIEW_PROJ_ASSN_STD table if this resource is a material resource.
ASSN_MATERIAL_BASELINEWORK	float	Refers to the AssignmentBaselineWork field in the MSP_VIEW_PROJ_ASSN_STD table if this resource is a material resource.
ASSN_MATERIAL_WORK	float	Refers to the AssignmentWork field in the MSP_VIEW_PROJ_ASSN_STD table if this resource is a material resource.

MSP_CUBE_ENTERPRISE_ASSIGNMENT_OUTLINE_n

There is one MSP_CUBE_ENTERPRISE_ASSIGNMENT_OUTLINE_n table generated for each existing ENT_ASSIGNMENT_CODEn in the MSP_CUBE_ASSN_FACT table.

Column Name	Data Type	Description
ASSN_OUTLINECODE_NAME	nvarchar(255)	The name of the Assignment Outline Code.
ASSN_OUTLINECODE_DESCRIPTION	ntext	The description of the Assignment Outline Code.
ASSN_OUTLINECODE_ID	integer	Refers to a valid ENT_ASSIGNMENT_CODEn in the MSP_CUBE_ASSN_FACT table.
ASSN_OUTLINECODE_PARENTID	integer	Refers to a valid ASSN_OUTLINECODE_ID in an MSP_CUBE_ENTERPRISE_ASSIGNMENT_OUTLINE_n table; set to 0 for -level codes without parents.

MSP_CUBE_ENTERPRISE_PROJECT_OUTLINE_n

There is one MSP_CUBE_ENTERPRISE_PROJECT_OUTLINE_n table generated for each existing ENTERPRISE_PROJECT_CODEn in the MSP_CUBE_PROJECTS table.

Column Name	Data Type	Description
PROJ_OUTLINECODE_NAME	nvarchar(255)	The name of the Project Outline Code.
PROJ_OUTLINECODE_DESCRIPTION	ntext	The description of the Project Outline Code.
PROJ_OUTLINECODE_ID	integer	Refers to a valid ENTERPRISE_PROJECT_CODEn in the MSP_CUBE_PROJECTS table.
PROJ_OUTLINECODE_PARENTID	integer	Refers to a valid ASSN_OUTLINECODE_ID in an MSP_CUBE_ENTERPRISE_ASSIGNMENT_OUTLINE_n table; set to "0" for -level codes without parents.

MSP_CUBE_ENTERPRISE_RESOURCE_OUTLINE_n

There is one MSP_CUBE_ENTERPRISE_RESOURCE_OUTLINE_n table generated for each ENTERPRISE_RESOURCE_CODEn in the MSP_CUBE_RESOURCES table.

Column Name	Data Type	Description
RES_OUTLINECODE_NAME	nvarchar(255)	The name of the Resource Outline Code.
RES_OUTLINECODE_DESCRIPTION	ntext	The description of the Resource Outline Code.
RES_OUTLINECODE_ID	integer	Refers to a valid ENTERPRISE_RESOURCE_CODEn in the MSP_CUBE_RESOURCES table.
RES_OUTLINECODE_PARENTID	integer	Refers to a valid ASSN_OUTLINECODE_ID in an MSP_CUBE_ENTERPRISE_ASSIGNMENT_OUTLINE_n table; set to 0 for -level codes without parents.

MSP_CUBE_PROJ_VERSIONS

This table gets all available project versions stored in the MSP_VERSIONS table and assigns them a unique ID to use with the Assignment or Resource cubes.

Column Name	Data Type	Description
PROJ_VERSION_UID	integer	Refers to a valid PROJ_VERSION_UID in the MSP_CUBE_PROJECTS table.
PROJ_VERSION	nvarchar(120)	The name of the project version, as indicated by the VERS_VERSION field in the MSP_VERSIONS table.

MSP_CUBE_PROJECTS

This table links specific information in the MSP_WEB_PROJECTS table with project versions and enterprise outline codes for use in Assignment and Resource cube generation.

Column Name	Data Type	Description
PROJ_UID	integer	Refers to a valid PROJ_UID in the MSP_WEB_PROJECTS table.
PROJ_NAME	nvarchar(255)	Refers to a valid PROJ_NAME in the MSP_WEB_PROJECTS table.
PROJ_PROP_TITLE	ntext	Refers to a valid PROJ_PROP_TITLE in the MSP_WEB_PROJECTS table.
PROJ_VERSION_UID	integer	The unique ID for the project version.
ENTERPRISE_PROJECT_CODEn	integer	Where n is represented by a number ranging from 1-30

MSP_CUBE_RES_AVAIL_FACT

The Resources Cube is made up of the Resource Availability Fact table and all of its associated dimension tables: MSP_CUBE_RESOURCES, MSP_CUBE_ENTERPRISE_RESOURCE_OUTLINE_n, and MSP_CUBE_TIME_BY_DAY.

Column Name	Data Type	Description
RES_ENTRUID	integer	Refers to a valid RES_ENTRUID in the MSP_CUBE_RESOURCES table.
TIME_ID	integer	Refers to a valid TIME_ID in the MSP_CUBE_TIME_BY_DAY table.
TIME_DATE	datetime	Refers to a valid TIME_DATE in the MSP_CUBE_TIME_BY_DAY table.
RES_AVAIL	float	This value is generated by comparing the resource availability table to the date range specified when building the Assignment or Resource cube. This value represents the total available time for a resource on a given day that falls within the specified date range.

MSP_CUBE_RESOURCES

Stores enterprise resource data based on specific information stored in the MSP_WEB_RESOURCES table.

Column Name	Data Type	Description
RES_ENTRUID	integer	Refers to a valid WRES_EUID in the MSP_WEB_RESOURCES table.
RESOURCENAME	nvarchar(255)	The name of the resource as specified in the RES_NAME field in the MSP_WEB_RESOURCES table.
ENTERPRISE_RESOURCE_CODEn	integer	The ID for the enterprise resource code; n is represented by a number ranging from 1-30.

MSP_CUBE_TIME_BY_DAY

Stores the time dimension for both the Assignments and Resource Availability cubes. This dimension is the date range selected when building the Assignment or Resource cube.

Column Name	Data Type	Description
TIME_ID	integer	The unique ID for the time dimension. Each day in the specified date range will have a unique ID.
TIME_DATE	datetime	The number of days in the time period; for example, if an OLAP cube is built around three days, then the value in this field would be 3.
TIME_DAY	nvarchar(32)	The name of the day of the week, for example: Monday.
TIME_MONTH	nvarchar(32)	The name of the month of the year, for example: August.
TIME_YEAR	integer	The year, for example: 2001.
TIME_DAY_OF_MONTH	integer	The day of the month (1-31).
TIME_WEEK_OF_YEAR	integer	The week of the year (1-53).
TIME_MONTH_OF_YEAR	integer	The month of the year (0-11).
TIME_QTR	nvarchar(2)	The fiscal quarter, for example: 1 for the first quarter.

Appendix II

Overview of Project Server security[2]

This topic is a centralized collection of security information from this installation guide as well as some general information about Microsoft Project Server security. Additional details and procedures for most of these items are described in separate topics for the subject in question.

Note

This information is primarily concerned with security as it relates to installing and configuring Microsoft Project Server. For information about security in Microsoft Project Web Access, see the "Manage Security" section of Microsoft Project Web Access Help for the Admin center.

Microsoft Project Server

- Directory security for the Microsoft Project Server virtual directory is set to Integrated Windows authentication.
- Directory security for the Microsoft Project Server virtual directory is set to grant access for IP addresses and domain name restrictions.
- File security for Pjdbcomm.dll (located in the Microsoft Project Server virtual directory) should be set to include Anonymous authentication if your organization still has users of Microsoft Project 2000.
- Directory security for the MSADC virtual directory is set for no access.

If the MSADC virtual directory already exists, does not change the settings for authentication methods.

- File security for Msdacs.dll (located in the MSADC virtual directory) is set to Integrated Windows authentication only.
- File security for Msdacs.dll (located in the MSADC virtual directory) is set to grant access for IP addresses and domain name restrictions.
- A Microsoft SQL Server user account to connect to an existing Microsoft Project Server database, or a SQL Server or Windows user account to create a new database is required to install Microsoft Project Server. If connecting to an existing database, the user account must be a member of the MSProjectServerRole role in the Microsoft Project Server database. If creating a new database, the user account must have sufficient permissions to create databases and user accounts.

- Microsoft Project Server stores information about the SQL Server user account it uses to access the Microsoft Project Server database in the registry. To prevent unauthorized access to the subkey \HKEY_LOCAL_MACHINE\SOFTWARE\Microsoft\Office\10.0\MS Project\WebClient Server, you should deny "log on locally" permissions for users on the Microsoft Project Server computer.

SharePoint Team Services from Microsoft

- The Microsoft Project Server computer and the SharePoint Team Services computer must be members of the same Windows domain or workgroup.

- The Microsoft Project Server computer and the SharePoint Team Services computer must use the same type of Windows authentication; for example, they must both use either Integrated Windows authentication or Basic authentication.

- If either Microsoft Project Server or SharePoint Team Services is configured to allow user access through the Secure Sockets Layer (SSL), both computers must support the https:// protocol so that Microsoft Project Server can communicate with SharePoint Team Services.

- Note The protocol used to connect to the Microsoft Project Server computer with Microsoft Project Web Access must be the same as the protocol used by Microsoft Project Server to communicate with SharePoint Team Services.

- For enhanced security, anonymous access should be disabled on each project subweb.

- Only Windows user accounts are supported for accessing SharePoint Team Services subwebs.

- A SQL Server user account to access the SharePoint Team Services database server when installing SharePoint Team Services is required.

- A Windows user account to access the SharePoint Team Services database from Microsoft Project Server is required.

- A Windows user account used by Microsoft Project Server for remote SharePoint Team Services administration tasks is required.

- Users with "Manage SharePoint Team Services" permission in Microsoft Project Web Access are added to the "Administrator (Microsoft Project Server)" role for the SharePoint Team Services root web and each project subweb.

Analysis Services

- By default, the OLAP cube database created by Microsoft Project Server has no database roles defined so that only users or groups specifically added have access to the cubes.

- A Windows user account that is a member of the OLAP Administrators group on the Analysis Services computer is required.

User access

- The Microsoft Project Server site must be set as trusted in Microsoft Internet Explorer.

- A SQL Server user account to access the Microsoft Project Server database from Microsoft Project Professional is required. Additionally, this user account must be a member of the MSProjectRole role in the Microsoft Project Server database.

- In order for users to log on to Microsoft Project Server by using Basic authentication, the authentication method for the Microsoft Project Server virtual directory and the file Msadcs.dll must be set, and Microsoft Internet Information Server (IIS) must be configured to use the SSL.

Microsoft Project Server supports the use of the Kerberos V5 authentication protocol for computers that are members of an Active Directory domain.

Note

Kerberos V5 authentication is not supported on Microsoft Windows XP Home Edition.

Users that log on to Microsoft Project Server by using Basic authentication cannot use the User Principal Name (UPN) format of account@domain.com, even if the the IIS computer is configured to allow the UPN format.

Tip

Windows user accounts are stored in the Microsoft Project Server database in the form domain\account, regardless of how they were entered.

Recommendations

In general, the following recommendations can be made for running Microsoft Project Server securely.

Corporate intranet users

- IIS should be configured to use SSL.
- The administrator account for Microsoft Project Server should be set to use Windows authentication.

Tip

To change the authentication method for the administrator account, point to Admin in the top link bar of Microsoft Project Web Access to go to the Admin center and then click Manage users and groups. Select Administrator from the dropdown list and then click Modify User. Click Windows Authentication, using the Windows User Account, enter information for a Windows user account (including e-mail address), and then click Save Changes.

Windows user accounts should be used instead of Microsoft Project Server user accounts.

To change the authentication method for user accounts, click Admin in the top link bar to go to the Admin center and then click Manage security in the side pane. Next, in the side pane under Security options, click User authentication. Click Windows Authentication only and then click Save Changes.

- Microsoft Project should be required to authenticate to the Microsoft Project Server computer before publishing.

Users of Microsoft Project 2000 will be unable to publish to the Microsoft Project Server computer.

> *Tip*
>
> To force Microsoft Project to authenticate when publishing, click Admin in the top link bar to go to the Admin center and then click Manage security in the side pane. Next, in the side pane under Security options, click User authentication. Select the Require Microsoft Project to authenticate to the Microsoft Project Server before publishing check box and then click Save Changes.

Extranet or cross-domain users

- IIS should be configured to use SSL.
- Windows user accounts should be used instead of Microsoft Project Server user accounts.

> *Tip*
>
> To change the authentication method for user accounts, click Admin in the top link bar to go to the Admin center and then click Manage security in the side pane. Next, in the side pane under Security options, click User authentication. Click Windows Authentication only and then click Save Changes.

- Enable Basic authentication for the Microsoft Project Server virtual directory and for the Remote Data Services ISAPI Library (Msadcs.dll) using the Microsoft Managment Console (MMC) snap-in for IIS.

> **Note**
>
> To enable Basic authentication for the Microsoft Project Server virtual directory, right-click the virtual directory in the left pane of the Internet Information Services window and click Properties. Click the Directory Security tab and then click Edit in the section for Anonymous access and authentication control. Select the Basic authentication check box and then click Yes when asked if you want to continue. Click OK twice to apply your changes and close the dialog box, and then click OK to close the Inheritance Overrides dialog box without making any changes.
>
> To enable Basic authentication for the file Msadcs.dll, select the MSADC virtual directory in the left pane of the Internet Information Services window. Right-click msadcs.dll in the right pane and then select Properties. Click the File Security tab and then click Edit in the section for Anonymous Access and Authentication Control. Select the Basic authentication check box and then click Yes when asked if you want to continue. Click OK twice to apply your changes and close the dialog box.

- If Microsoft Project Server user accounts must be used, Basic authentication to the IIS computer is still recommended.

  Users are authenticated twice, once to the IIS computer and again to Microsoft Project Server.

Tip

Extranet users should connect to the Microsoft Project Server computer by using a Web address appropriate for their authentication method. Using a domain of fabrikam.com, for example:

- Users connecting by using Windows user accounts should connect to www.fabrikam.com/projectserver/lgnbsc.asp
- Users connecting by using Microsoft Project Server user accounts should connect to www.fabrikam.com/projectserver/lgnps.asp

Appendix III

Overview of clustering and distributed configurations with Project Server[2]

Some of the improvements for Microsoft Project Server include support for a distributed configuration of Microsoft Project Server components and clustering Microsoft Project Server computers.

Distributed configuration

This type of configuration involves distributing different components of Microsoft Project Server to several computers to increase overall performance for organizations where large numbers of users and heavier server loads are expected and scalability is an important issue. The components that may be distributed away from the Microsoft Project Server computer are:

- Microsoft Project Server database

  A Microsoft SQL Server database may also be part of a cluster (failover clustering is a feature of Microsoft SQL Server Enterprise Edition).

- Analysis Services

  Moving the online analytical processing (OLAP) portion of the Portfolio Analyzer feature to a separate computer can significantly increase performance.

- SharePoint Team Services from Microsoft

  Provides support for the documents and issue tracking features of Microsoft Project Server.

- Session Manager service

  The Session Manager service replaces ASP sessions in Microsoft Project Server.

- View Manager service

  The View Manager service controls, along with resource availability information and the OLAP cube, generation of the project information displayed in the Project Center, a process which can be extremely processor-intensive.

> ***Note***
>
> Not all of the features and components described above may apply to your installation of Microsoft Project Server.

Tip

For more information about distributing Microsoft Project Server components, see the Deployment section for Microsoft Project Server in the Microsoft Project 2002 Resource Kit at: http://go.microsoft.com/fwlink/?LinkId=4326

Clustering

With the elimination of ASP sessions in Microsoft Project Server, clustering multiple Internet Information Server (IIS) computers running Microsoft Project Server is now possible. The method of clustering you use is independent of Microsoft Project Server, whether you choose hardware (for example, through a router or a switch) or software (such as Network Load Balancing) clustering technology.

Session Manager service

The Session Manager service tracks which user is engaged in what actions in which area of Microsoft Project Web Access. It replaces ASP sessions for Microsoft Project Server and, when used in a clustered environment, should be deployed on its own server outside the cluster. This allows users to be directed to any one of the clustered application servers.

View Manager service

The View Manager service controls when and how the Microsoft Project OLE DB provider and other server components are used to generate the data for building project views in Microsoft Project Web Access, for example, when a project is published from Microsoft Project Professional. It also controls the publishing of resource availability data and building of the OLAP cube. The View Manager service should be deployed on its own server outside the cluster.

Because of the system resource requirements for generating view data, the View Manager service can also play a part in a distributed configuration for your Microsoft Project Server installation. See the items about Analysis Services and the View Manager service in the "Distributed configuration" section above.

Microsoft Project Server database

Although the Microsoft Project Server database may be part of a database cluster, it should be deployed on its own server outside the IIS cluster.

---

1. Microsoft Project Server Database Information. svrdb.htm. Microsoft Corporation, 2002.
2. Microsoft Project Server Installation Guide. Microsoft Corporation, 2002.

Index

A

B

B

C

E

F

G

H

I

L

M

N

O

P

R

S

T

U

V

W

X

0-595-24060-7

www.ingramcontent.com/pod-product-compliance
Lightning Source LLC
Chambersburg PA
CBHW080151060326
40689CB00018B/3942
* 9 7 8 0 5 9 5 2 4 0 6 0 9 *